Advertising Works 20

Proving the payback on
marketing investment

Case studies from the
IPA Effectiveness Awards 2011
Limited to campaigns with an annual marketing
communications budget of up to £2.5m

Edited and introduced by
Charlie Snow
Convenor of Judges

First published 2011 by Warc
85 Newman Street, London W1T 3EX
Telephone: 0207 467 8100
Fax: 0207 467 8101
Email: enquiries@warc.com
www.warc.com

A CIP catalogue record for this for book is available from the British Library

ISBN: 978-1-84116-224-9

Typeset by HWA Text and Data Management, London
Printed and bound in Great Britain by the MPG Books Group

Contents

Foreword

Lindsey Clay
Managing Director, Thinkbox

One of the things Thinkbox shares with the IPA is a commitment to and obsession with effectiveness.

This is why Thinkbox has sponsored the IPA Effectiveness Awards for each of the six years it has existed (which pales into insignificance when compared to the IPA's commitment to these Awards spanning over 30 years).

We want to shine more light on effectiveness, test it, learn about it, share it and of course, for us in particular, to have an even greater understanding of the vital role that TV plays at its heart.

So we feel a near spiritual connection and empathy with all those celebrated in these pages; those midnight oil burners who have pored over the data in order to prove the specific contribution that their communication has made to the success of their respective brands and organisations.

The reason we're so obsessed is because nothing is more important in advertising than effectiveness; actually making a difference. It is the card in your hand that trumps everything else: cost, innovation, accountability, efficiency. Effectiveness – driven by creativity and great thinking – beats them all.

But it doesn't get any easier as time goes on. The complexity of the new communication landscape is much written and talked about but what this means for advertisers is an ever-increasing series of options and permutations as to how they can go about fulfilling their objectives. Navigating this requires gallons of midnight oil.

This year's winners are a perfect demonstration of the variety of options available and ways that advertisers and their agencies have achieved success. Whether, like Ovaltine, it is by focusing limited resources in one medium (TV sponsorship) and doing that one thing brilliantly, or, like the Colombian Ministry of Defence, employing a creatively conceived but classically executed integrated, multi-media campaign to reduce terrorism.

So, congratulations to all the Award winners. It may be a more complex and challenging communication environment, but what the winners show is that there are many routes to success and our understanding of how to use them better together is improving all the time – thanks in no small part to these Awards. We should all be obsessed with how effectiveness works and, to help fuel that obsession, you can always get a regular fix or some inspiration at www.thinkbox.tv.

Sponsors

The success of the 2011 IPA Effectiveness Awards is in no small part down to its sponsors, and the IPA would like to thank the companies listed here for their continuing support. We are particularly grateful to Thinkbox, its overall sponsor, for their commitment to sponsor this competition.

IN ASSOCIATION WITH

facebook

 Clear Channel

campaign

Acknowledgements

Many people worked hard to make the Awards a success, especially the following: Richard Exon, Chairman of the IPA Value of Advertising Group, Charlie Snow, Convenor of Judges and Lorna Hawtin, Deputy Convenor of Judges.

At the IPA, the core team were: Bryony Clare, Danielle Davies, Tessa Gooding, Kathryn Patten, Sophie Walker and Sylvia Wood.

We also owe a debt of gratitude to:

The IPA Awards Board

The Awards Board is made up of past, current and future Convenors of Judges of the IPA Effectiveness Awards, the Chairman of the VAG and key representatives from the IPA Secretariat. It meets twice a year and its role is to review and agree on the direction of the IPA Effectiveness Awards competition.

IPA President, Nicola Mendelsohn	Karmarama
IPA Chairman of VAG, Richard Exon	RKCR/Y&R
1988/90 Convenor of Judges, Paul Feldwick	
1992/94 Convenor of Judges, Chris Baker	
1996 Convenor of Judges, Gary Duckworth	
1998 Convenor of Judges, Nick Kendall	
2000 Convenor of Judges, Tim Broadbent	
2002 Convenor of Judges, Marco Rimini	
2004 Convenor of Judges, Alison Hoad	
2005 Convenor of Judges, Les Binet	
2006 Convenor of Judges, Laurence Green	
2007 Convenor of Judges, Richard Storey	M&C Saatchi
2008 Convenor of Judges, Neil Dawson	HMDG
2009 Convenor of Judges, Andy Nairn	MCBD
2010 Convenor of Judges, David Golding	Adam & Eve
2011 Convenor of Judges, Charlie Snow	DLKW Lowe
2012 Convenor of Judges, Marie Oldham	MPG Media Contacts
2013 Convenor of Judges, Lorna Hawtin	TBWA\Manchester
IPA Director General, Paul Bainsfair	
IPA Director of Communications, Tessa Gooding	
IPA Events Senior Manager, Kathryn Patten	
1982/80 Convenor of Judges, Simon Broadbent *(d)*	
1986/84 Convenor of Judges, Charles Channon *(d)*	

Acknowledgements

The IPA Value of Advertising Group:

Richard Exon (Chairman)	RKCR/Y&R
Bridget Angear	AMV BBDO
Les Binet	DDB Matrix
Jonathan Bottomley	BBH
Lucas Brown	Total Media
Ken Dixon	Newhaven
Simeon Duckworth	Mindshare
Nick Emmel	Dare
Graham Fowles	Publicis
Lorna Hawtin	TBWA\Manchester
Gavin Hilton	RAPP
Sophie Maunder-Allan	VCCP
Richard Morris	Carat
Marie Oldham	MPG Media Contacts
Charlie Snow	DLKW Lowe

The Judges

Charlie Snow
Convenor of Judges
Director of Communications Strategy
DLKW Lowe

Lorna Hawtin
Deputy Convenor of Judges
Disruption Director
TBWA\Manchester

STAGE 1: INDUSTRY SPECIALISTS

Roger Banks
Managing Director, Incite

Clare Bruce
CEO, Nunwood

Ali Bucknall
Ali Bucknall Planning and Research

Matthew Dearden
CEO, Clear Channel

Karen Fraser
Director and Head of Strategy,
Credos and The Advertising Association

John Kearon
Founder, CEO and Chief Juicer,
BrainJuicer Group

Andrew Melsom
Managing Director and Founder,
Agency Insight

Doug McConchie
Head of Consulting,
Bellis-Jones Hill

Roger McKerr
Founding Partner, Davies+McKerr

Ruth Saunders
Managing Partner, Galleon Blue

Kate Waters
Strategy Partner, Now

Laurie Young
Consultant

STAGE 2: CLIENT JURY

Lord Black of Brentwood
Chairman of Judges
Executive Director, Telegraph Media Group

Andy Bolden
European Media Director,
GlaxoSmithKline

Elizabeth Fagan
Executive Marketing Director, Boots UK

Duncan MacCallum
Founder, MacC Comms

Betty McBride
Director of Policy and Communications,
British Heart Foundation

Torsten Schuppe
Marketing Director UK and Ireland, Google

Russ Shaw
Former Vice President and
General Manager for Mobile, Skype

Robert Tansey
Group Brand Marketing Director,
BSkyB

Simon Tilden
Global Category Director of Advertising,
Diageo

Catherine Woolfe
Head of Marketing Communications,
E.ON

Introduction

By Charlie Snow
Director of Communications Strategy, DLKW Lowe
Convenor of Judges 2011

For anyone more used to tweet-sized chunks, I'll kick off with the 140 character introduction:

> *This book cld easily be called '**Advertising**(social media,sponsorship,website, app,email,and remarkable experiential)Works 20' #ipavarietyshow*

For anyone with a slightly longer attention span, here's the fuller version.

It's a pretty extraordinary and dynamic marketplace we're all operating in at the moment. On the one hand, huge opportunities are opening up before us, with an amazing array of channels in which to employ communications spend, and yet on the other hand, that very spend continues to be squeezed from all sides, seemingly closing down the opportunities.

The 2011 papers in this publication reflect these modern times perfectly, and the tension between increased choice and restricted money. What you will find here are some truly inventive ways of using small communication budgets, ways that have all proven to be effective.

One of the hopes in setting up the restricted budget Awards in the odd numbered years was that they would encourage entries with less conventional communications approaches. And 2011 has certainly delivered in this area.

Amongst many gems, you have the story of an iPhone app for a charity for the homeless with a total spend of just £6,000 (the smallest ever entered into the Awards); you have a social media campaign for the country of Iceland where within a day, over a quarter of the whole Icelandic population had participated; you have the story of Ovaltine who with TV sponsorship sought to change the market in which it was operating; you have Marie Curie Cancer Care who made the bold decision to use advertising to ask people to collect money rather than give money; and you have a truly remarkable piece of experiential activity in the jungles of Colombia that moved and inspired both sets of hard-nosed judges. So much so, that it is the deserved winner of the Grand Prix. And whilst the last restricted Awards in 2009 saw a media agency win the top prize for the first time, 2011 sees the first non-UK company – Lowe-SSP3 – take the honours, which is a tremendous achievement.

Lowe-SSP3's paper is an extraordinary story of communications being used as a *"powerful yet fundamentally peaceful weapon of war"*. I won't spoil it for you. But to give you a flavour, I remember one of the client judges on the day saying that he now uses this case study if he's ever in a situation where one of his team has come to him with a *"very brave"* communications idea, to which he is now able to reply *"you call that brave, I'll show you brave..."*

But it's not just about these selected papers. There's the extraordinary experiential events in the town of Sandwich to savour from Walkers, the real-time comments from first direct customers on digital posters, a website redesign, an email campaign, clever sponsorship ideas, a radio campaign and of course the continued effective use of television...indeed, throughout this book you will find inventive communications ideas that have been proven to work. In many ways, this could be described as a breakthrough year for the Awards, with such variety on show.

In recent years there has been much Plannery debate in the committees about the very name of the fine organisation that is the Institute of Practitioners in Advertising – with its highly respected Effectiveness Awards: *"surely it should be the Communications Awards?" "Shouldn't the name be changed from the Institute of Practitioners in Advertising to the Institute of Practitioners in Communications?"*

People can get very antsy about all this. It's all academic. It doesn't matter, it's all advertising, it's all trying to sell stuff or change people's behaviour. It's just that the advertising palette has got broader, and hence the definition of advertising has got broader too.

All good institutes provide great learning for its members, and there's certainly much here for today's practitioners to take away and use. The extra chapters in this book pick up on some of the key themes that emerge from the collective entry.

In his chapter, Jim Marshall explores the issue of budget setting within a multi-media, multi-channel and multi-tasking world. He discusses the challenges that this world poses on tight budgets, looking at how to go about selecting multi-media and how to carve up what is invariably a limited budget. Jim also explores the question as to whether it's still effective to concentrate resources on one single medium or channel – and you will see that some of the successful papers prove this to be true.

Byron Sharp and Kate Waters discuss the two key roles for marketing: building the mental and physical availability of brands. Some of the 2011 papers have demonstrated how communications have indirectly driven physical availability by establishing and maintaining distribution (e.g. Jungle Formula). But what is more interesting are the campaigns that have been designed deliberately to have a more direct role in driving distribution, for instance Marie Curie, where the role for communications built an increased network of collectors, and Walkers from the private sector who grew the quality of distribution by encouraging the retailers to stock crisps next to sandwiches. The authors ask whether these times specifically lead strategists to develop campaigns designed specifically to take on both objectives.

Lorna Hawtin tackles how to measure the effectiveness of experiential activity, which has clearly become more central to communications campaigns, in a large part due to the rise of social media. Using learning from the best papers, Lorna offers invaluable advice for how to approach the tricky task of measuring experiential activity, particularly encouraging people to bear in mind all the audiences: participants, spectators and recipients alike.

Linked to Lorna's chapter, Roger McKerr explores how organisations harness people power to achieve their objectives, by engaging and allying with their audiences (or particular elements within their audience) rather than simply seeing them as recipients and end users of communications. Roger notes that several of the most successful participation-led entries use consumer participation as a platform for reaching out to less engaged consumers or non users. Adopting a people-led brand voice provides the authenticity and credibility for organisations to reach out on a much broader basis to engage prospects and to build market share.

Laurie Young, someone with decades of client-side experience, sees this year's Awards as evidence that marketers are getting their minds around the best use of social media. He points out that many are building these fast changing tools into campaigns alongside other media to engage with audiences and brand loyalists; but they are developing new organisational capabilities to do so.

To finish we have Ruth Saunders, one of the sharpest judges on the industry jury with her McKinsey attuned perspective and experience, who offers sound advice on how to demonstrate effectiveness in today's world. She offers an insider's view of the judging experience and shows some of the pitfalls that many authors fall into. Looking at where some papers fell down in the judging process, Ruth advises on how to measure business performance, set the right benchmarks, discount other variables and forge as strong a link between communications and business results as possible.

In conclusion, I would like to offer a personal thanks to all the judges that took part. The discussions were passionate and of a very high quality befitting these highly respected Awards. Above all, thank you to everyone who entered this year – the winners have certainly added to the bank of learning.

Whilst 2011 has been a step-change in many ways, with many new communications solutions being measured, it's still just the start of an exciting new era. In terms of measurement, there is so much more that can be achieved and improved on, especially in the digital space. And that's what makes these Awards so challenging and exciting. The IPA looks forward to many more papers that push the boundaries, further inspiring and helping advertising practitioners in the years to come.

SECTION 1

Prize winners

SPECIAL PRIZES

BEST INTERNATIONAL
Program of Humanitarian Attention to the Demobilised

BEST SOCIAL VALUE
Program of Humanitarian Attention to the Demobilised

BEST SOCIAL BY DESIGN
first direct

BEST NEWCOMER
Marie Curie Cancer Care

BEST CHANNEL PLANNING
Aquafresh Kids

BEST NEW LEARNING
Marie Curie Cancer Care

BEST DEDICATION TO EFFECTIVENESS
first direct

GRAND PRIX

Lowe-SSP3 for Program of Humanitarian Attention to the Demobilised (pp. 41–56)

IF CHRISTMAS CAN COME TO THE JUNGLE, YOU CAN COME HOME.
DEMOBILIZE. AT CHRISTMAS EVERYTHING IS POSSIBLE.

Cover the tree with lights.

GOLD AWARDS

Publicis for Depaul UK (pp. 57–69)

DLKW Lowe for Marie Curie Cancer Care (pp. 71–89)

WCRS&Co/Engine for Ovaltine (pp. 91–109)

SILVER AWARDS

MediaCom and Kids Industries for Aquafresh Kids (pp. 113–135)

Mindshare for first direct (pp. 137–161)

VCCP for Jungle Formula (pp. 163–176)

Abbott Mead Vickers BBDO for Organ Donor Register (pp. 177–192)

The Brooklyn Brothers for Promote Iceland (pp. 193–221)

BRONZE AWARDS

LIDA for East Midlands Trains (pp. 225–242)

AKQA for Fiat (pp. 243–259)

Tullo Marshall Warren for Lynx (pp. 261–270)

PHD Media for McCain (pp. 271–287)

Abbott Mead Vickers BBDO for PepsiCo Walkers (pp. 289–315)

Abbott Mead Vickers BBDO for *The Economist* (pp. 317–329)

SECTION 2

New learning

Chapter 1

Media planning in the digital age

By Jim Marshall
Chief Client Officer, Aegis Media

In the last 10 years or so the way that people consume media and advertising has fundamentally changed. The internet and digital technology have changed everything, even the way that people live their lives. In the past, the challenge for the media planner was to design a media strategy and construct a media plan normally around a pre-determined creative approach, a pre-set budget and a target audience that could be found reasonably easily (and in some abundance) in a single or limited number of media channels. Today, not only has the world of media become a far more complex environment as the media channels have expanded, fragmented and merged, but also the definition of a media channel has expanded to such a degree that the industry has created a number of new categories: it now talks about the media in terms of 'bought, owned and earned media'.

Consequently, the media planner must identify which of these channels, and in what combination, will deliver the most effective communication. This in turn has redefined the entire process of budget setting, channel selection and even the role of creative to the point where there is a strong argument that advertising doesn't necessarily have to start with an ad – it could be a web site, an event or even just a dialogue with consumers on social media sites such as Facebook, Twitter, etc.

Of course the 'old/traditional' media are far from dead or even dying. Even though some are finding it a bit of a struggle, such as newspapers whose circulations continue to decline, the power of the 'old media' should not be underestimated – newspapers are still read by more than 50% of the UK population every week and over 80% every month. And of course many are in rude health – TV audiences continue to increase and, in spite of the doom merchants who predict a move to time-shift viewing and a high incidence of 'ad avoidance', many millions continue to watch live TV every day and the commercials that appear in those programmes (and indeed commercials that appear in recorded programmes). Additionally, digital technology is creating new distribution opportunities for the 'old' media which is having the effect of both generating access to incremental audiences and 'blurring the lines' between the media channels – digital radio channels accessed through the TV set, newspapers on the iPad and video on demand (VOD) through the internet.

So, in a world of 'bought, owned and earned' media channels and where there appears to be a limitless array of media options, how are modern media strategies and plans constructed?

There are a number of rules (or arguably guidelines/trends) that should be applied to the process now. These fall under the following headings:

1. Multi-media/multi-channel approach

In 1759, Dr Johnson said: "Advertisements are now so numerous that they are very negligently perused." (No doubt in a hundred years time the ad industry will be laughing about the meagre number of advertising opportunities in the twenty-first century!)

However, we really do live now in a world of multi-media, multi-channel and multi-platform communications, where the consumer can dip in and out of their chosen media (and commercials they carry) based on their personal interests, choices and availability. Furthermore, many audiences are adept at multi-tasking in their media behaviour, for example they are online and texting at the same time as they are watching television or listening to the radio. So in order to reach and engage with potential consumers it is increasingly necessary to adopt a multi-media approach, utilising a combination of media that reflect their customers' behaviour and preferences.

Interestingly, this trend is confirmed by IPA Effectiveness Awards winners over the last 20 years. In 1990 the winners were on average using just two media channels, in 2000 it increased to slightly over four, but in 2010 it had increased to over nine. Recent winners in this year's Awards, such as Walkers, first direct and Aquafresh have demonstrated a highly effective multi-media approach.

However, it should be noted that there continue to be successful campaigns using a single or dominant medium. *The Economist* outdoor campaign is a good example of this, but *The Economist* has a strong history and legacy in the medium, it also used an interactive texting devise offering free trial and, of course, it benefits from exposure on the newsstands. So while they will continue, single medium executions will undoubtedly prove to be exceptions in the future.

2. Integration

Clearly, in the modern world of joined up media channels, integration is key. But what does it really mean and require in terms of media planning?

Nowadays, consumers expect their favourite media, whether feature films, TV or radio programmes, newspaper or magazine articles, etc, to provide additional information, activities and interactivity. So their experience doesn't begin and end with just the programme or article. They want to know more, they want to comment on or discuss it, and often they want to do or buy something associated with it. The modern digital media world is designed to deliver this to consumers, whether it's providing catch-up TV, YouTube, a mobile application or additional information online: whether texting, blogging, Twittering, joining an online forum or Facebooking; and whether it's a coupon, direct mail, telephone number or a purchase online.

Consumers regard brands and their advertising in exactly the same way – if they like them, they want more information about them, they want to talk about them and (ideally) they want to buy them. Effective communications leverage all these opportunities, and most successfully in combination, i.e. the combination of 'bought, owned and earned' media.

3. The increased importance of the consumer

Digital technology and the internet specifically have resulted in a subtle but increasingly significant shift of emphasis in media planning, from structuring a plan around a selected medium or media, and then maximising the delivery against a core target audience, to much more precision in defining the target and where that audience can be most effectively reached across the various media and within segments of the individual media.

Targeting of course has always been a fundamental requirement and skill in the process of media planning, but today it has taken on greater precedence for a number of reasons.

First, as the media have expanded and fragmented, it has become increasingly possible to buy into media that deliver (albeit smaller overall audiences) but audiences which are often of a very specific profile and/or consumer type. Consequently, it is possible to 'hone' the targeting and plan/buy media that deliver a higher content of the advertiser's key consumers.

Second, the internet and the web, through interactivity, audience profiling, data analysis and tagging, offer potentially very precise targeting opportunities. It is now possible to go far beyond age, sex and socio-economic targeting to the extent that pre-determined consumers can be set as the target audience (e.g. credit card purchasers, buyers of 'C class' cars, etc) and further 'behavioural targeting' can be applied, where purchasing history will indicate a future propensity to buy.

Third, research data is becoming both more sophisticated and much more 'consumer centric'. Historically, and still today, industry media research focuses entirely and exclusively on the individual media – BARB for TV, NRS for print, RAJAR for radio, etc. This is beginning to change with the research bodies needing to incorporate 'digital consumption' of their various media, with BARB needing to cover not just the incremental digital TV channels but also video on demand and eventually viewing online, the NRS covering both offline and online readership. However, more importantly, the recent development of the IPA's TouchPoints research, has potentially revolutionised the opportunity to plan across all media with a far more consumer-based approach. Not only does TouchPoints fuse all the standard media research, facilitating multi-media planning with consolidated cross media audience data, and coverage and frequency estimates, but it also provides insights into people's purchasing and shopping behaviour along with and linked in to their overall media consumption.

So we really have moved from an era of 'mass media' and a somewhat amorphous approach to targeting to a time when it is both desirable and possible to be far more precise and selective in setting and delivering communication targets.

4. New value definition

Value has always been at the heart of what any smart media practitioner does, whether a media strategist, account manager, planner or buyer. The new digital age has already brought significant benefits with advertising prices generally declining over the last 10 years or so, with the rapid increase in commercial media channels. But we are also seeing a re-evaluation of how media value is defined and quantified. Of course the old/standard definitions still very much apply and, quite correctly, are rigorously pursued in the media planning process.

However, 'old value' is being supplemented by additional value measures. So the value of a TV campaign will still be judged and analysed on a CPT (cost per thousand) basis and in terms of the comparative cost versus other media, but it will also be evaluated in terms of its ability and efficiency in generating search enquiries, YouTube uploads, Twitter comments, etc. While, in turn, the many internet providers are dismissing the 'traditional' measures of value and claiming that they are irrelevant when they are actually delivering measurable visits, enquiries and even sales. And of course there is the challenge of putting a value on Facebook fans, Twitter followers and advocates of a brand or product wherever they may choose to express themselves.

In spite of the difficulties in developing new value models, this is now a fundamental part of the media strategy and planning process, as the latest set of IPA Effectiveness Award winners have demonstrated.

Summary

I have to confess that the themes I have expressed here (and some of the specific words) have been 'lifted' from a book that Hamish Pringle and I have recently co-authored on UK media. (Incidentally, its title is *Spending Advertising Money in the Digital Age: The Media Flow*, it is published in early December 2011 and available at a very reasonable price from Amazon and better book shops.) Anyway, having got the ad out of the way and also having rightly credited Hamish, I should say that the main themes of the book are: digital has and continues to change the whole world of media and advertising, and where previously the media were structured and utilised in a linear and generally 'siloed' fashion, they are now merging and overlapping, creating a 'media flow'. This means that the old world of boundaries between media is fast disappearing and, most importantly, people's media behaviour is also changing as they are able to dip in and dip out of their chosen media on an increasingly discretionary basis. Though the new 'digital world' is still developing and evolving (the anticipated growth of connected TVs next year will further accelerate this), many of the previous media planning approaches and processes will start to become obsolete.

As with any changing environment, developing new approaches requires an appetite for innovation and experimentation. It also requires trial and error – albeit thoughtful and research/data-based trial and error – because the media world is still very much in transition. In these circumstances it needs 'pioneers' who will develop and find new media planning solutions (either doing the same thing differently or doing different things), which is very much the same way as advertisers learnt to use commercial TV effectively in the second half of the twentieth century.

This is exactly what the best IPA Effectiveness Awards papers demonstrate, whether in their use of the more traditional media channels i.e. TV, newspapers, outdoor, etc and/or in their use of the newer channels and platforms i.e. social media, mobile, e-commerce, etc.

Chapter 2

Growing by growing distribution

By Kate Waters
Strategy Partner, Now

Byron Sharp
Professor of Marketing Science
Director, Ehrenberg-Bass Institute

How does advertising work?

The purpose of brand advertising is to affect the buying behaviour of consumers. Don't let anyone tell you otherwise. The billions of dollars spent on brand advertising are spent to protect and build sales; logically, this can only happen by affecting buying behaviour and by increasing or restoring the probability that a consumer will choose your brand on any given purchase occasion.

Yet advertising is a weak force in the sense that it doesn't have the ability to change our opinions the way that recommendations from family and friends (and even authority figures) can. People tend not to pay advertising anywhere near as much attention as marketers would like, and when they do engage with it, consumers aren't push-overs – they largely discount persuasive claims (they know advertising is a biased message trying to sell them something). Ask yourself, of the probably hundreds of advertisements that you were exposed to yesterday, how many did you pay close attention to, and how many changed your mind about a brand? From a persuasion perspective the vast majority of advertising looks completely ineffectual.

So how does advertising work then? The answer is that it largely works without forcing people to consider and change their opinions. And this is why much advertising can get away with being very 'soft sell' with few or no claims of product superiority (or just standard or vague claims that the brand is merely good – e.g. *"a bank you can trust"*, *"our restaurant features fine wines"*).

People have a tendency to see advertising for brands that they already use, and are less likely to notice advertising for brands that they do not use. It's very common for people to report, with some surprise, that after buying a car they notice lots of advertising for the brand they bought that they did not see previously. This is because we have a tendency to pay more attention to things we like, and we have more developed memory structures for brands we use so it takes less mental effort to process advertising for brands we buy. Consequently users of a brand are two to three times more likely to recall its advertising than non-users of the brand (Sharp *et al.*, 2001).[1] This means that advertising is particularly good at refreshing existing memories; it can do this rather quickly and without us giving the advertising much dedicated attention or deep mental processing. So advertising has a natural advantage in encouraging existing loyalties – encouraging people to continue doing what they already do.

The weak force of advertising helps maintain our loyalties, helping to prevent us forgetting about brands that we occasionally buy. And it helps us learn about new features and new brands. The gentle nudges of advertising are an important part of a competitive marketplace. Advertising works for marketers because it is a cost-effective way of communicating with many buyers.

Mental and physical availability helps brands grow

Brands grow when they gain mental and physical availability – when they become easier for more people to buy them at more times and in more places.[2] So more people buy brands more often when it becomes easier for them to do so. Very often they are totally oblivious of this effect; that's why people say advertising doesn't affect them. And we must remember that the changing behaviours for most individuals are often trivial (even if together they mean millions of pounds of revenue) – large shifts in market share are often due to most buyers moving from buying once a year to twice, a change which they scarcely notice. The effect on their mental availability has been small and largely non-conscious, and their change in actual repeat-buying also rather small.

Advertising's primary role is to support and build *mental* availability, but it also supports and can even help build physical availability. Search advertising, it can even be argued, directly provides physical availability.

Physical availability is tremendously important because people generally hold repertoires of brands they buy, not one special brand. Or, put another way, they are loyal to (some of) the brands that are in front of them. But mental and physical availability work together – people bring their brains into the store. They don't see an awful lot of what is available to them. What they do see depends on mental availability. So brands need both.

Brands without extensive physical availability face the disadvantage that much of their advertising effort will be wasted because it will reach consumers who have very little opportunity to buy. Also the advertising will lack impact because it will not be reinforced by people seeing the brand in stores.

Building mental availability

Being noticed in a store, recognised on shelf or on screen, or recalled as an option to buy depends on our ability to retrieve memories relevant to the brand in that context.[3] Therefore, a key advertising task is to reinforce and deepen the associations that are already there, and occasionally build new associations, that will increase the propensity of the brand to be thought of in relevant buying situations. Doing so increases the brand's *mental availability* – that is its propensity to be noticed and/or thought of in buying situations.[4]

Most advertising works in this way, creating or reinforcing distinctive assets that consumers learn to associate with the brand. In turn, these assets help consumers to see the brand's packaging or store front – so long as they are reinforced and their memories kept fresh by advertising. Direct Line's red phone, the meerkat for Compare the Market and 'a glass and a half' for Cadbury Dairy Milk are all examples of assets that advertising has created or reinforced to build mental availability.

Using advertising to grow physical availability

Using advertising to support physical availability or distribution is not unusual. Many FMCG brands, particularly small ones, use their consumer campaigns to justify their existing listings in retail, or help make the case for broader reach. However, in most cases, the distribution objective is secondary, and little effort is made to evaluate the contribution of the advertising in meeting it, less still on quantifying the impact. (A notable exception from the IPA Databank is Peperami, where 23% growth was attributed to the increase in distribution that resulted from the success of the advertising among consumers).

Four of this year's entries have a story to tell about physical availability in addition to the impact of advertising on consumer demand or mental availability: Jungle Formula, Rubicon, Walkers and Marie Curie Cancer Care.

Jungle Formula provides evidence of how advertising can increase distribution through an *indirect* mechanism: the success of the consumer campaign and the timing of it in early summer motivated retailers to stock up the brand, resulting in an increase from 59 distribution points to 73. Unfortunately, there is no analysis of the impact that this distribution increase is likely to have on future sales, but it will undoubtedly be significant.

A new development in the 2011 entries is the use of advertising to exert a *direct* influence on physical availability, by making distribution gains an explicit role for communication.

The Rubicon paper identifies the trade as a key audience for communication, recognising that even if the communication cut through to a consumer audience, the brand could only grow by having an equally significant impact on the trade. The 20:20 cricket campaign was unusual in having a high degree of integration between the trade and consumer activity, and as a result it not only engaged the trade emotionally, making the brand relevant and meaningful to them, it also led distribution gains of 22% for the brand. In one case, where the retailer built a mini 'Stade de Rubicon' as part of the trade campaign, sales increased by an impressive 76%.

Perhaps the best example from this year's entries of using communication to increase physical availability is the Marie Curie case. Here, the commercial task was to increase the amount of money raised during the Great Daffodil Appeal. The conventional strategy was to use advertising to prompt people to give money. However, the 2010 campaign took the brave step of recruiting collectors, rather than donors. In doing so, the charity was able to increase the physical availability of the brand, making it easier for more of the general public to donate. The results provide compelling evidence of the power of advertising that works in this way: 5,219 additional collectors were recruited, a year-on-year increase of 47% that matched the effect seen when the charity was chosen as Tesco's charity of the year in 2008, and over £630,000 of incremental income was generated.

So should we all immediately redefine the focus of our advertising from building mental availability to physical availability? Arguably, small brands like Jungle Formula and Rubicon, or charities such as Marie Curie Cancer Care, are special cases. With small brands which don't invest in advertising very often, a campaign acts as good justification for increasing distribution. With charities, the use of volunteers means physical availability is not limited to physical locations, so it is perhaps easier to manipulate distribution. So are there opportunities for bigger commercial brands to use advertising to improve physical availability?

The Walkers case provides the evidence. However, rather than seeking to increase the breadth or reach of distribution, Walkers focused on the quality or depth of its distribution. The Sandwich campaign sought to increase sales of crisps with sandwiches and was explicitly designed to increase both mental and physical salience. 10,000 new 'meal deals' were created in stores, bringing sandwiches and crisps closer together and therefore making the combination easier to buy for consumers.

Why now?

The cases described above are fascinating in and of themselves. But even more interesting is *why* this trend for using advertising to influence physical availability has emerged in this year's entries.

An obvious hypothesis is that the challenge of a small budget forces agencies and clients to be more creative in how to use it. So, if you haven't got sufficient budget to grow market share through your share of voice,[5] a good alternative is to use the advertising budget in a more focused way to reach a small number of people or organisations who can in turn influence hundreds or thousands more – analogous to the targeting of 'influencers' online or 'early adopter' segments beloved of tech brands.

Alternatively, one could argue that the recent economic climate is in part responsible for fuelling this trend. And perhaps this is because a dual strategy, where advertising is used to grow mental *and* physical availability, is simply a more efficient use of funds. When times are good and markets are buoyant, advertising works hard enough if it just grows mental availability. But when times are harder, and all forms of marketing investment are challenged, including budget for things like new product development which would typically be used to justify additional listings, using whatever funds are available to perform this dual role is the most efficient strategy for growth.

What can we learn from this?

What these papers show is that advertising can work in a number of different ways to influence physical availability – both indirectly by using consumer campaigns to help persuade retail/the trade to increase distribution, but also in some cases to target potential distributors directly. More importantly, the evidence for how brands grow suggests that this could be a very effective communications strategy.[6]

Moreover, a strategy that seeks to increase physical availability as well as mental availability promises not only effectiveness but efficiency too – a two birds with one stone strategy. And for the smart planner, therefore, two ways to demonstrate advertising accountability in these increasingly pressured financial times.

Notes

1 Sharp, B., Beal, V. and Romaniuk, J. (2001) First steps towards a marketing empirical generalisation: brand usage and subsequent advertising recall. Proceeedings of the Australia & New Zealand Academy of Marketing conference 2001. Albany, New Zealand: Massey University.
2 Sharp, B. (2010) *How Brands Grow*. Oxford: Oxford University Press.
3 This memory retrieval is a function of the strength of the brain's associative network, which is determined by: the uniqueness of the memory node relative to other nodes (Meyers-Levy, 1989); the number of pathways between two nodes (Unnava and Burnkrant, 1991); and repeated use (Anderson, 1983, Martindale, 1991). (Meyers-Levy, J. (1989) The influence of a brand name's association set size and word frequency on brand memory. *Journal of Consumer Research*, **16**, pp. 197–207. Unnava, H.R. and Burnkrant, R.E. (1991) Effects of repeating varied ad executions on brand name memory. *Journal of Marketing Research*, **28**, pp. 406–416. Anderson, J.R. (1983) A spreading activation theory of memory. *Journal of Verbal Learning and Verbal Behavior*, **22**, pp. 261–295. Martindale, C. (1991) *Cognitive Psychology: A Neural-Network Approach*. Pacific Grove, CA: Brooks Cole.)
4 Romaniuk, J. and Sharp, B. (2004) Conceptualizing and measuring brand salience. *Marketing Theory*, **4**, pp. 327–342.
5 The excess share of voice 'rule' is described in Binet, L. and Field, P. (2007) *Marketing in the Era of Accountability*. London: IPA/Warc.
6 Future papers exploring how advertising builds distribution could add significant value to the IPA Databank by attempting to quantify the impact of distribution gain on current and future sales, since this is something that few papers have attempted to date.

Chapter 3

"Tell them and they'll forget; show them and they may remember; involve them and they'll understand"

By Lorna Hawtin
Disruption Director, TBWA\Manchester

This year, many of the most powerful and interesting submissions to the Effectiveness Awards have centrally featured experiential elements. A discipline which has emerged from its largely tactical role to become a much more central part of brand strategy, is finally being celebrated amongst the IPA community for its effectiveness, it would seem. But why so late to the party?

One thing is clear; the sudden appearance of experiential on the IPA Effectiveness Awards' horizon is a reflection of a growing curiosity towards these types of activities amongst a broader range of agency types and clients. The vast majority of this latest crop of cases, whether it's the mobilisation of advocates on behalf of Iceland or Marmite, or the 'celebrity event' of the Walkers' Sandwich campaign, or even the FARC Christmas tree installations, have been submitted by agencies who would probably not count themselves as experiential specialists.

Experiential emerging as a strategic driver

Let's face it, from the minute you pick up a product or utilise a service, you are experiencing it. And there's nothing more memorable, nor authentic, than experiencing a brand in all its rich sensory detail; even in its simplest forms, the deli counter chunk of cheese or the humble test drive. So in some senses, brand behaviour has always been experiential.

Furthermore, it creates a lasting sensory, informational and somatic imprint in the minds of customers, which is hard to replicate. This is what enables it to reach out to elusive customer groups; more readily transferring messages and values which are difficult to convey or less powerful via other means. For example, the best bricks and mortar retailers, such as Hollister, have recognised the unforgettable viral power of an immersive experience; an experience their online competitors will find difficult to match.

This is perhaps why experiential and its resulting content is challenging the 'advertising' idea as the new beating heart of brand-behaviour strategy. A point illustrated by campaigns such as the Homebase 'makeover' and T-Mobile campaign, which both overtly leverage this relationship.

In a world where people strive to enrich both themselves and their existence, a branded experience can readily deliver for the consumer too. Exclusive access to a branded 'happening' offers the consumer life-enhancing content and social currency that they can play out into their networks and across their own personal 'media'. For instance, it only took a few weeks for over half the Icelandic population to become personally involved in the campaign, demonstrating how experiential content can ricochet via social media networks.

And it is arguably this ever-increasing appetite for *content* and the widespread adoption of social sharing mechanisms, which has shown clients and agencies that experiential happenings can generate significant ripple effects that echo well beyond the immediate participant and the immediate time frame. Experiential is increasingly a *mass-reach* mechanism (albeit, for some, a seemingly costly one). A fact which is drawing attention to the 'medium' and forcing agencies and clients of all shapes and sizes to think very seriously about what experiential might really do for their business, beyond brand building amongst a niche audience or driving immediate sales via sampling.

So what can we observe about the measurement of experiential from the cases prepared for this year's Awards? And what obstacles still remain in the quest to understand the value it can add to the bottom line? Key questions, given that experiential is still often viewed sceptically beyond the marketing department.

In a 2008 survey (2008 Marketers Survey – Jack Morton Worldwide), 70% of marketers claimed experiential was extremely/very important for their brands moving forward, but still 79% said their ability to measure and demonstrate experiential ROI represented a key barrier to successfully deploying it for their brands. A greater investment in understanding *how* it can drive profit is likely to be the key to convincing wary clients and providing meaningful forward planning insights for the industry.

As Pete Bachelor, Planning Director at Arc UK comments:

What we need to do now is make sure we have the variety of measurement tools and techniques ready to build client confidence in the effectiveness of these activities. We need more shared knowledge on the performance of experiential activity and we welcome anything that builds more science into the measurement approaches we have at our disposal.

Why so few industry benchmarks?

One of the difficulties in drawing any centralised conclusions on this theme, is that experiential has become somewhat of a 'catch all'. Encompassing everything from demos to events, to PR stunts, to ambassador and community programmes, to game playing, to sampling; the sheer breadth of activities claiming some form of experiential DNA presents a challenge to anyone hoping to draw broader insight or create wider models for the industry as a whole.

Also, as experiential has gained salience amongst the marketing community, the discipline has been adopted by a wide range of agency types. This is probably contributing to the lack of a central point of view for the medium as a whole. The IPA has already spotted this issue and is addressing the challenge by creating an industry-wide dialogue regarding the discipline.

This fragmented identity is reflected in the breadth of experiential activities evidenced in this year's Awards papers, the varied nature of the objectives, and the various means by which they have been measured.

■ On the one hand, we see experiential uniting a population and rewarding their participation in the Iceland case.
■ The Colombian FARC campaign used experiential installations to interrupt guerrillas whilst manoeuvring in the forests of Colombia to encourage them to demobilise.
■ Walkers used experiential to create rich content, social currency and to establish a clear occasion for Walkers crisps – the lunchtime sandwich.

Each of these campaigns relies to a greater or lesser extent on experiential activity, but requires a totally different evaluation method in line with its role in campaign activities and the specific behaviours they sought to influence. As with any type of activity, clarity of objectives seems to be the obvious prerequisite for effective measurement.

It would seem that the ephemeral nature and limited relative investment of one-off or smaller-scale experiential activities will continue to make it difficult to justify further (and to some, disproportionate) investment in evaluation methods such as research, panel development, or control groups. Evaluating the impact of the FARC experiential efforts, by parachuting researchers into the jungle, however fitting, would have indeed been an extreme and costly approach to the evaluation of their campaign.

Although on-site or 'at point of experience' research appears to have played a key role in measurement historically, there is a very real concern that the data collection process itself, i.e. research, detracts from the quality of the experience, or indeed, muddies the effects it is trying to measure. What is the impact of someone interrupting your experience and asking you to rationalise what you've just experienced? Equally, the fact that you've been recruited on to a long-term panel is likely to substantially affect subsequent purchasing or advocacy behaviours around the brand.

The link between experience and long-term sales effects remains elusive

Even in cases where the intermediate effects have been measured, the holy grail remains to link intermediate shifts in brand relationship, knowledge, intimacy, and claimed purchase intent to harder measures: frequency of transaction, loyalty, active advocacy, product investigation and, ultimately, trial. This is easy when you can track immediate sales resulting from point of purchase sampling or voucher redemption codes, e.g. Tennent's can easily evaluate the amount of beer purchased at the T in the Park, but with how much confidence can they isolate subsequent purchase shifts to direct versus indirect experiential content?

Mass-reach brand activities such as advertising solve this problem by looking to market level analytics. However, linking data from the point of experience to the point of consumption becomes much harder when an event/activity has a smaller immediate reach and perhaps a more extended purchase or decision-making cycle.

Take, for example, the challenge to link the Colombian demobilisation campaign with actual demobilisations. Following the impact of the Christmas message, demobilisation itself may have happened over the course of months, even years. The case addresses this challenge by referencing verbatim claims made by demobilised soldiers regarding the power of the campaign and its role in their decision, but it is hard to make the link conclusive or to fully quantify, or predict its eventual effect. The only approach left is to draw a line and eliminate several other factors that could have explained the specified results such as: lack of changes in demobilisation efforts, underlying trends, army/police anti-guerrilla activity, changes in political stance by FARC, changes in leadership, the weather etc.

Because desired behaviours often play out in a geographically and chronologically dispersed way, only by being able to isolate a robust sample of individuals who've been exposed, will we be able to definitively understand *how* the effects unfold, and what value the experience has added in commercial terms. This will remain difficult to do definitively without the development of substantial ongoing panel studies, or via detailed and expensive econometric work. They may present a more rigorous approach to isolating effects, but these methodologies, familiar in the evaluation of other disciplines, currently seem the exception rather than the rule for experiential.

We must redefine the sphere of influence to calculate ROMI

Participants have traditionally been the focus of experiential evaluation, i.e. those people who have had a direct, one-to-one exchange with the activity. Typically measured onsite, studies analyse the number of exchanges and their quality, i.e. profile of participants, length of exchange, emotional/informational take-outs, word-of-mouth intentions, net promoter scores, brand beliefs etc. All this helps to build some understanding of the perceptual impact of the activity. But this type of immediate and targeted measurement will omit key contributors to ROMI and may have led to a serious underestimation of the commercial value of such activities.

In addition to participants, there is very often a large number of additional first-hand *spectators* who tend to be overlooked in measurement terms. Spectators are those that are not interacting personally with an experiential activity, but who may witness or be in the vicinity. Some suggest 70% of those exposed fall into this category and researchers are now employing analysis of conscious and sub-conscious take-outs to help understand this very effect. What is the relative quality of a spectator's experience and its impact on their behaviours, and thus the bottom line and how can this be included in ROMI models?

But latterly, there is even more potential beyond the spectator and the participant which ought to be factored in. In a world where social media facilitates the ripple effect, what of the *recipient* audience, i.e. those who experience the event via word-of-mouth rather than in person, or via the subsequent marketing outreach of the brand? If their second-hand exposure to the experiential activity leads them to shift behaviour in favour of a brand, those sales need to be recognised and accounted for in evaluation and return on investment terms.

Research by the Word of Mouth Marketing Association suggests that participants go on to pass on their experience to between four and 10 people and spectators to between one and three people. It seems there may be some sense in assigning a first, second, third and subsequent generational value to people touched by an experience, but we are little closer to being definitive as to what that might be. This all supports the view that experiential return on investment might indeed be much greater if we can identify and measure the behaviours of *all* of the individuals who ultimately become influenced by an activity.

And this is something we've seen emerging in this year's papers. The Iceland Tourism campaign describes the mobilisation of the home nation to create a 'recipient level' effect amongst potential *foreign* tourists. Similarly with the Walkers example, a single event was designed in a way that it could be amplified as content way beyond the boundaries of the town and the immediate timeframe of the activity, to influence the marketplace as a whole. The reach of the activity was clearly substantial enough to undertake a macro-level analysis of ROMI from a data point of view.

Furthermore, the focus of supporting mediums was to amplify the reach of experiential content, thus placing experiential at the heart of these campaigns. Where the boundary between experiential and amplification is blurred in this way, it seems entirely valid to evaluate ROI at a campaign level, rather than by discipline.

Walkers Sandwich campaign demonstrates this perfectly. Their analysis leads with the response amongst townspeople of Sandwich and journalists, and then goes on to show social media take-up of the idea. Ultimately they then look at shifts in the percentage of all out-of-home sandwiches eaten at lunch with a packet of Walkers, and econometric analysis as evidence of the strategy coming to fruition. It would not make sense in this case to divorce the cost for the event itself from the costs of amplification, making their macro approach to ROMI analysis credible.

So if this year's cases are anything to go by, we should expect to see experiential emerging as a strategic fulcrum and content driver for brands, putting human experience back at the heart of brand behaviour. But the challenge remains to justify that role and lend credibility to the recommendations of the future. And this will only happen if we commit to evaluation, working together with our clients to isolate and learn from our experiential activities as an industry. Only then will we have the evidence with which to convince clients, after all, "Tell them and they'll forget; show them and they may remember; involve them and they'll understand."[1]

Notes

1 Chinese proverb.

Chapter 4

Harnessing 'people power'

Can participation-led approaches impact beyond a brand's current fanbase?

By Roger McKerr
Founding Partner, Davies+McKerr

Participation has been a buzz-word for a long time in the world of marketing and brand communications. It seems as though clients and agencies have been constantly experimenting with participative brand communication approaches since the arrival of the internet on the mainstream consumer scene some 15 years ago.

And over the past couple of years the extent of usage and experimentation has gathered pace as participative, interactive channels of communication have exploded and become so much more capable and user-friendly, whilst 'traditional' media such as TV and print are increasingly consumed 'on demand' or in other user-driven formats across an array of digital devices.

In fact, it's possible to feel that we're going through a 'tipping point' that is seeing a decisive shift from the dominance of interruptive, self-contained communications towards the emergence of participative, interactive relationships as the dominant force in the brand communication landscape.

So shouldn't we all be jumping on board the participation train?

To some extent, the jury has remained 'out' on the commercial marketing effectiveness of participation-focused campaigns. The IPA's recent study of the effectiveness of different marketing communication models, *Datamine.03: New Models of Marketing Effectiveness*,[1] analysed 256 case studies entered into the Effectiveness Awards over the past seven years. It aimed to analyse how communication channels were used in different ways, and to assess and understand the effectiveness of different approaches that were emerging.

Their findings identified four different models of brand communication:

1. Campaigns showing **No Integration** (utilising a single channel or utilising multiple channels but with no integration evident between them).
2. Campaigns showing **Advertising-led Integration** (utilising multiple channels and organising the communication around an advertising-led concept at *"a visual, promotional, icon or idea based level"*).
3. Campaigns showing **Brand Idea-led Orchestration** (utilising multiple channels and organising the communication around an underlying brand concept, benefit or need state platform, enabling them to vary creative execution over time and across media whilst retaining consistency at a thematic level).
4. Campaigns showing **Participation-led Orchestration** (utilising multiple interactive channels with the aim of integrating the brand communication into people's lives, creating a common dialogue, co-creation or conversation).

The findings contained in the study are much too rich and extensive to summarise here. However, a few key conclusions emerged which are notable as we consider the participation-led entries in the 2011 Awards.

First, that campaigns organised at a 'Brand Idea' level emerged as the most effective case histories overall, highlighting the continued importance of anchoring communications in a meaningful and enduring brand concept, even if the creative expression of that concept varies considerably. Clearly it's just as important as ever to identify the underlying brand proposition for your audience and to use that as the consistent anchor point for effective communications.

Second, that overall *"the less-participatory campaign models seem still to be the most effective on most harder sales measures"*.

In fact, the analysis showed that campaigns from the 'No Integration', 'Advertising-led Integration' and 'Brand Idea-led Orchestration' groups were all *considerably* more effective in terms of hard business results than 'Participation-led' campaigns (see Figure 1).

Even allowing for the fact that there were fewer participation-led awards entries to analyse over the seven-year period (meaning the findings for this model may be slightly less robust), and that the effects of participation-led campaigns might have been more difficult to measure, the notion of the 'new kid on the block' lagging so far behind the tried and trusted models of brand communication in terms of discernible commercial effect is, at the very least, thought-provoking.

Third, the effectiveness results that could be claimed by participation-led awards entries were largely related to market share defence. Participation appeared to work best as a means of engaging existing loyalists, shoring up or enriching their relationship with the brand. But it seemed to struggle as a model when it was applied in pursuit of other goals, for example gaining share, acquiring new customers, or profit gain.

To some extent the findings of the *New Models of Marketing Effectiveness* study also back up a growing sense of scepticism amongst the marketing and planning

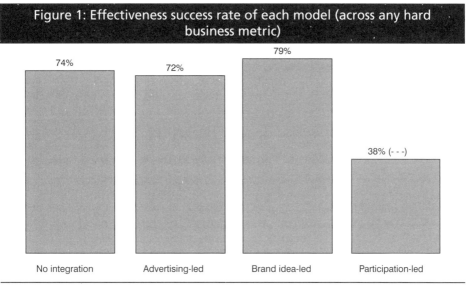

Figure 1: Effectiveness success rate of each model (across any hard business metric)

74% No integration
72% Advertising-led
79% Brand idea-led
38% (- - -) Participation-led

Source: *Datamine.03: New Models of Marketing Effectiveness*

community about the application of participation-led campaigns and the potential over-reliance on them when seeking to create broader communication impact than deepening engagement with existing 'fans'. As Tom Morton put it in a recent *Campaign* article,[2]

> *When a biscuit asks you to stage a filmed time trial, something has fallen far off the scale.*

Or as the *New Models of Marketing Effectiveness* authors identified, there's an inverse correlation between the participation demands the campaign puts on consumer attention and the campaign's ability to impact on non-user behaviour (see Figure 2).

Nevertheless, rather than get too negative about the participation-led model we need to remember that interactive media is increasingly predominant, that participation is here to stay and that the landscape for its usage and application is emergent and developing.

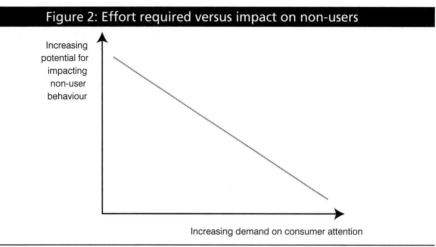

Figure 2: Effort required versus impact on non-users

Increasing potential for impacting non-user behaviour

Increasing demand on consumer attention

Source: *Datamine.03: New Models of Marketing Effectiveness*

Overall, a rough tot-up of the number of participation-led entries in this year's small-budget Awards suggests that this model continues to grow in terms of usage. In the last small-budget Awards (2009), 7% of entries were classed as participation-led by the *New Models of Marketing Effectiveness* authors, whilst in the following big-budget Awards (2010) 16% of entries followed this model. According to my rough estimate[3] 18% of this year's small budget entries were orchestrated around a participation-led idea, more than double the number in 2009.

So what do this year's participation-led awards entries tell us about the potential role that this model can play and how participation can be applied?

Perhaps most importantly it is interesting to note that several of the most successful participation-led entries have used consumer participation as a platform for reaching out to less engaged consumers or non-users. Rather than seeing participation as an end in itself, aiming to strengthen existing relationships with loyalists and fans as a means of defending share, they have sought to actively enrol engaged consumers or to leverage their existing engagement and used their participation as a communication asset to engage prospects against more expansive commercial objectives.

For example, 'Inspired by Iceland' demonstrates that a participation-led campaign can break the rules both in terms of seeking to create mass-participation, rather than exploiting the participation of a small number of influencers, and by seeking to enrol prospects on a global basis off the back of the initial participation drive.

The 'Inspired by Iceland' case shows how Iceland's tourism industry was facing meltdown with chronically negative consumer sentiment towards the country as a destination following the eruption of the Eyjafjallajökull volcano in April 2010, which served to deepen the problems already being experienced due to the credit crunch and ensuing recession from 2008.

Faced with a significant predicted decline in tourism across the key summer period, and with a strong sense of scepticism towards conventional Icelandic tourism advertising, the campaign instead sought to engage the entire Icelandic nation as advocates for Icelandic tourism.

Figure 3: Prime Minister's address via 'Inspired by Iceland' website

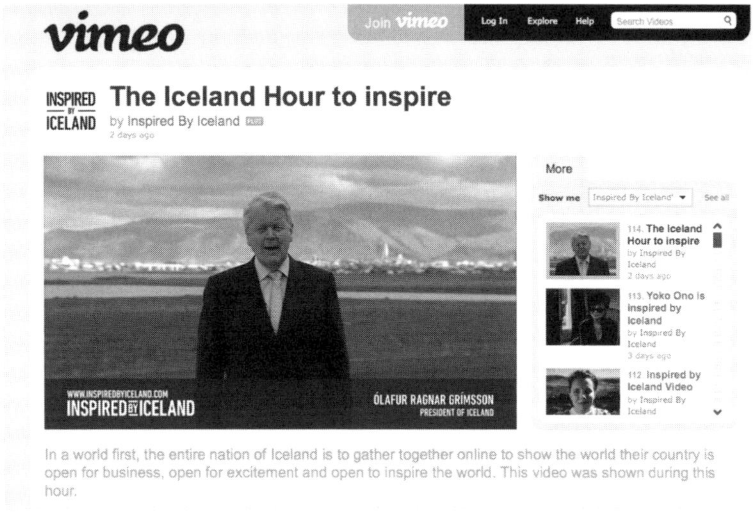

Source: Promote Iceland

The campaign connected to the Icelandic citizens' shared interest in a much needed successful tourism season by stopping the country for an hour and appealing for their participation. It also provided them with the tools to participate and reach out to prospective travellers abroad with real, live positive stories.

Figure 4: Example of social networking on 'Inspired by Iceland' website

Source: Promote Iceland

Notably, by the end of the first day, 27% of Icelanders had sent a positive video story from the 'Inspired by Iceland' site to someone they knew abroad and 1.5 million people (mostly foreign potential tourists) had downloaded a video from the site. Between June and August the live webcams on the site (showing that Iceland was not indeed covered with ash) had been viewed 60 million times.

Clearly, this was not only participation on a massive scale, but also participation that produced a broad based effect on the audience of prospective tourists. The result was that the country avoided the forecast 22% decline in visitor numbers and actually ended the season with modest growth in visitors.

The Marie Curie entry is an example of achieving participation with relatively conventional methods.

Faced with a tougher environment for charitable donations, a much smaller budget than competing cancer charities and the loss of a major donation distribution point in Tesco, which had previously nominated Marie Curie as its charity of the year, the charity determined to spend 25% of its budget asking its most engaged supporters to participate in collecting funds for the annual Great Daffodil Appeal, rather than simply donating funds. The remaining 75% of an already small budget was then spent reaching out to potential donors via advertising and PR so that the participation of the new, larger army of collectors could be effectively utilised.

Figure 5: 2010 Marie Curie poster 'Give us an hour. It will help someone in their final hours'

Source: Marie Curie Cancer Care

The results achieved by asking more engaged supporters to participate as collectors and reach out to donors, rather than devoting all investment towards encouraging donation, were impressive as Marie Curie achieved their highest-ever level of street collections and their most successful Great Daffodil Appeal ever.

The first direct entry also demonstrates how the participation of more engaged customers can be leveraged to attract and persuade the less engaged. In this case, the engaged customers were already participating in online forums, discussing their experience and assessment of first direct as a banking service.

Figure 6: Example of first direct live visualisation of feeling

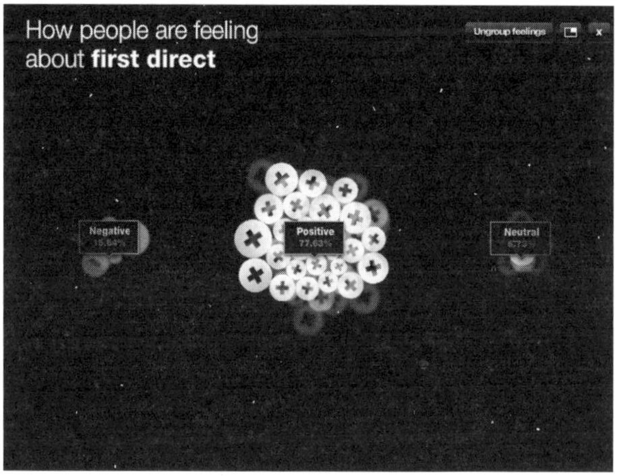

Source: first direct

Whilst the campaign encouraged and facilitated this online dialogue and expression of sentiment, first direct's stroke of brilliance was to resist the temptation to simply deepen their dialogue with these engaged and, on the whole, very positive customers, and instead to find highly innovative ways to broadcast their online conversations to a wider audience of prospects. In doing so they reached prospects with a highly credible and novel voice at a time when banks were far from popular.

There is a key learning about authenticity here from the first direct case, and indeed from 'Inspired by Iceland'. In both cases, by leveraging the participation of positively engaged advocates and customers, they were able to find a more credible, relatable and effective voice for their brand communication message. Both of these brands faced problems with direct, first-voice communications. Neither the Iceland government nor the banking sector brands were especially trusted or highly regarded at the time, and conventional advertising from either brand would probably have been dismissed with a good deal of scepticism.

Participation with positively engaged advocates and customers was a vital means of finding a more potent and effective standpoint from which to disseminate the brand message to the prospect audience. Again, this shows another way in which participation-led campaigns can deliver advantages when seeking to reach out to non-users or less engaged consumers who are likely to be more sceptical about what a brand has to say.

In summary, the landscape for participation continues to change rapidly, and whilst the ability of participation-led campaigns to strengthen and deepen ties with existing, highly engaged users is already well documented in studies such as *New Models of*

Marketing Effectiveness, there are signs that brands are increasingly finding ways of exploiting participation towards more expansive commercial ends.

So ask not only what you can do to enrich your relationship with participating consumers in pursuit of greater loyalty and market share defence, but also what you can do to leverage participating consumers as a brand communication asset in their own right, to reach out on a much broader basis to engage prospects and to build market share.

Notes

1 Kate Cox, John Crowther, Tracy Hubbard and Denise Turner (2011), *Datamine.03: New Models of Marketing Effectiveness*, London: Warc.
2 Morton, T. 'Participocalypse: why we can't be bothered to join in.' *Campaign Soap-Box*, July 2011.
3 Note the *New Models of Marketing Effectiveness* authors have not assessed this year's papers in terms of which model they would classify them as.

Chapter 5

Social by Design

Social networking comes of age

By Laurie Young
Consultant

2011 is the year that new media and social networking really came of age. The world watched as ordinary people found their voice and courage to face down guns in Tunisia, Egypt, Syria and Libya. Similarly, it was appalled by the behaviour of London rioters but moved by the crowd-prompted clean-up campaigns that soon followed in places like Croydon and Ealing. Two powerful forces, youth and technology, made these possible; and they are forcing social media into mainstream marketing.

These iconic moments are symptomatic of the fact that social networking tools have moved from geeky enthusiasts and teenagers' bedrooms into normal life. There are now vast numbers of buyers who search the web for potential products on mobile devices. Twitter has become a major phenomenon which people follow and then connect with blogs to develop conversations. Facebook has emerged as the dominant digital channel amongst many. It is used to access video, photos and conversation with communities. A good number of people are now so fused to their smartphones that they refer to them during meals and bedtime. They use them to browse the web, email (even when near their computer) and buy goods. As a result, 'apps' have become common currency, with several hundred thousand in Apple's AppStore and many now paying for them. Although most seem to be forgotten soon after downloading, people do not want to be left out of this fast developing world. And, as 85% of iPhone users are well-heeled people under 45, this is an irresistible demographic for any ambitious brand manager.

To exploit this fast-changing morass of communication mechanisms, marketers must stay up with the human dynamic underneath it. These media are fast being adopted into the lifestyle of many people on the planet creating new communities, new concepts and new attitudes to life. Yet it's too easy to make assumptions and form daft biases. For instance, although younger people reach for the web as easily as breathing, many older, retired people (with a little more time on their hands) have also assimilated this technology. They will Skype middle-aged sons and daughters (who are too busy juggling careers and young families to be as proficient with fast developing tools) and hold Facebook conversations with their grandchildren. In the USA, social network use has doubled in over-55s. And usage changes as people get to grips with it. In their annual survey the *McKinsey Quarterly* found that 50% of online consumers were advanced users of smartphones, social networking tools and internet videos. They also demonstrated that people under 24 were abandoning email, texts and phone calls for these new tools.

It is no surprise, then, that the 2011 IPA Effectiveness Awards reflect an increasing interest in the use of social media. Until now, its appearance in some campaigns has been experimental and faddy but this year's entries demonstrate hard-headed attempts to integrate these tools into mainstream programmes tackling serious problems. Lynx, for instance, were looking for engagement with their brand users when they decided to put more emphasis on social media. Apparently, the deodorant market is becoming increasingly commoditised and Lynx's large-scale campaigns gain new buyers but do not necessarily stimulate loyalty.

Their experience reflected McKinsey's findings. The initial use of email as a response mechanism was poor. So, as the target market was 16 to 24-year-old males, they decided to manage recruitment via Facebook. As with other marketers reaching for social media, they tackled new communication issues and had to build new organisational capability. For instance, they created a 'conversation calendar' and employed a full-time 'social editor' to manage Facebook interactions. They discovered that the best interaction was at the weekend and had to change working practices. Yet the Lynx campaign shows that social media is as much about volume as any other communication medium. They put the Facebook page at the centre of the overall marketing strategy, with all other media featuring it as the call to action.

Walkers (another powerful and familiar brand with hugely successful mass campaigns) incorporated social media into a campaign aimed at tackling a specific issue. The Lineker campaign is one of the longest-running celebrity programmes and is based around the thought that 'these crisps are so good they can make a nice guy nasty'. Yet, as the firm wanted a strategy for single-pack sales, they thought the campaign was not the best vehicle to deliver a very specific message. So, they developed a proposition that: *A sandwich is more exciting with Walkers.*

Through a series of surprise events, held over three days in the town of Sandwich, they set out to grab attention by combining TV with news coverage and compelling online content. They featured different celebrities fulfilling typical roles in the town (such as Frank Lampard coaching the football team, Jenson Button driving a cab and Pamela Anderson working in a pub). They wanted to capture the surprise and excitement of the locals for TV and online video content. However, the celebrities were chosen because of the size of their Twitter fan bases in order to stimulate viral communication about the event and reach a larger audience.

Viral communication was the aim of many of these campaigns because it is the phenomenon behind much of the success of social networking tools. It is the transportation of an idea from person to person and a powerful way of energising brand engagement. It was made famous through the writings of people like Malcolm Gladwell and Seth Gordon. They charted the effect of word-of-mouth in spreading new ideas, especially new products or brands, and gave focus to the different types of audiences who play important roles in spreading an idea ('connectors' and 'mavens'). This prompted some marketers to deliberately amplify chatter and to create programmes aimed specifically at significant viral audiences like Apple's 'super users'.

Marmite's submission was a great example of an intent to create and engage with brand advocates; using viral marketing through social media to launch new products. They knew that their product was both vehemently loved and hated. So, they wanted to tap into the intensity of those who loved it, to engage with an influential and highly passionate group of fans, and spread the message amongst those 'in the know'. Involvement was to be aspirational, a badge of honour for the serious Marmite consumer to wear proudly. They were involved in the new product's development as well as the campaign itself, making them feel a sense of responsibility. Yet it was designed so that they would talk avidly about it to others through social media.

The campaign involved the invention of a quirky Victorian world called 'The Marmarati'; and, again, showed a balance between new media and established methods. Recruitment involved social media outreach and Facebook but was backed by personal invitations sent via direct mail. Those who replied attended a luxurious event, with Marmite cocktails, canapés and an air of mystery. They were then invited to a private Facebook group to allow their dialogue to continue, and to enable the distribution of follow-up material. As a result of this competent blend of communications techniques, the new Marmite XO product was successfully launched and sold out within days, despite there being no significant paid media. In four months the campaign generated 150 blogs (reaching an estimated 2.4 million online readers) and over 6,000 Twitter updates. Yet it had a powerful lasting result: the creation of a community of loyal brand advocates. Marmite's own 'super users', 'mavens' who want to be involved and are available to help launch future products.

These campaigns demonstrate that, just because it is new, this form of communication need not be given overdue importance. It needs to be part of the experienced, hard-nosed communications discipline and aligned with other methods of reaching markets. Of course marketers need to be open-minded and explorative of the new but they need to keep a hard headed perspective of how their human buyers actually behave. Some pundits have, for instance, got some aspects of the social media phenomenon seriously wrong. They have argued that viral campaigns ought to be the main method of marketing in the twenty-first century and that other media aimed at mass audiences ought to be ditched. They cite the fact that broadcast TV networks are disrupted and argue that companies should focus on 'early adopters' who will spread the message to others on the web, virally. It does, though, seem over the top to throw out mass advertising, to neglect communication tools that have a 100-year track record of building brands amongst the majority in mass markets. The IPA Awards seem to reflect the more sober approach of experienced communicators, in line with evidence from the USA, that big-budget marketing companies are returning to highly targeted broadcast methods, but integrated with online, digital and new media strategies.

Yet, the phenomenon of crowd sourcing and the tendency to behave enthusiastically, as a herd, does open up some remarkable possibilities. One entry that was audacious in this ambition was 'Inspired by Iceland'. Turning to it amongst the pile of entries, most judges were expecting a routine campaign aimed at selling frozen foods. But this was something else. The planners set out to engage a whole country in solving a major problem, and they used social media to do it. When the Eyjafjallajökull volcano erupted in April 2010, it brought European air traffic to a complete standstill; a further body blow to the Icelandic economy after the traumas of the credit crunch. 'Inspired by Iceland' was specifically created to harness the tendency of people to respond as a group through social media. Rather than doing what the leisure industry normally does (advertise to potential tourists) they decided to stimulate Icelanders to share their stories with the world; to create a 'virtual social movement'. The entire nation gathered online to tell the world how much they love their country and why people should visit. There was a live TV address by the prime minister after which thousands spread positive messages across Facebook and Twitter. Friends of Iceland were filmed and their stories posted on the website. This prompted people around the world to get involved and post their own stories. By the end of the first day 1.5 million people had downloaded different videos from the website and nearly a third of the nation had sent a video to someone abroad.

The winner of the 'Social by Design' award demonstrated a masterly command of the power of social networking tools to tap into the energy of a community, especially when integrated with first-rate communications skills. There have been so many case studies and awards for first direct that a number of judges were surprised that their strategic problem was quite serious. Despite their wonderful reputation, they were losing differentiation, brand awareness was down and they were failing to significantly acquire new customers. On top of that, their industry was fast becoming loathed by the British public. They needed a communications platform that separated them from the pack and, once again, communicated the strength of their great service.

Rather than trying to talk at their intended audiences, first direct set out to use viral communications, to exploit the fact that their customers were already talking about their service. It is a precept of service marketing that people tell others about a good service experience. So the campaign strategy was to amplify their voices. The team said that, like so many others, it's changed the way they thought about social media and put it at the centre of the communications strategy.

The idea was something no other brand had ever done and something no other bank would or could dare consider: to broadcast the views and opinions of customers live. first direct live harnessed the latest data visualisation techniques, social media and participation concepts to project customers' views on its service. The programme mined and collated data from forums, blogs, comment threads and social networks. By visualising both negative and positive sentiment, the bank moved away from presenting their chosen message to the world to something very risky: an unedited reflection of the views of a customer community.

The online ads pulled data feeds from 20,000 online news sources, over eight million blogs and more than 100,000 message sources (boards, forums, Usenet news groups and the campaign's microsite). This data was then visualised and updated live to all online ad units. The online ads clicked through to a dedicated microsite. There was a live banner on their home page which reflected sentiment and invited customers to get involved. Visitors to the microsite were able to provide live comments, positive and negative, on Talking Point, showing how people were feeling about the brand.

The results were stunning. They justified the risk and made them the deserved winner of the prize. In a loathed sector, where brand awareness was stagnant, they changed the perception of their company with a relatively small share of spend. At the same time, they reversed a decline in positive media coverage and re-established a lead position in the market. Service and innovation scores all improved by one third. As a result they were able to pull away from the pack. Brand consideration amongst those taking out a new current account (or switching) doubled; and their share of these accounts substantially increased. Advertising, traditional media and social media are all converging, first direct Live is a first rate example of how these are so powerful when professionally combined to full effect.

There is no doubt that modern consumers are turning in greater and greater numbers to social networks, blogs, tweets and online video. A number of the IPA entries demonstrated that deploying social media as a sensible part of campaigns, integrated with other communications, allows marketers to tap into something very human and very powerful. Several said that 'brand engagement' was the main reason they reached for social media because of the number of touchpoints and the potential for timely dialogue about a brand. Yet this rather gentle phrase does not really capture the potential of social media to tap into the raw, almost animalistic urge of people to behave as a crowd.

'Engagement' is what Tunisians felt when a fruit seller burnt himself to death and how London residents fumed the day after their city burned, but it does not capture the depth of sentiment. Social media connects with something fundamental in human nature: the need to belong. Whether it is tattooing the Harley Davison brand on their bodies, being seen in Harvey Nicks for tea or being tempted to join in with an unruly crowd, people gleefully find ways to be part of a herd (or, just as powerfully, do not want to be left out). They have demonstrated that social media are new tools to express, explore and develop this need. As a consequence, the best marketers are learning to use this phenomenon effectively, building the organisational capability to make it part of business as usual. They are integrating social media into other elements of the marketing communications mix and finding new, effective ways to connect with audiences.

Chapter 6

Proving the effectiveness of campaigns

By Ruth Saunders
Managing Director, Galleon Blue

Introduction

As a past writer of IPA papers, I was surprised by how much, as an IPA judge, I willed each paper to be a winner in its own right. As I started to read each one I wanted it to be a good read, a compelling case, packed with fresh new insight and learning. A case that makes me proud to be in the world of brands, and one that makes the time being an IPA judge worthwhile.

This year, we focused on campaigns with less than £2.5m spend. Often, people say *"how can I prove the effectiveness of my campaign with such a low level of spend and so little money for research and econometric models?"*. As a judging team, we were blown away by the creativity of some of the papers in using evidence to prove the case, even if the spend level was less than £100k, proving beyond doubt how even campaigns with small budgets can have a lasting effect on company success.

That said, some cases could have been so much better if written well, and so we thought it would be helpful to lay out what it takes to write a great IPA paper and some of the common pitfalls that writers fall into that can be easily avoided.

Writing a great IPA paper

So the best papers have two important elements:

- a campaign with a compelling business case, i.e. one that really has driven a significant return (be it in sales and profitability, or in charity donations or, in the case of government advertising, in real behavioural change) over the short and longer-term (if possible), and at a material level;

■   a clearly written, succinct paper that proves beyond reasonable doubt that the campaign has been effective, and clearly demonstrates the reasons why the campaign was successful.

There is no point in submitting an IPA paper if there isn't a compelling business case, as the data won't be there to back it up. The best cases tend to be so strong that they can show the uplift in growth in multiple ways, for example using: basic sales and market share, charity donations or behavioural change data; quantitative research such as customer purchase funnels and brand image shifts; qualitative research using customer quotes; other anecdotal evidence such as supplier and industry expert quotes or PR.

They also demonstrate the short-term effectiveness as the campaign breaks, as well as the longer-term one due to fundamental shifts in customer behaviour.

Similarly, if the paper isn't written clearly then the judges won't find it compelling enough to give it the top mark. Obviously, as the reader, we want the paper to be a joy to read by flowing easily. If the argument is convoluted and difficult to follow then the paper is by nature weaker. The best papers start with a clear introduction, outlining what they were trying to achieve, what they did to make it happen and then showing how the campaign delivered against each of the objectives.

Additionally, in some cases, we felt that the case was strong but that there was a vital piece of information missing that could most probably have been included. For example, one paper showed positive shifts in purchase funnel behaviour and a strong ROI, but didn't include any overall sales or market share data, and so it was hard to know if the campaign had really grown the business on the metric which counts most, sales; a piece of data that could probably have been included. This was obviously frustrating for the writer of the paper but it was frustrating for us too, as we want as many strong cases to go through as possible, and this piece of data probably existed.

Common pitfalls

When judging an IPA paper, we focus on whether the campaign has, beyond reasonable doubt, generated a significant and profitable commercial return and in turn shareholder value. Thus, we focus primarily on two key measures:

1.   Are the results sizeable? Was there a significant uplift in sales, charity donations or behavioural change, both during the campaign and longer-term? Did the investment pay back at an attractive level?

2.   Is the proof overwhelming? Is the growth primarily down to the campaign, rather than other variables?

Thus, there are a number of issues that writers need to be mindful of when writing their paper, and, to that end, here are some of the more common pitfalls that this year's entrants fell into that future writers should avoid.

Setting the right benchmarks

First, it's important to set tough benchmarks against which to measure the success. The weak papers tend to measure success against soft internal objectives, such as: *"We aimed to sell 10,000 units"*, with little justification on whether 10,000 is high or low; or *"we changed our targets versus last year"* with little rationale as to why.

In contrast, strong papers tend to set tough objectives, such as: internal ones that are significantly higher than those achieved in the previous year with the same spend; external ones that are significantly higher than those achieved by competitors with the same or higher spend.

If the benchmark is a subjective measure with no rationale as to why it is tough to achieve then the paper cannot be awarded a high mark.

Measuring the business performance

Most importantly, it's important to show how the campaign has benefitted the business, i.e. how it has driven profitable top and bottom line sales growth, an increase in charity donations or a meaningful shift in customer behaviour. Many papers undersell themselves here for a multitude of reasons:

- **Some papers don't show how the campaign has driven growth.** Some show how it has changed the brand image, without showing the campaign's impact on sales or share. Some show how the campaign has increased click-throughs and pay-per-views, but don't go on to show the sales impact. Some very cleverly use test and control panels to show how the campaign increased the percentage of people buying within their small subset, but then don't go on to show the impact the campaign had on total brand sales. And some rely solely on an ROI measure that may look impressive, but can be difficult to unpick in terms of what it really achieved and how it was calculated.

- **Some papers show how the campaign has driven growth, but are not proving that the growth is profitable** (i.e. they return a significantly higher level of money than was invested). Obviously companies can choose how best to invest their money to generate the highest return on investment (ROI), and thus if the campaign is only just breaking even then it's probably not the best use of company money. Some papers showed a profitable ROI, but at a level that was so low that it makes the investment questionable. Others used unproven assumptions on what the future repeat purchase levels will be to turn a negative short-term ROI into an unrealistically positive longer-term one, and thus make a case that is more fantasy than fiction.

- **Some papers show how the campaign has driven short-term but not sustainable longer-term growth.** We all know that when a campaign is on air, measures such as sales tend to increase. Just by making the brand more visible usually translates into higher sales or charity donations. The issue is when the campaign comes off air, do the sales plummet back to pre-campaign levels or has the campaign significantly shifted customer behaviour to the extent that customers continue to buy the brand even when it isn't being advertised.

The best papers demonstrate not only the sales effect when on air but also the post-campaign sales effect, showing how the campaign has really shifted customer behaviour for the better.

Proving the link

Third, it's important to prove that the campaign was a primary driver of the growth by ruling out all other possible variables. The weaker papers tend not to do this.

- **The best papers don't rely solely on black box econometric models;** instead they use a multitude of more transparent data and anecdotal evidence (e.g. customer and supplier quotes) to clearly show the campaign effect. To do this, papers need to show pre-, during and post-campaign data to show that the growth or behavioural change started when the campaign broke. Importantly, if any growth or behavioural change happens before the start of the campaign then this needs to be explicitly accounted for, something that weak papers often brushed under the carpet.
- **The best papers systematically work through and discount any other variables** that might have caused the growth (e.g. price changes, distribution growth, promotions, new product launches, weather, competitor changes). Some weak papers failed to admit to and discount an important variable, in one case the launch of new products into the line, and in another, the other communication activity that was happening on the brand at the same time. Judges tend to be better at spotting these things than some writers give us credit for.
- **The best papers feature campaigns that people believe are working.** They tend to be ones that have real customer insight that clearly shows why the campaign has been more successful at shifting customer behaviour. Additionally they tend to be ones that have run a number of times, as the company has seen and believes in the campaign's effectiveness. This in turn helps the writer show the longer-term campaign effectiveness, which makes the case even more compelling.

In conclusion

Strong IPA papers are a joy to read. They clearly show the power of brands and advertising, and thus why ambitious CEOs, Boards and Government organisations need to invest in their marketing and brands if they want to achieve step change growth.

It's a credit to the industry that every year so many clients and agencies commit to demonstrating the effectiveness of their campaigns, even when spend levels are low, as was the case this year. To that end, we encourage more marketers and advertisers to take up the challenge.

However, at the same time, we encourage writers to focus on the most compelling cases, i.e. ones with campaigns:

- that are proven to drive significant profitable growth, both in the short and longer term;
- that can discount other variables and thus prove the power of the campaign in driving the growth;
- that have delivered an impressive return, one that is material;
- that have compelling customer insight and fresh, new learning that others can apply;
- that we as an industry can be proud of.

My biggest top tip to any new writer is an easy one: before starting, read the highest awarded IPA papers over the past few years to see what it takes to make a compelling case. The top performers really do shine, and it would be great if your paper did too.

SECTION 3

Gold winners

Chapter 7

Program of Humanitarian Attention to the Demobilised

FARC Operation Christmas campaign

By Mihir Warty and Jane Dorsett, Lowe and Partners; Marialejandra Urbina and Juan Pablo García, Lowe-SSP3

Credited company: Client: Colombian Ministry of Defence

Editor's summary

This paper demonstrates how Colombia successfully demobilised members of the oldest guerrilla group in the world, Fuerzas Armadas Revolucionarias de Colombia (FARC), which commits a terrorist act on average once every three days. Insight revealed that Christmas is the most sensitive period for this group. Consequently 'Operation Christmas' was created; two anti-guerrilla contingents and two Black Hawk helicopters travelled into the jungle to cover trees with 2,000 LED lights, alongside banners exhorting the guerrillas to lay down their arms. The message successfully encouraged 331 FARC members to demobilise and re-enter society. The year-on-year reduction in guerrilla numbers is estimated to return over £2.3m to Colombian government through tax receipts, a £11.35 ROMI, and the benefits to Colombian society and economy through a reduction in FARC's illegal 'fund raising' is estimated to be £1m in the first year. This paper stood out as an incredible testament to the problem-solving power of creativity. The judges admired the inventive efforts to quantify the impact of demobilisation and isolate the effects under unique and limiting circumstances.

1. Introduction

This entry is about Colombia's 60 years of struggle against the oldest guerrilla group in the world, *Fuerzas Armadas Revolucionarias de Colombia,* or **FARC**. 8,000 guerrillas are in action, committing a terrorist act on average once every three days.

We were asked to create an idea to demobilise them. To invite them to recover their life, their freedom.

Delivering demobilisation messages to the guerrillas is a very difficult task. The remaining guerrillas are hardcore fanatics. They eschew conventional media in the main and connecting with them is fraught with danger and risk.

Insight from group sessions and interviews revealed that Christmas time is the most sensitive and emotional period for guerrillas. Consequently we created Operation Christmas: two professional anti-guerrilla contingents, 2,000 LED lights, and two Black Hawk helicopters travelled into the jungle to find and cover giant trees (75 feet tall) with Christmas lights. Placed alongside the guerrillas' strategic walking paths the lights would come on when they approached, with banners exhorting them to lay down their arms becoming visible too.

The powerful and timely messaging encouraged 331 FARC guerrillas to demobilise and re-enter society – a 30% uplift on the previous year.

The year-on-year reduction in guerrilla numbers is estimated to return over £2.3m[1] to Colombian government through tax receipts, an £11.35 return on marketing investment. At a wider level, the benefits to Colombian society and the economy through a reduction in FARC's illegal 'fund raising' is estimated to be in excess of £1m in the first year alone. And looking even more broadly, the innovative concept and its impact gained huge awareness, both within Colombia and internationally.

2. New learning

Communications tasks don't come much tougher than this. This gives hope to anyone faced with a communications challenge that is seemingly impossible, i.e. an audience with fully entrenched behaviour – hardcore guerrillas; and a really difficult to reach audience, people in the jungle.

This paper demonstrates that you can use communications to achieve the impossible:

1. Through real understanding of your audience and by making a genuine connection, in this case identifying and utilising the emotional connection guerrillas make with Christmas; and
2. By delivering a remarkable and unconventional creative solution to bring Christmas to the jungle by putting lights on trees.

3. Background

What is FARC?

The *Fuerzas Armadas Revolucionarias de Colombia* (Revolutionary Armed Forces of Colombia), also known by the acronym of **FARC,** is a revolutionary guerrilla organisation based in Colombia.[2] It is the largest and oldest (60 years) insurgent group in the Americas with an estimated 8,000 current members.[3] FARC's stated goal is to overthrow the current democratic government of Colombia. As such it is denoted as a violent non-state actor (VNSA) and considered a terrorist group by the Colombian government, the United States Department of State and the European Union.[4] From 1999 to 2008 the FARC, together with the associated ELN guerrilla group, was estimated to control between 30 and 40% of the territory in Colombia, an area bigger than the size of England.

FARC funds itself principally through ransom kidnappings, extortion and taxation of the illegal drug trade. It has been estimated that FARC supplies more than 50% of the world's cocaine.[5] Since 1996, Free Country Foundation has registered more than 3,000 kidnaps committed by FARC and sister organisation ELN.

Colombia's guerrilla war has caused more than 40,000 deaths since 1990, most of them civilians.[6] On average FARC commits a terrorist act once every three days.[7] As a result of FARC activity Colombia now has more landmines than any other country in the world, maiming on average three Colombians each day.[8] The largest concentrations of FARC guerrillas are believed to be located throughout the south-eastern parts of Colombia's 500,000 square kilometers of jungle and in the plains at the base of the Andean mountains.

The demobilisation effort to 2010

Since 2002, the PAHD (the Colombian Ministry of Defence's Program of Humanitarian Attention to the Demobilised) has been striving to promote the demobilisation of guerrillas and enable them to return to a conventional, civilian life. In the past few years efforts have included a government advertising campaign created by Lowe-SSP3 broadcasting appeals on radio and television during big football games. These appeals use testimonials of former FARC members – some recorded and broadcast the very day the guerrilla member turned him or herself in. Another initiative involved flying to towns and villages considered vulnerable to FARC influence and setting up fêtes to attract local youngsters and highlight to them the dangers of joining up.

Alongside this messaging, in a process known as 'reinsertion', the government has been offering amnesty and trying to reintegrate into society many of these battle-hardened guerrillas. About 50,000 former members of outlawed guerrilla and militia groups are being re-educated in schools and colleges; practical job training and psychological support are also available.[9]

2010 situation

Numbers have been reduced to a hard core of around 8,000. However, as Figure 1 below shows, recent efforts have yielded diminishing returns and the rate of demobilisations has fallen:

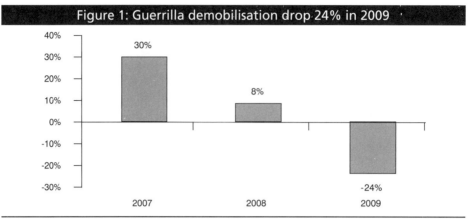

Figure 1: Guerrilla demobilisation drop 24% in 2009

Source: Colombian Ministry of Defence

Demobilisations have become more difficult, firstly, because the remaining guerrillas are those with higher ideological convictions and secondly, they have been responding to the PAHD communication tactics by locating in more isolated rural areas and reducing their internal communications (e.g. banning the use of personal radios except by commanders). Consequently there was an emerging need during 2010 to reinvigorate the demobilisation effort and take it to this increasingly hard to reach audience.

4. Marketing challenge

Campaign objective

Due to the sensitive nature of the subject and the constantly changing landscape, the PAHD has never set numeric targets for the number of guerrillas that should quit as a result of their activity. However, their challenge – and therefore the campaign challenge – is to stem the recent decline in demobilisations and reach an increasingly hard to reach – and hard to convert – audience.

The campaign task was therefore to build a message for demobilisation in this context and to make sure that guerrilla members received it.

Scale of the task

The difficulties involved in this challenge cannot be underestimated and fall into three main areas:

1. The campaign needs to resonate extraordinarily strongly, in order to generate a change in behaviour amongst hardcore individuals who may have held particular views for years, even decades.
2. The campaign needs to touch an audience who by definition is incredibly hard to reach and outside the access of conventional media channels.
3. The campaign needs to operate successfully in highly dangerous locations and a fragile situation.

Insight applied

Despite the difficulties involved it was recognised early on that insight from ex-guerrillas was needed in order to generate an effective campaign. As a result group sessions were held to identify key insights that could be utilised. The major theme that emerged was that in this highly religious Catholic society, Christmas is the time when many guerrillas begin to think about the idea of quitting. They feel too far removed from their homes, families and children. The awareness of Christmas even being close, with carols and fireworks, makes them feel nostalgia towards civilian life.

Creative strategy

The insight identified above led to the creation of a strategy to take Christmas and the power of its sentiment to the heart of FARC's jungle strongholds.

Creative solution

Lowe-SSP3 therefore created Operation Christmas. The operation ran for four days in December 2010 in the Macarena, Meta region of Colombia, where 52% of the guerrillas are based. The first step was for military intelligence to identify paths used by the guerrillas to transport food, clothes and medicine. Then the military would fly over the jungle to spot large (75 foot-plus) trees adjacent to these strategic guerrilla walking paths.

The next step, with the help of two professional anti-guerrilla contingents and two Black Hawk helicopters, was to cover the selected tree with 2,000 Christmas lights (Figure 2). Adjacent to the tree, military light mechanisms were put in place that detected people's movements and thus lit the trees as guerrillas approached. Finally, beside the tree, large banners were held with our emotive message:

IF CHRISTMAS CAN COME TO THE JUNGLE, YOU CAN COME HOME.
DEMOBILISE. AT CHRISTMAS EVERYTHING IS POSSIBLE.

It should be noted that in order to make the programme work, the Colombian Army ceased all other activity in the zone being utilised. Military actions against FARC stopped and it was agreed that Operation Christmas would not be used to identify and attack guerrillas, only to invite them to demobilise.

Initially the operation looked to light one tree but its success – in terms of demobilisations and media coverage – led to the operation being extended to cover a further nine trees (see Figure 3).

The success also led to a TV commercial being produced of the operation activity, subsequently broadcast on prime time television during Christmas (Figure 4). Although media access amongst guerrillas is limited, TV remains the most common form of media used by guerrillas and the coverage would also be seen by their families, who in turn would exert some pressure for their demobilisation (Table 1).

Operation Christmas in action

Figure 2: Work on Black Hawk helicopters and soldiers, production and agency team before take-off to the jungle

Source: Lowe-SSP3

Creative

Figure 3: Christmas lights on trees

Source: Lowe-SSP3

Figure 4: Television

Source: Lowe-SSP3

Table 1: Media plan

Launch of campaign	17 December
End of campaign	31 December
Channels	RCN (35%) and Caracol TV (65%), both leaders in national TV
Schedule	Early (25%), day (10%), prime (60%) and late time (5%)
Number of spots on air	27

Source: Lowe-SSP3

Campaign costs

Table 2 provides a breakdown of the overall campaign costs.[10]

Table 2: campaign costs	
Area of spend	**Cost**
TV airtime	$82,595
Campaign production costs	$25,000
Agency fees	$10,000
Military Operation cost for 10 trees (2 hours x 2 Blackhawk helicopters, 2 contingents of FUDRA – 6 commanders and 54 soldiers – per tree)	$183,550
Total campaign cost (at £0.62:$1 conversion rate)	$301,145 (£186,710)

Source: Lowe-SSP3

5. Campaign results

Success measures

As mentioned above, the client – the PAHD – has not historically set targets for demobilisations. As a result we worked with the client to identify the sort of metrics which would help judge whether the campaign would be a success:

- Number of demobilisations taking place during December 2010 to January 2011.

In addition to the 'direct' metrics outlined above, a number of 'externalities' were also identified that would illustrate the wider impact of the campaign:

1. international and national media coverage of the operation;
2. website links and referrals to the project; and
3. social media coverage of the project.

Direct metrics

331 guerrillas demobilised

From campaign launch in December 2010 until 25 January 2011, 331 guerrillas demobilised, a 30% uplift on the previous year. This uplift is against the trend which saw an annual 24% reduction for demobilisations in 2009. Guerrillas themselves report that the campaign had a considerable impact, and this is recognised by the Colombian National Security (Figures 5 and 6).

Figure 5: Impact of Operation Christmas – demobilised guerrillas

Even if someone couldn't see one of the trees, they had a power to become gossip amongst the guerrillas and for us this is more effective than everything

Our command wasn't angry because of this message. It was different to the other propaganda we had seen... he was touched

We definitely knew all of the strategies the Government had done, but we never expected something like this

Source: Colombian Ministry of Defence

Figure 6: Impact of Operation Christmas – Colombian government

For about four years we have been working with Lowe on a campaign to draw fighters out of FARC, as part of the government's demobilisation programme. We have tried to bring Lowe's sharp advertising tools to bear on a pretty unique problem: how to open a guerrilla's eyes to the fact that they can have a different and better life. The 'Operation Christmas' advert was the cherry on the cake.

Sergio Jaramillo, National Security Advisor and former Vice-Minister of Defence

Source: Colombian Ministry of Defence

Externalities

As well as the direct effect on FARC guerrillas the campaign also had a broader impact, and to some degree changed the context for the ongoing conflict. The idea touched the hearts of the entire country and was shown all over the world.

International and national media broadcasted the operation (Figure 7).

Figure 7: International and national media broadcasts

Source: CNN.com; Telegraph.co.uk

Over 60,000 views on YouTube in two days (Figure 8).

Figure 8: YouTube videos

Source: YouTube.com

More than 2 million links referred to the project (Figure 9).

Figure 9: Online links referring to the project

Source: Lowe-SSP3

More than 400 links on Facebook and Twitter appeared (Figure 10).

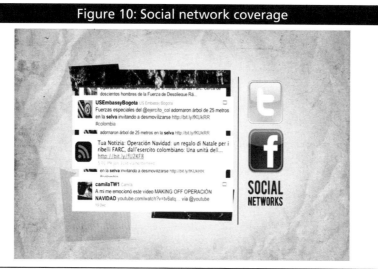

Figure 10: Social network coverage

Source: Lowe-SSP3

The impact of viral coverage

The campaign, and all of the press and social media coverage, has had a unique 'humanising' effect which led to three wider shifts in perception and behaviour:

1. The guerrillas increasingly feel they are still part of society, of their families, even though they have chosen to leave that role. It makes them feel wanted and nostalgic.
2. Crucially, it raises the military's disposition to welcome the demobilised 'enemy' by reminding them that these combatants are as human as they are after all.
3. By touching the hearts of ordinary Colombians, it helps smooth the reinsertion into society process by destroying some barriers that society has against accepting demobilised guerrillas in their workplaces or in their neighbourhoods.

6. Eliminating other factors

Other potential influences on increased demobilisation can be ruled out as having a significant effect:

1. There was no other major change in demobilisation efforts

All other demobilisation activities were carried out as in previous years.

2. Underlying trend in demobilisations was not a factor

As we have already seen, the rate of demobilisations has slowed with a 24% reduction in the numbers demobilising in 2009 (see Figure 1).[11]

3. Army/police anti-guerrilla activity has not changed significantly during this period

Whilst there have been changes in political leadership in Colombia during 2010, there has been no change in the status of FARC as a terrorist group or in activity to reduce their presence.[12]

4. FARC's political stance has not changed during this period

The underlying political positioning of FARC and its aims have not altered during this period and will not have caused individuals to demobilise.

5. There have been some changes in FARC leadership in 2010 but these are not significantly different to those experienced in previous years

Although there were changes in leadership at FARC during 2010 (for example, FARC military leader, Mono Jojoy, was killed in a large-scale military assault in September), such changes have occurred in previous years.[13]

6. There was no major change in international support for FARC during 2010

The most significant recent shift in external support came about in 2008 when Venezuelan President Hugo Chavez condemned FARC's strategy of armed struggle and kidnapping, encouraging them to lay down their arms. This was a shift from his earlier calls to governments (across Latin America) to take the FARC-EP off their lists of global terrorist groups.

7. There was no major change in public support for FARC during 2010

The most significant recent public rallies and protests against FARC took place in 2008, not recent enough to have sparked any shift in demobilisations during Christmas 2010.

8. Although Christmas 2010 was wetter and cooler than in 2009 the differentials are unlikely to have triggered significant demobilisations (Table 3).

Table 3: Weather averages for Villavivencio, Christmas 2010 vs. Christmas 2009					
	Average temperature (0c)	Number of rainy days		Average temperature (0c)	Number of rainy days
December 2010	27.3	12	January 2011	28.5	4
December 2009	29.4	2	January 2010	30.5	0

Source: Tutiempo.net

We therefore conclude that Operation Christmas was the primary driver for increased demobilisations on Christmas 2010.

7. Payback

The benefits to Colombian society from reducing the number of FARC guerrillas are huge. They include tangibles such as:

1. a reduction in casualties;
2. an increase in government income tax receipts as the guerrillas return to civilian working life;
3. a reduction in the costs to Colombian society incurred through reduced FARC 'fund raising' (generated from taxation of the illegal drug trade, ransom, kidnappings and extortion of large landholders, multinational corporations, and agribusiness).

Beyond these tangible and quantifiable benefits to Colombia there are broader, intangible effects. Families and individuals in affected areas feel safer, travel and transportation is more feasible and businesses feel more confident to invest. The wider perception of Colombia as a nation – for tourism, business and cultural purposes – is also enhanced.

In order to calculate payback we could consider the impact of the entire 331 reduction in guerrillas as we have shown that there are no factors outside the campaign that might have driven these guerrillas to demobilise. However, as we know that Christmas is a trigger time for demobilisations, we consider the most conservative effect which is the 30% year-on-year uplift in the numbers demobilising: Christmas 2010 saw 331 guerrillas demobilise, 78 more than in 2009. 78 fewer guerrillas represents a 1% reduction in the total number of FARC guerrillas (Table 4).

Table 4: Reduction in FARC forces – year-on-year comparison		
	Christmas 2010	Year-on-year comparison Christmas 2010 vs. 2009
Estimated FARC forces	8000	8000
Reduction in FARC forces through demobilisation	331	78
Demobilised as a % of total estimated forces	4.1%	1.0%

Source: Colombian Ministry of Defence

We go on to consider the impact and benefit to society of this 1% reduction in FARC guerrillas.

1. A reduction in Colombian casualties

According to a December 2010 report[14] 357 members of the Colombian security forces died in combat between January and September 2010. An additional 1,382 government soldiers or policemen were wounded during the same period, with the report estimating that the total number of casualties could reach 2,500 by the end of the year. A 1% reduction in these numbers would see three fewer members of the Colombian security forces killed, 13 fewer wounded soldiers and 24 fewer annual casualties in total (Table 5).

Table 5: Reduction in casualties – effect of a 1% reduction in FARC guerrillas	
	Effect of a 1% reduction in FARC guerrillas (Christmas 2010 vs 2009)
Members of the Colombian security forces killed (Jan–Sept 2010)	357
Pro rata reduction in security forces killed	3
Government soldiers or policemen were wounded	1382
Pro rata reduction in wounded soldiers and policemen	13
Total 2010 predicted casualties	2500
Pro rata reduction in total predicted casualties	24

Source: Colombian Ministry of Defence; Lowe and Partners

2. An increase in government income tax receipts

A direct benefit from ex-guerrillas re-entering civilian life and the workforce is an increase in income tax receipts. The average lifetime salary per demobilised guerrilla is estimated to be $47,668. Seventy-eight demobilised guerrillas will deliver incremental tax receipts of over $3.7m or £2.3m. Deducting campaign costs, net payback is £2.1m. This shows that FARC Operation Christmas campaign is delivering a ROMI[15] of £11.35 for every £1 invested (Table 6).

Table 6: Payback – benefits to society from income tax receipts	
$ Government income from taxation per ex-guerrilla Lifetime value (at net present value)	$47,668
$ PAYBACK:	
Increase in Government income from taxation from 78 guerrillas Lifetime value (at net present value)	$3,718,109
£ PAYBACK:	
Increase in Government income from taxation from 78 demobilised guerrillas Lifetime value (at net present value)	£2,305,228
£ Campaign Cost	£186,710
£ Net payback	£2,118,518
£ ROMI	£11.35

Source: Colombian Government; Lowe and Partners calculations

In order to cover the cost of the campaign, only seven guerrillas[16] would have had to demobilise rather than the 78 the campaign realised.

3. An increase in savings to society through reduced FARC financing

FARC receives most of its funding – which has been estimated to average some $300 million per year[17] – from taxation of the illegal drug trade, ransom, kidnappings and extortion of large landholders, multinational corporations, and agribusiness. From taxation of illegal drugs alone, FARC has been estimated to receive approximately 60 to 100 million dollars per year.[18]

If we exclude the taxation of illegal drugs, the benefits to Colombian society and the economy through a reduction in FARC 'fund raising' is estimated to be in excess of £1m in the first year alone (Table 7).

Table 7: Payback – savings to society	
	Effect of a 1% reduction in FARC guerrillas
FARC funding excluding taxation of illegal drugs pa	$200,000,000
$ PAYBACK: Reduction in FARC fund raising from 78 demobilised guerrillas	$1,950,000
£ PAYBACK: Reduction in FARC fund raising from 78 demobilised guerrillas	£1,209,000

Source: Lowe and Partners

How else might Operation Christmas funds have been deployed?

Given that production costs and agency fees were pro bono, the net media cost for Operation Christmas is $266,845. If these funds had been deployed against additional military personnel, FUDRA[19] would have had an additional 20 professional soldiers or five captain-commanders.[20] With 5,000 in the FUDRA military, this would have represented an increase of +0.4% soldiers or +0.1% captains.

We feel it is unlikely that these increases would have delivered 331 demobilisations, not only as the increase in forces would be marginal, but any increased FUDRA presence is unlikely to be able to reach the target audience to deliver the message given that the guerrillas are entrenched in highly dangerous jungle territory and any connection with the guerrillas is fraught with danger and risk.

8. Conclusion

This entry is about Colombia's 60 years of struggle against the oldest guerrilla group in the world, FARC. It is the story of how communications can act as a powerful yet fundamentally peaceful weapon in war.

It shows how coupling insight, creativity and endeavour encouraged 331 FARC guerrillas to demobilise and re-enter society – a 30% uplift on the previous year. This year-on-year reduction in guerrilla numbers is estimated to return over £2.3m[21] to Colombian government through tax receipts, a £11.35 return on marketing investment.

At a wider level, the benefits to Colombian society and the economy through a reduction in FARC's illegal 'fund raising' is estimated to be in excess of £1m in the first year alone. And looking even more broadly, the innovative concept and its coverage has helped humanise the conflict and its combatants, making an end to the struggle all the more hopeful.

Notes

1   The payback section later in the paper explains how we have made these calculations.
2   FARC is not the only guerrilla group operating in Colombia, nor is it the only group invited to demobilise. The Ejército de Liberación Nacional (ELN) and Ejército Popular de Liberación (EPL), are

the other major groups who often operate alongside FARC. For the purposes of this paper we refer to FARC as this was the key target for this campaign.

3 Colombian government estimate cited by BBC (http://news.bbc.co.uk/1/hi/world/americas/7217817.stm).

4 FARC is on both the US State Department list of foreign terrorist organisations as well as the EU list of terrorist groups.

5 US Department of Justice, 2006 (http://www.justice.gov/dea/pubs/pressrel/pr032206a.html).

6 UN estimate reported by Reuters, 4 April 2007.

7 A compendium of 557 terrorist acts between 2002–7 attributed to FARC and reported in the foreign press.

8 International Landmine Monitor report that up to 100,000 landmines have been buried in Colombian soil.

9 *The Independent*, 21 March 2010 (http://www.independent.co.uk/news/world/americas/after-the-revolution-why-are-farcs-young-soldiers-laying-down-their-guns-1922847.html).

10 Agency fees and production was provided pro bono but the equivalent costs have been calculated using standard Colombian production/agency costs.

11 Source: PAHD.

12 For example, President Juan Manuel Santos was elected in 2010, having served as Minister of Defence under the previous President, Alvaro Uribe.

13 For example, in March 2008, FARC's second-in-command, Raúl Reyes, was killed by the Colombian military. In September 2007, Tomas Medina Caracas, said to be in charge of the FARC's drugs and weapons smuggling operations, was killed by Colombian troops. In March 2005, senior commander Omaira Rojas Cabrera was extradited to the US and imprisoned in 2007 on drug trafficking charges.

14 Source: Corporación Nuevo Arco Iris.

15 Return on marketing investment.

16 $48,009 × 0.62 (£ conversion) = £29,765 × 7 = £206,879 vs. £186,710 campaign costs.

17 Source: Robert C. Neville (2001), *The Human Condition*, New York: SUNY Press. pp. 74–76.

18 Jeremy M. Weinstein (2007), *Inside Rebellion: The Politics of Insurgent Violence*, Cambridge: Cambridge University Press, p. 291.

19 FUDRA – La Fuerza de Despliegue Rápido is Colombia's Rapid Deployment Force. FUDRA is a rapid-reaction force tasked with conducting counterinsurgency operations throughout the country. Its motto is 'any mission, any place, any time, in the best way, ready for victory'.

20 FUDRA average contract salary of 18 months: professional soldier $13,500, captain-commander $54,000.

21 Lifetime value (net present value) of income tax receipts from 78 ex-guerrillas re-entering the workforce.

Chapter 8

Depaul UK

iHobo

By Andy Lear, Ginger Professor and Benjamin Worden, Publicis
Credited company: Client: Depaul UK

Editor's summary

For a number of years Depaul UK has attempted to recruit younger donors to counteract its shrinking donor base. Previous press and radio campaigns yielded only modest results. In 2010, Depaul UK developed an iPhone application that could help it reach out to a younger audience. iHobo required users to take care of a virtual homeless person for three days. Despite no paid media coverage the app was downloaded 600,000 times, delivering 95 times more new donors than previous campaigns. It has added 1,021 young people to the Depaul UK database who have a potential combined lifetime donation value of as much as £1.5m. This was an exciting paper which really captured the imagination of the judges, applying gaming codes to charity communications, and offering many new learnings. It is the lowest ever budget entered into the IPA Awards.

Introduction

There are more than 300,000 apps in Apple's UK AppStore.[1]

80% of these are forgotten within a day of downloading.[2]

This is the story of one that burned brightly, but also endured.

By doing so it helped to transform the long-term commercial fortunes of the relatively unknown homelessness charity behind it – Depaul UK. iHobo breathed new life into a formerly shrinking donor database, will bring in lifetime donations of up to £1.5m, and could generate a potential ROI of £250 for every £1 spent.

Previous papers have shown how an engaging app can play a supporting role in big budget TV-led campaigns.[3] This paper goes one step further, demonstrating what can be achieved when an app takes a central, starring role, with nothing to rely on but its own engaging content.

It was a bold move by Depaul UK – switching its entire £6,000 budget out of a press campaign and into an app, with no paid-for media support. Putting your faith in content alone is a frightening prospect for any brand, whatever its budget. In an attempt to temper that fear for future developers, this paper will offer some learnings not just on what iHobo achieved and how it did so, but why it was such a success.

A charity with a mature donor base

Depaul UK helps young people who are homeless, vulnerable and disadvantaged. Like most charities, Depaul UK relies on voluntary donations in order to be able to fund the valuable work that it does. And like the vast majority of charities, the marketing budgets it can employ to bring in those donations are very small.

With a loyal donor base Depaul UK raised £1.4m through corporate support, trusts, events, investments and individual donors in 2009. However, for a number of years, a demographic time-bomb has been ticking away inside that base of individual donors. The vast majority of people who donate to Depaul are over 65.

These older donors are a great asset to Depaul, but there's an obvious problem: how do you ensure that those older donors are replaced by younger donors at a sufficient rate to continue to support your activity?

Haven't we been here before?

This wasn't a new problem.

Every year Depaul UK set out to recruit new, younger donors through advertising, but every year the outcome would be the same – a net decrease in donor numbers, due to a limited media budget and the inevitable shrinking of an ageing donor base.

In recent years Depaul UK worked with Publicis to create small scale print and radio campaigns encouraging younger people to become donors or register to join the database of potential donors (Figure 1).

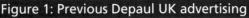

Figure 1: Previous Depaul UK advertising

Although print and radio are perfectly good as a means to reach young affluent people, with a limited media budget the limitations are obvious. Whereas larger charities such as Shelter have the funds necessary to reach 'critical mass' through conventional media channels, Depaul simply does not.

As a result, all previous campaigns enjoyed limited success, typically recruiting around 50 new donors each year – not enough to counteract the number of older donors that the charity was losing each year.

Making homelessness impossible to ignore

Not only was the fundraising campaign failing to refresh the donor base, the issue itself was slipping out of view.

Homelessness is an uncomfortable and complex problem that surrounds us all, but research shows that there are plenty of other causes that people would rather donate to first (Figure 2).

To make matters worse Depaul UK's desired audience (25–45 year olds) are particularly emotionally hardened to homelessness as an issue; they've grown up with it all around them, so to them it feels like an unchangeable fact of life. Impossible to change, but quite possible to ignore in the context of a busy life full of more pressing things to think about.

Unless we could make homelessness impossible to ignore we would have no hope of recruiting the new young donors Depaul UK so desperately needed.

The brief was as much of a media challenge as it was a creative challenge:

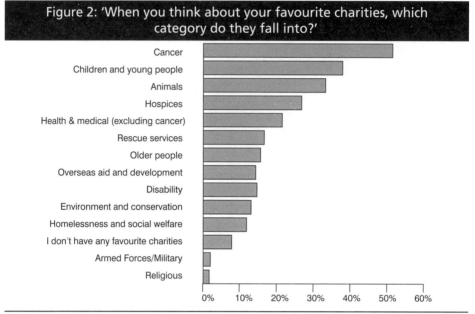

Figure 2: 'When you think about your favourite charities, which category do they fall into?'

Source: Future Foundation/nfpSynergy, Charity Awareness Monitor, 2010

- What sort of channel could deliver the in-depth engagement required to get people to wake up to the problem?
- Which medium would allow us to give a more realistic depiction of the realities of youth homelessness?
- How could we make our target audience find time to take in the message we wanted to communicate when their lives are so full of distractions?
- What kind of idea would help us to outgrow the limitations of our media budget?

We alighted on a smartphone app as both a more effective way to reach the audience *and* raise the issue:

- genuinely interruptive – this audience finds it easy to look the other way when they see a homeless person on the street, but calls, text messages, and e-mails to their smart phone are impossible to ignore;
- potential for more prolonged, more meaningful contact;
- engaging mobile content, if passed on, would give us the opportunity to reach far further on our budget;
- iPhone owners fit Depaul UK's target donor profile perfectly – 85% of iPhone users are under the age of 45, and people with higher incomes over-index massively in terms of ownership (Figure 3).[4]
- under 45s are twice as likely to download applications than older iPhone users.[5]

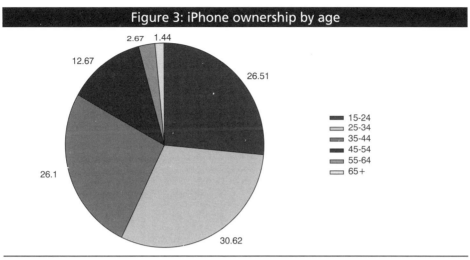

Figure 3: iPhone ownership by age

15-24
25-34
35-44
45-54
55-64
65+

Source: TGI Q3 2010

The engagement power of gaming

Psychological research has shown that gaming around a particular subject could increase empathy and identification with that subject.[6]

In addition, a prominent analysis of user behaviour around apps showed that gaming and entertainment apps have longer shelf-lives, with users more likely to engage with them over several days or weeks rather than just a single day.[7] Adopting the principles of gaming could help us achieve the longer-term engagement we were after (Figure 4).

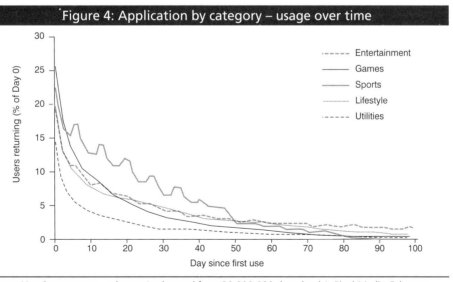

Figure 4: Application by category – usage over time

Entertainment
Games
Sports
Lifestyle
Utilities

Source: 'AppStore secrets – what we've learned from 30,000,000 downloads', *PinchMedia*, February 2009

Meet iHobo...

iHobo was a remarkably simple concept. To get people to see the complexity of the problem we asked them to download an app and take care of a virtual homeless person on their iPhone for three days (Figure 5).

Figure 5: iHobo iPhone app

If they helped him out he'd be ok. If they neglected his calls for help, his condition would deteriorate, he'd get cold, lonely and hungry. Eventually he'd sell his possessions and turn to hard drugs (the fate of three out of four young homeless people).[8] He might even overdose.

To ensure the highest possible levels of engagement, the app developers made three breakthroughs:

1. To make the character feel as real as possible iHobo was the first iPhone application in the world to use live action footage rather than CGI.
2. To produce a piece of content that was truly interruptive iHobo used Apple's newly-developed push alert technology. iHobo wasn't just there when you wanted to play the game – he was with you 24 hours a day, sending you alerts to ask for food, protection from the cold, or just a few friendly words.
3. iHobo was the first app to include a one click 'text to donate' mechanic within it (Figure 6). This allowed people to do something tangible to help real homeless people, and to add their names to the Depaul database, thereby serving the long-term objective of refreshing an ageing donor base.

Figure 6: 'Text to donate'

The app was seeded with two influential technology bloggers who'd also been involved in the beta-test (TheNextWeb and Mashable) – true experts on iPhone apps with an established following. They downloaded iHobo, played it for three days, and begun to tell their followers all about the experience, hailing it as 'a tamagotchi with a social conscience'.[9]

What it achieved – (1) massive consumer engagement

It rapidly became a download phenomenon.

- Within a week iHobo had reached the top of the iTunes free app chart. It dwarfed downloads of paid apps from multinational brands like Coca-Cola and Sky (Figure 7).

Figure 7: iTunes top free apps

- To date, iHobo has been downloaded more than 600,000 times.
- Figure 8 shows just how rapidly the phenomenon spread. But it also shows just how long iHobo continued to have an impact amongst the audience. **Almost a year after it was first launched, it is still being downloaded 2,781 times a week,** at no additional cost to Depaul UK. In stark contrast to a typical press campaign whose impact wanes quickly after viewing, iHobo's influence just grows and grows.

Figure 8: iHobo weekly and total downloads

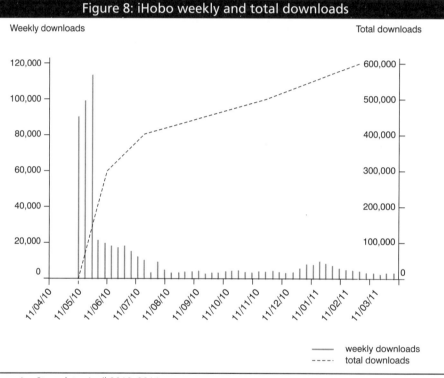

Weekly downloads   Total downloads

------- weekly downloads
----- total downloads

Source: AppStore data, April 2010–2011

Consumer engagement didn't stop at downloading:

- 74% of downloaders went on to talk to other people about iHobo after they'd played it.[10]
- iHobo has been tweeted about more than 7,000 times.[11] Even a year after launch it's still being tweeted about more than 50 times a week.
- But perhaps the most startling measure of just how deeply iHobo engaged the audience is the number of downloaders who felt compelled to give it a rating and/or leave a comment about it on the AppStore after downloading/ experiencing it. Simply put, the best apps – be that the most useful, the most innovative, the most moving – secure the most ratings. Conversely, apps that leave people indifferent secure very few ratings. Figure 9 puts iHobo's UK AppStore ratings into context.

Figure 9: Apple UK AppStore Ratings

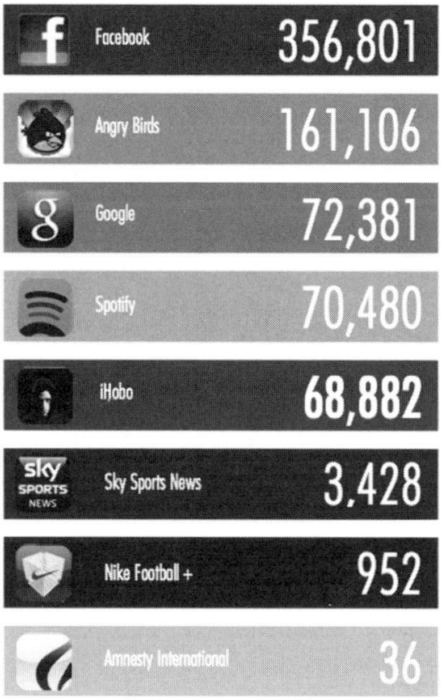

f	Facebook	356,801
	Angry Birds	161,106
8	Google	72,381
	Spotify	70,480
	iHobo	68,882
sky SPORTS NEWS	Sky Sports News	3,428
	Nike Football +	952
	Amnesty International	36

With a budget of just £6,000 iHobo generated the same degree of consumer involvement (as measured by AppStore Ratings) as leading apps from Google and Spotify.

- With this rising groundswell of participation, awareness of Depaul UK rose to unprecedented levels: monthly traffic to the Depaul UK website has increased by 59%.[12]
- Awareness of Depaul UK is more than three times higher amongst those who've downloaded iHobo, and downloaders are more than twice as likely to donate to Depaul UK.[13]
- What's even more impressive about this awareness is the degree to which it has endured. This research study (Figure 10) took place a full year after the original launch of iHobo (and the peak of downloads), yet for 48% of downloaders the awareness iHobo had built was retained.

What it achieved – (2) a revitalised donor database

- iHobo generated seven times more money through in-game donations alone than previous advertising campaigns had ever achieved, attracting 4,758 new young, affluent donors.
- More importantly 1,021 of these donors volunteered their contact details and consented to being contacted by Depaul in future for fundraising purposes.
- As a result, iHobo delivered 95 times more new donors and 20 times more new additions to the database than previous activity, meaning that Depaul's donor base actually expanded for the first time in years.

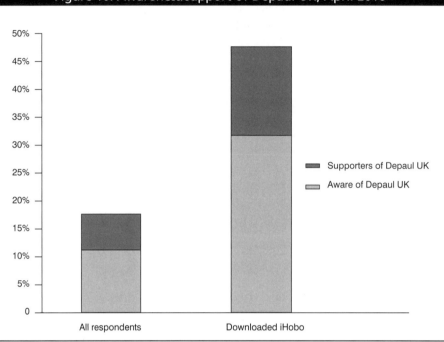

Figure 10: Awareness/support of Depaul UK, April 2010

Source: Depaul UK website analytics 2010

What it achieved – (3) a remarkable long-term return

- Setting aside that the instant donations more than covered the development costs, iHobo enabled Depaul to acquire 1,021 new database contacts at a cost of just £5.88 per acquisition. Given that Cancer Research UK and the British Heart Foundation recently admitted paying over £100 per acquisition through street and doorstep fundraising, iHobo represents an incredibly effective means of building a donor base for the future.[14]
- Based on current donor behaviour (the average Depaul UK supporter gives £49 a year), these 1,021 new young, affluent database contacts could have a lifetime value to Depaul UK of more than £1.5m.[15]
- **On the basis of a cost per acquisition of £5.88, and a potential lifetime value of £1,470 per supporter,** this represents a potential ROI of £250 for every £1 spent.

Isolating other factors

Overall it seems likely that the broader context would have hindered rather than helped Depaul UK in reaching its objectives:

- 52% of charities stated that the recession had had a negative impact on donations.[16]

- Sympathy with the issue of homelessness rises in colder months, but iHobo went live at the end of a warmer than average April 2010 so it seems unlikely that the weather at the time of launch had an impact.
- Depaul UK receives limited press coverage, and the period prior to the launch of iHobo was not exceptional in this respect. There was no other significant coverage at the time that could have amplified the impact of the campaign itself.[17]

Why did it work?

It's clear that iHobo had a public impact that far exceeded its minuscule budget, and that it has helped transform the long-term commercial fortunes of Depaul UK.

But why did a solitary app with no media budget have such an effect?

The rich stream of behavioural data and spontaneous audience feedback around apps allows us to answer that question:

1. Endorsement was crucial

- Beta-testing and seeding iHobo with two key bloggers with a combined following of over 2.7 million people clearly drove a large uplift in downloads shortly after launch. Their views continued to be reposted/retweeted weeks, even months, after they were first made.
- Our endorsers changed over time. Two weeks after launch, prominent charity and third sector bloggers began to champion iHobo and gave downloads a second wind.

2. Engagement beats shock value

We can use the 68,882 AppStore ratings as a representative view of public sentiment towards iHobo. Whilst a small number of comments suggested that people felt that the app was in poor taste, the vast majority of reactions to iHobo were in fact overwhelmingly positive, particularly after the third sector bloggers spoke out in its favour.

iHobo drove an incredibly deep interaction over three days and nights each time people played it. Tweet activity suggests this could be up to eight or nine times in some cases, a total of 27 days of engagement.

Below is a sample taken from a typical 4-day period of tweet activity at the height of the buzz. It shows just how deeply players were feeling for the homeless person in their care, even playing/tweeting about it in the middle of the night:

my iHobo is dead again. That's the sixth time he's died

Tue 15 Jun, 21:32

Every time I go on my ihobo app i just want to cry cuz i know there is a homeless person out sleeping on the streets right now :-(

Tue 15 Jun, 15:28

My ihobo died. God I'm gutted

Tue 15 Jun, 01:37

I'm hopeless at looking after my ihobo

Mon 14 Jun, 18:13

I hate not being able to let my ihobo live more than 2 days

Mon 14 Jun, 17:32

ihobo gets annoying... once he dies after the 8th or 9th time

Mon 14 Jun, 01:34

Right, now that ihobo is all tucked in & peacefully sleeping I can go to sleep

Sun 13 Jun, 23:15

I think Harry the ihobo just died <3. Got a new one, I promise I'll take better care of him

Sun 13 Jun, 21:38

My ihobo is scared he might have HIV he's glad I'm here now

Sun 13 Jun, 17:37

I think it's time to download ihobo again, it's so sad though

Sat 12 Jun, 20:36

Help meee, my ihobo turned into a druggie, what am I meant to doo?

Sat 12 Jun, 17:25

- The scale and level of engagement iHobo created cannot be overstressed. Over the course of a year, from a single investment of £6,000 it created over 600,000 rich digital experiences, which in more conventional digital channels would have cost £2.4m.[18]

3. iHobo educated as well as entertained

- The messaging within the app clearly shifted perceptions from young homeless people being '*a* danger' to young homeless people being '*in* danger'. People who had downloaded the app were twice as likely to empathetically understand that young homeless people would find themselves unable to go to school or get a job, and half as likely to think that homeless people were destined to pose a threat to society and turn to crime.[19]
- From this we can hypothesise that iPhone users who downloaded and played iHobo had less negative, more informed views towards homelessness after their experience with the app.

Conclusions

In an age when paid-for media is less dominant than ever, this paper offers more proof for the widely-held belief that, with sufficiently engaging content, brands can offset a small – or in this case non-existent – media budget.

But more than that, the success of iHobo shows just what mobile apps can achieve on their own. Done well, they can take centre stage in a brand's marketing plan, multi-tasking in a way few media channels can manage: they can drive a response; they can drive mass engagement (in fact they can drive a depth of engagement more traditional media could only dream of); and far from being a quick hit soon forgotten, they can have a long-term enduring impact, touching new audiences and continuing to pay back months, even years, after their initial launch.

Notes

1 'Apple AppStore UK metrics Q4 2010 edition', AppManifesto.com, 29 December 2010.
2 'AppStore secrets – what we've learnt from 30,000,000 downloads', *PinchMedia*, February 2009.
3 Barclaycard 'Sliding our way into a greater share of the future', IPA Effectiveness Awards, 2010.
4 'Mobile phones and networks – reigniting the replacement cycle', *Market Intelligence,* Mintel UK (January 2010) p.101. Graph taken from TGI Q3 2010.
5 'Mobile phones and networks – reigniting the replacement cycle', *Market Intelligence,* Mintel UK (January 2010) p.101.
6 K. Facer, R. Joiner, D. Stanton, J. Reid, R. Hull and D. Kirk 'Savannah: mobile gaming and learning?' *Journal of Computer Assisted Learning,* vol. 20 (2004), p. 403.
7 'AppStore secrets – what we've learned from 30,000,000 downloads', *PinchMedia*, February 2009.
8 *Youth Homelessness and Substance Use: Report to the Drugs and Alcohol Research Unit*, Emma Wincup, Gemma Buckland and Rhianon Bayliss, 2003.
9 'iHobo iPhone app: Tamagotchi with social conscience', Cult of Mac, 10 May 2010.
10 Depaul UK/OnePoll iHobo usage survey, April 2011.
11 iHobo Media Analysis Platform, Feb 2011.
12 Depaul UK website analytics 2010.
13 iHobo usage survey, Depaul UK/OnePoll, April 2011.
14 BBC News 'Charity Millions "go to fundraising companies"', 26 August 2010. http://news.bbc.co.uk/1/hi/programmes/newsnight/8946145.stm.
15 Assumes 'lifetime value' equals a relationship of up to 30 years.
16 Data from Charities Commission Research. For full details see http://news.bbc.co.uk/1/hi/uk/7946518.stm.
17 Depaul UK PR monitoring.
18 Publicis Modem Benchmarking. This calculation is based on using a more conventional digital approach to delivering this kind of experience – a display advertising campaign driving people to a microsite with a downloadable game. To get 600,000 downloads we'd have needed 6,000,000 people to clickthrough to the site where it was held, based on an average 10% download rate. To get 6,000,000 people to clickthrough we'd need a massive 120,000,000 impressions (assuming the normal 5% clickthrough rate). Based on a standard cost per 1000 impressions of £20 we'd need to spend £2.4m on display advertising to have the same impact as iHobo.
19 iHobo usage survey, Depaul UK/OnePoll, April 2011.

Chapter 9

Marie Curie Cancer Care

How Marie Curie Cancer Care benefited from using advertising to ask people to collect money rather than simply give money

By Anna Hutson, DLKW Lowe and Jane Dorsett, Lowe and Partners
Credited companies: Media Agency: Maxus; Client: Marie Curie Cancer Care

Editor's summary

Faced with enormous pressures on charitable giving, Marie Curie redeployed a small part of its 2010 advertising budget to ask people to collect money for their Great Daffodil Appeal, rather than simply give money. Celebrity supporters produced two radio executions and online content, asking the public to sign up an hour of their time to collect, recruiting an extra 5,219 collectors. These collectors generated an additional income of £634,583, delivering a payback of £2.45 for every £1 spent. This equates to an extra 8,808 nursing hours for the terminally ill, thus enabling 228 patients to spend their final days at home. The judges were drawn to this paper's strategic central thought – to build distribution rather than donations. Furthermore, the rigour of the analysis left the judges in no doubt that marketing communications had created a significant and proven return, coupled with long lasting future benefits for the organisation.

1. Introduction

This is the story of how a very small communications campaign that ran in the first two months of 2010 recruited over 5,000 extra people to collect for Marie Curie Cancer Care's Great Daffodil Appeal. In fact, it was achieved with a total campaign outlay of just £184,000, the smallest budget so far entered for an IPA Small Budget award.[1]

We will show how the 5,219 collectors that were recruited by the campaign generated an additional income of £634,583, delivering a ROMI of £2.45 for every £1 spent. This equates to an extra 8,808 nursing hours for the terminally ill, thus enabling 228 patients to spend their final days at home.[2]

2. New learning

This paper shows how you can reap rewards by challenging the advertising norms in a sector. In particular, it's a story of changing the role for advertising.

The vast majority of charity campaigns ask people to *give* money. This campaign asks people to *collect* money, therefore increasing the opportunities for people to give. In marketing terms, this is the equivalent of using advertising to build distribution.

3. Background

What is Marie Curie Cancer Care?

Marie Curie Cancer Care is a charity specialising in providing free, hands-on nursing care for the terminally ill, as well as emotional and practical support for their families and carers. Its remit now goes beyond cancer patients to all the terminally ill.

Although Marie Curie runs nine hospices, the main focus is on providing specialist palliative care to the two thirds of the population who would prefer to die at home surrounded by the people and things they love. Currently only a quarter is able to.[3]

To maintain and grow its service, Marie Curie relies on the generosity of the public. Its main fundraising event since 1986 has been The Great Daffodil Appeal.

The Great Daffodil Appeal (GDA)

This appeal runs every March: local fundraisers galvanise their supporters to raise money and seek donations from local businesses, raising an average of £4.5m (2005–2009).[4] Just over a quarter of income comes from manned street collections.[5] The charity relies on volunteers to take to the shopping centres, stations and streets with their collecting tins and hand out daffodil pins on receiving donations from the public.[6] The average donation is £1.

Communications are used before and during March to help boost the profile of Marie Curie, and encourage donations.

4. 2008 and 2009 communications campaign – setting the context

The communications strategy

A communications campaign ran in 2008 and 2009 to support the GDA. It set out to do two things:

1. Improve the understanding of Marie Curie

Recent research showed that although the charity had high prompted awareness (77%),[7] there was limited understanding of its remit.

So we set out to explain the remarkable work that the Marie Curie nurses do: helping the dying and their families get through the emotionally, and often physically, stressful time of a loved one's last days peacefully, with dignity and warmth.

2. Improve the association with the daffodil

The research also showed that only 16% of adults associated the daffodil with Marie Curie.[8] If we could imbue the daffodil with symbolic meaning, like the Royal British Legion has done for the poppy, we could aid recognition and support for the appeal.

So within the creative treatment we deliberately raised the profile of the daffodil to become the campaign visual. This look and feel was adopted for the street collectors' boxes to create synergy through to 'point of donation'.

The media strategy

The target for the campaign was women aged over 45, especially the more well-off. They represent the core supporters, and tend to be the key carers when someone becomes terminally ill.

The two key media were leisure-based magazines (e.g. *Hello*, M&S magazine and Sunday supplements), and easy-listening radio (e.g. Heart and Classic FM). We wanted to break through the warm atmosphere with our sobering messages about how Marie Curie helps people die with dignity (Figures 1–3).

Around £500k was spent on the campaign each year.

Figure 1: 2008 and 2009 collector box

Figure 2: Examples of 2008 and 2009 creative work

Figure 3: 2009 radio – 40"

'Stephen Mangan – Guitar'

SFX: Stephen Mangan playing a recognisable tune (badly) throughout

Steve: When my mum was dying of cancer I used to play this to her.

Really badly.

The Marie Curie Nurses who were looking after her said that no one should be made to suffer like that.

I said I do the jokes around here.

The Nurses were fantastic. They chatted to her for hours, even when she couldn't talk herself anymore.

One of them, Angela, even showed us how to move her gently without hurting her and they let us know it was ok for her to eat whenever and whatever she wanted.

Because mum was at home, we could talk to her about really personal things in private.

Marie Curie Nurses made that possible and they did it for us for free.

Please join me and show your support for them by wearing a daffodil this March.

For more information visit www.mariecurie.org.uk/daffodil

It was thanks to Marie Curie Nurses that my mum spent her last days at home, with dignity....
And with my guitar playing.

The results of the 2008 and 2009 communications campaign

The campaign was deemed to be a success. TNS research commissioned at the end of March 2009 showed that:

People were more aware of the advertising, and of Marie Curie:

■ The campaign achieved its highest ever result for advertising awareness at 32%, up 9 percentage points (ppt) from the pre-2008 campaign.[9]
■ Spontaneous awareness of Marie Curie increased 13ppt to 42%.

People better understood the charity's remit:

■ People's understanding that Marie Curie is about 'home nursing for the dying' rose from 34% (pre-2008) to 42% (2009).[10]

People were more likely to associate the daffodil with Marie Curie:

■ Spontaneous association of the charity with the daffodil increased 12ppt to 30%,[11] its highest ever level.

2008 and 2009 income

The income trend for 2008 and 2009 was stable despite predictions of a slump in charitable giving. In 2008, income was significantly boosted by Marie Curie becoming Tesco's charity of the year, with extra collection points provided at their 2,115 stores (see Figure 4).

Collections held at Tesco stores in March 2008, as part of Marie Curie Cancer Care's Great Daffodil Appeal, raised £536,000 for the charity.[12]

Income dropped back slightly in 2009, once this partnership ended.

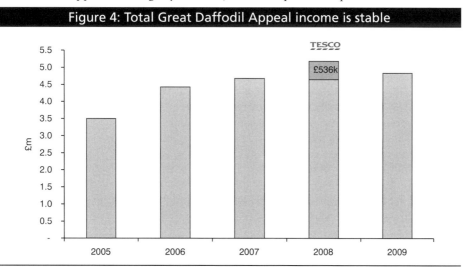

Figure 4: Total Great Daffodil Appeal income is stable

Source: MCCC; GDA income 2005–2009

5. 2010: Introducing a new strand to the campaign

2010 – A big challenge

By the time it came to developing the communications strategy for 2010, we continued to face a huge challenge on three fronts:

1. Overall donations to UK charity were in decline

2008/09 had seen a 10% year-on-year (YOY) fall in donations (see Figure 5):

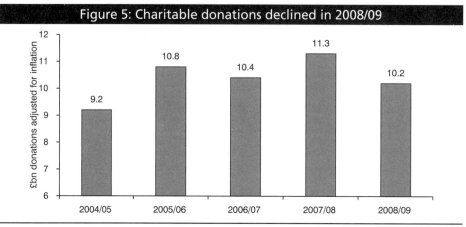

Figure 5: Charitable donations declined in 2008/09

Source: NCVO/CAF; estimated amounts given to charities in the UK by individuals, 2004/05 to 2008/09 adjusted for inflation

2. The economy wasn't getting any better

The election was imminent in May; economic Armageddon dominated public debate, and our stalwart middle England supporters were seeing their savings and retirement funds shrink.

3. We were being consistently outspent by our competitors

Although the key competitors' annual advertising budgets had reduced over the years, in 2009 Marie Curie's budget was still only about a third of that of Cancer Research UK and Macmillan (see Figure 6).

All of which forced us to think even harder about the most effective use of the money.

A new communications strategy

To take up the challenge set before us, we decided to redirect some of the advertising budget to achieve a new objective. In marketing terms, we wanted to use advertising to build distribution – increasing the opportunities for people to give. Could we somehow use advertising to replicate the Tesco effect of 2008?

Instead of using advertising to ask people to **give** money to Marie Curie, we would use advertising to ask people to **collect** money for Marie Curie.

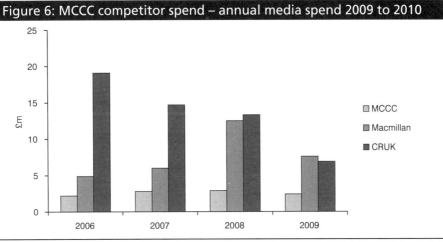

Figure 6: MCCC competitor spend – annual media spend 2009 to 2010

Source: Nielsen

As this had never been done before by Marie Curie, about a quarter of the 2010 Great Daffodil Appeal media budget was assigned to the task.

The campaign objective

Just over a quarter of GDA income comes from manned street collections – 26.7%.[13] The average number of collectors per year (2005–09) is 12,782, and their average collection is £94.[14] The campaign was tasked to pay for itself in year one, with a view to delivering a profit in year two – the charity believes that 46% of new collectors return for at least one year of collecting (see Table 1).[15] To cover the media costs of the campaign in the first year, we would need to recruit just over one and a half thousand collectors – an 11.6% uplift on the number of collectors in 2009.[16]

Table 1: Collector campaign target

Year 1
£150k (media spend) ÷ collector average of £94 (2005–2009)
= 1,596 new collectors to break even

Year 2
46% returners = 638 collectors × average collection of £94
= £60k worth of new donations

The creative work

The creative work asked people for an hour of their time to collect money for Marie Curie. To view this hour in a new perspective, we framed it against the final hours of someone who is dying:

Please, give us an hour. It will help someone in their final hours.

Marie Curie's PR department galvanised celebrity supporters to produce two radio executions and online content, getting them to ask the public to sign up to collect for an hour – the twist being that it is normally the public asking celebrities for a signature.

The campaign deliberately set a target for people to help them understand just how many collectors were required. Marie Curie was confident that it would get between 13,000–14,000 collectors via the usual means;[17] we needed to get an extra 1,500 to break even, so we put forward a stretch target of 20,000.

The media strategy

We continued to target our core supporter group of women aged 45-plus. Radio formed the core of the campaign (two-thirds of the media spend), using stations such as Classic, Magic, Heart, LBC and Smooth (see Figure 7).

Radio was supported with online advertising; a PR film was also developed as extra content to help the recruitment and was placed on the Marie Curie YouTube channel (see Figures 10 and 11). Posters were also supplied for the 180 Marie Curie charity shops, nine hospices and regional offices (see Figures 8 and 9).

The ads ran during January and February to sign up collectors.[18] The total cost of the campaign was £184,151 (including media, production and agency fees) (see Tables 2 and 3).

Examples of 2010 creative work

Figure 7: 2010 radio – 40"

'Jane Horrocks'

SFX: Crowd noise and camera flashes as if at stage door.

Fan: Miss Horrocks, can I get your autograph?

SFX: Crowd noise fades behind VO.

Jane Horrocks: You can love, but only if you give me yours too.

That's right, now I'm the one collecting signatures.

I'm helping Marie Curie Cancer Care sign up 20 000 collectors for their Great Daffodil Appeal this March.

Put your name down to spend just one hour with a collecting tin giving out daffodils, and the money you raise will provide more nursing care to terminally ill patients in their own homes.

Call 0845 601 3107 or visit mariecurie.org.uk/daffodil to sign up.

Your local fundraiser is ready to contact you.

Please, give us an hour. It will help someone in their final hours.

'Stephen Fry'

Stephen Fry: I've amassed over a million followers on Twitter. I'm a natural at collecting people.

Which is rather good as that's what I'm doing for Marie Curie Cancer Care. I'm helping them collect 20 000 collectors for their Great Daffodil appeal this March.

Sign up to spend just one hour holding a nice yellow collecting tin and giving out daffodils and the money you raise will help to provide more nursing care to terminally ill patients in their own homes.

Call 0845 601 3107 or visit mariecurie.org.uk/daffodil and sign up with me.

Your local fundraiser is ready to contact you.

Please, give us an hour. It will help someone in their final hours.

Figure 8: 2010 poster used in Marie Curie Cancer Care shops

Figure 9: Hospice poster

Figure 10: 2010 online

Figure 11: 2010 online PR film – various celebrities invite people to sign up to be a collector

Table 2: Collector media plan 2010

			January			February		
Media	**£000**	**Delivery**	11	18	25	1	8	15
Radio	100	41% @ 4.66						
Online	50	31m impressions		14 Jan–10 Feb				

Table 3: Campaign costs

Total media	£150,347
Campaign production costs	£23,673
Agency fees	£10,131
Total campaign cost	£184, 151

The Collector campaign results

The campaign:

- recruited a record number of collectors;
- who in turn made a record contribution to the Great Daffodil Appeal;
- which resulted in the most successful GDA ever.

More collectors were recruited

Against the Collector campaign's key objective of increasing the number of street collectors or 'distribution points', we saw a year-on-year uplift of 6,503 to over 20,000, 47% more than in 2009 and 59% more than the average for the last five years (see Figure 12).[19] Our break-even target was an 11% uplift vs. 2009.

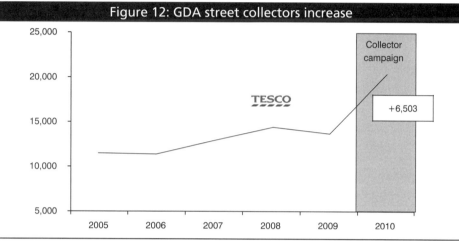

Figure 12: GDA street collectors increase

Source: MCCC; GDA street collectors 2005–2009

Increased income from the collectors

Donations from street collections increased year-on-year by £477,977 to £1.7m, the highest ever level, outperforming 2008, a year of exceptional results with Tesco contributing nearly a third of the collections total (Figure 13).

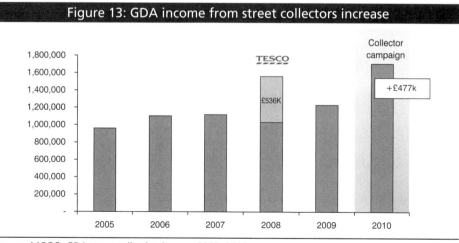

Figure 13: GDA income from street collectors increase

Source: MCCC; GDA street collection income 2005–2010

The most successful GDA ever, with the highest contribution from street collections

Overall donations for the Great Daffodil Appeal increased by £731,698 to £5.6m, its highest ever level; with street collections delivering their highest ever percentage at 31%, 6ppt ahead of 2009 and 5ppt ahead of the 2005–09 average (Figure 14).[20]

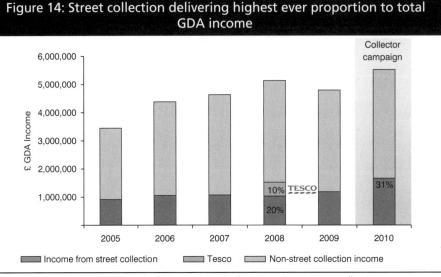

Figure 14: Street collection delivering highest ever proportion to total GDA income

Source: MCCC; total GDA income split between street collection and non-street collection

How we know the record results were down to the campaign

Due to the low investment in the campaign, we do not have any tracking research at our disposal.

However, we do have other strong evidence that enables us to attribute the increase in collections to the campaign.

Collector recruitment correlates with radio activity

First, we can see a very strong correlation between regional radio impacts and recruitment. The higher the weight, the greater the uplift in new recruits (Figure 15).

Online activity increased

Across the campaign period we saw:

- A 16% year-on-year increase in website visits to 135,771 visitors;
- 3,386 views of the celebrity video on YouTube;
- 1,664 click throughs from our banner ads, which was +45% more efficient than a comparable 2010 Marie Curie online campaign.[21]

New recruits only registered via the phoneline, Facebook or online

All new recruits registered via the national advertised phone number, Facebook or the web address during January and February, as opposed to their local regional branch which is the normal means of registration (see Figure 16).

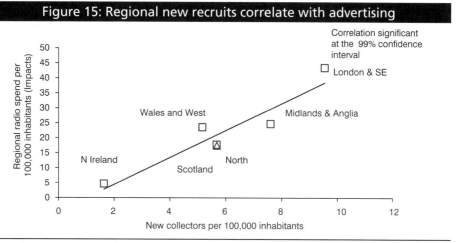

Figure 15: Regional new recruits correlate with advertising

Source: MCCC/Maxus/ONS; 2010 regional advertising spend per UK inhabitant and new collectors per UK inhabitant

Eliminating other factors

All other potential influences on collector recruitment can be ruled out:

1. There was no change to the normal recruitment efforts

The campaign was the only change in Marie Curie's recruitment efforts. All other recruitment activities were carried out as normal by local fundraisers and within the 'Shine On' supporter magazine. Marie Curie had no new consumer facing partnerships.

2. The regular GDA advertising activity could not have had any effect

The main GDA spend comes in March, after the Collector campaign. All collectors need to have registered by the end of February.

3. We continued to be outspent by our two main rivals in the two months of our activity

In January and February 2010, Cancer Research UK took 79% share of voice, and Macmillan 13%, with Marie Curie trailing in third with 8%.[22]

This situation was reflected in the overall annual spend figures (Figure 17):

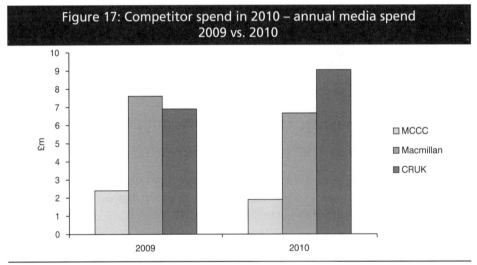

Figure 16: All new recruits registered via dedicated phoneline,
Facebook or online

Dedicated phoneline

Facebook

Website

Source: MCCC; new recruits, method of registration 2010

Figure 17: Competitor spend in 2010 – annual media spend
2009 vs. 2010

□ MCCC
▨ Macmillan
■ CRUK

Source: Nielsen

4. There was no sudden rise in the incidence of cancer deaths in the time period

Latest published data from CRUK says that deaths from cancer have declined by 20% between 1978–2008. We have no reason to believe there has been a significant uplift since 2008. Incidence has remained steady for a decade.[23]

5. There were no high profile cancer deaths

The most recent incident was Jade Goody's much publicised death from cancer. She died in March 2009, and was cared for by Marie Curie nurses – proceeds of her book go to Marie Curie.[24] But at the time of this campaign, January/February 2010, she was not prominent in the media.[25]

6. Changes to seasonal conditions were minimal in March

Compared to the equivalent month in 2009, March 2010 was colder, less sunny and equally wet – so improved weather was not the reason for the improved collector turn-out (see Figure 18).

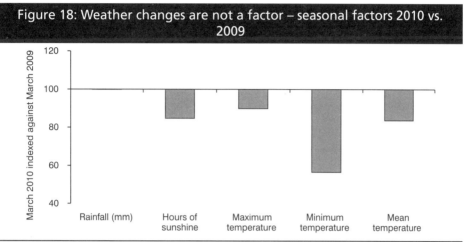

Figure 18: Weather changes are not a factor – seasonal factors 2010 vs. 2009

Source: http://www.metoffice.gov.uk/climate/uk/datasets/#

We can therefore conclude that the Collector campaign was the primary driver for increased street collectors and collections in 2010.

Calculating payback

We have calculated financial payback based on the best practice expounded in the COI's Payback and Return on Marketing Investment (ROMI) in the Public Sector.[26] Whilst not a public sector campaign, a charity campaign faces similar challenges in proving effectiveness and calculating ROMI.

The three methods deployed are:

1. a year-on-year analysis (2010 vs. 2009);
2. a comparison with the previous five year average (2005–2009);
3. trend analysis based on the underlying growth in street collectors (2005–2009).

1. A year-on-year analysis (2010 vs. 2009)

Initial payback calculations focus on the 47% uplift in street collectors. By delivering 6,503 additional street collectors, the campaign delivered a £477k uplift in year one. Assuming a 46% retention rate for year two,[27] and applying a discount factor of 3.5% to calculate the net present value, we see a two year 'lifetime value' of £690,151 in incremental donations.

Deducting total campaign costs, net payback is £506k which is over eight times our pre campaign target of £60k. This shows our campaign as having a ROMI of £2.75 for every £1 invested (Table 4).

Table 4: The Collector campaign ROMI year-on-year	
	Year-on-year (2010 vs 2009)
Incremental street collectors	6,503
Total payback year 1	£477,977
Total payback by end of year 2	£690,151
Total campaign cost	£184,151
Net payback	£506,000
ROMI	£2.75

2. A comparison with the previous five year average (2005–2009)

In order to include the Tesco effect in our payback calculations, we have also compared the number of 2010 street collectors with the five year average. This analysis shows a two year campaign payback of £738,642.[28] After deducting total campaign costs, this shows our campaign as having a ROMI of £3.01 for every £1 invested (Table 5).

Table 5: The Collector campaign ROMI 2010 vs. 5 year average (2005–2009)	
	2010 vs 5-year average (2005–2009)
Incremental street collectors	7495
Total payback year 1	£511,560
Total payback by end of year 2	£738,642
Total campaign cost	£184,151
Net payback	£554,490
ROMI	£3.01

3. Trend analysis based on the underlying growth in street collectors (2005–2009)

The underlying five year trend for GDA street collectors shows that numbers are growing at around 758 per year. We have factored in this rising trend which has in part been driven by the core campaign and from being Tesco's charity of the year in 2008 (Figure 19).

Regression analysis predicts just over 15,000 collectors for 2010. Given that we saw over 20,000 collectors, this analysis shows an uplift of 5,219 for the Collector campaign, delivering a two year payback of £634,583 and a ROMI of £2.45 for every £1 invested (Table 6).[29]

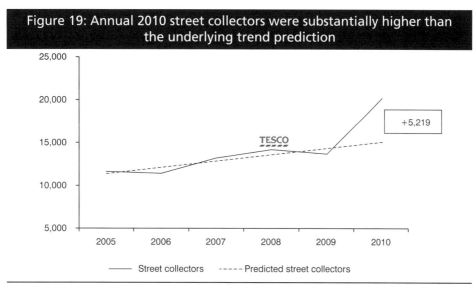

Figure 19: Annual 2010 street collectors were substantially higher than the underlying trend prediction

TESCO

+5,219

——— Street collectors   - - - - Predicted street collectors

Source: MCCC; 2010 predicted collectors based on 2005–2009 regression analysis

Table 6: The Collector campaign ROMI 2010 vs. predicted trend (2005–2009)

	2010 vs. predicted trend (2005–2009)
Incremental street collectors	5,219
Total payback year 1	£439,492
Total payback by end of year 2	£634,583
Total campaign cost	£184,151
Net payback	£450,431
ROMI	£2.45

As this delivers the most conservative ROMI for the campaign, and excludes the underlying trend, it is the ROMI we are most comfortable with and is used in the benefit returns analysis to follow.

We are unable to find many comparable campaigns to benchmark ourselves against other than the Barnardo's 2001 IPA Effectiveness Grand Prix winner. At £2.45, our campaign ROMI compares favourably to Barnardo's £9m donor recruitment campaign, which utilised press, direct mail and professional recruiters to deliver a £2.16:1 ROMI.[30]

Benefit return of the campaign

As a charity, Marie Curie does not have a traditional profit margin or a financial profitability measure. Instead it measures return on marketing investment through the benefit given to the individuals and families that they help.

For every £1 donated, Marie Curie spends 34p on administration, fundraising and operational costs. So, 66p goes directly to helping the terminally ill.[31] Discounting our two year net payback of £450k[32] at 66%, the Collector campaign delivers an additional £297,285 in 'profit'.

Against media spend of £184k, this £297k 'profit' delivers a £1.61 profit ROMI which compares very favourably with charity industry benchmarks on recruitment activity returns, as most recruitment activity is undertaken at an initial loss with charities achieving a return of only 50–70p for every £1 invested.[33]

The £297k generated by the Collector campaign equates to an additional 8,808 hours of free nursing care; allowing an additional 228 terminal cancer patients and their families to be given the choice of where and how to spend their final days.[34]

Finally

The success of the 2010 Collector campaign has given Marie Curie the confidence to reinvest at a higher level in 2011.[35] As a result, the number of registered new collectors is up 55% on 2010.[36]

A central register of collectors is now being developed, enabling Marie Curie to reactivate collectors more efficiently year-on-year, and encourage them to recruit their friends. In time, we will be able to look at the real lifetime value of our new recruits, not just the two year value.

Notes

1 Source: IPA Effectiveness Small Budget Awards 2009; campaign spends range from £219k for the ghd website redesign to £2.4m for Morrisons 'Let's Grow' campaign.
2 The payback section at the back of the paper explains how we have made these calculations.
3 Source: MCCC.
4 Source: MCCC.
5 The average contribution between 2005–2009 from street collections to the Great Daffodil Appeal was 26.4%.
6 Daffodil pins are offered to anyone making a donation. They are given free and should not be regarded as being sold or given in exchange for a donation.
7 tns omnibus 2006; sample 2,000 GB adults.
8 tns omnibus 2006; sample 2,000 GB adults.
9 Source: tns omnibus, March 2009; 2,000 GB adults.
10 Source: tns omnibus, March 2009; 2,000 GB adults.
11 Source: tns omnibus, March 2009; 2,000 GB adults.
12 Tesco press release 1 April 2009.
13 Source: MCCC.
14 Average street collection generates £93.56, source: MCCC.
15 Source: MCCC.
16 There were 13,774 collectors in 2009. 1,596 = 11.6%. Source: MCCC.
17 Recruitment is carried out each year by local fundraisers, and within the supporter magazine 'Shine On'.
18 From March, we reverted back to the 'Education' campaign we had run in 2008 and 2009, to continue to encourage donations to the GDA.
19 Source: MCCC, GDA street collectors: 2010 = 20,277,2009 = 13,774 (uplift 2010 vs. 2009 = 47%); average 2005 to 2009 = 12,782 (uplift 2010 vs. average 2005 to 2009 = 59%).
20 Street collections accounted for 25% of total GDA income in 2009. Source: MCCC.
21 Source: MCCC. Just under half, 46%, of collectors return to collect the following year.
22 In Jan/Feb 2010 Cancer Research UK spent £1.9m and Macmillan spent £250k on media. Source: Nielsen.
23 Source CRUK: http://info.cancerresearchuk.org/prod_consump/groups/cr_common/@nre/@sta/documents/generalcontent/018070.pdf.
24 Coverage of Jade Goody's death prompted a 12.5% increase in cervical cancer checks. Source: NHS Information Centre, October 2009.

25 A documentary of her life was screened 22 March 2010 after campaign activity had stopped.
26 Source: http://coi.gov.uk/blogs/bigthinkers/wp-content/uploads/2009/11/coi-payback-and-romi-paper.pdf.
27 Source: MCCC. Just under half, 46%, of collectors return to collect the following year.
28 Assuming a 46% retention rate for year two, and applying a discount factor of 3.5% to calculate the net present value.
29 Based on an incremental 5,219 collections, collecting an average £84.21 in donations (the 2010 average).
30 Source: IPA. The Barnardo's Grand Prix winning case study was a £9m donor recruitment campaign featuring press, direct mail and professional face-to-face collectors. ROMI was based on a 4-year lifetime value.
31 2010 MCCC costs (administration, fundraising and operational costs) as a percentage of voluntary income = 34%, source: MCCC Annual Report and Accounts 2009/10.
32 £634k 2-year payback less £184 campaign cost = net payback of £450k.
33 Source: http://www.charityfacts.org/fundraising/fundraising_costs/index.html. 'Whilst undertaking this work does still typically generate a very satisfactory return, it does so only over the full term of the relationship developed with each supporter'.
34 Source: http://www.mariecurie.org.uk/en-gb/your-money/ The hourly cost of nursing is £33.75 (£40.5m spent on nursing care delivers 1.2m nursing hours = £33.75 per hour). 1.2m nursing hours allowed 31,000 to be given the choice of where and how to spend their final days = an average 39 hours per person.
35 The media budget for 2011 is £200k.
36 Source: MCCC.

Chapter 10

Ovaltine

Small slice, big pie: how moving from a milky sleep aide to a daytime break drink paid dividends for Ovaltine

By Ric Nicholls, WCRS&Co/Engine
Credited companies: Media Agency: ZenithOptimedia; Client: Twinings

Editor's summary

This paper shows how Ovaltine moved from being second (of two) in the malted sleep aide market to gain over 1% of the £1.65bn daytime hot drink market. Faced with a category in steep decline, Ovaltine needed to recruit younger drinkers and enter a new market space. Using a six-month sponsorship of ITV3 daytime and various creative solutions, Ovaltine established itself in a different occasion and grew rapidly as a consequence. It has been estimated the campaign will generate up to £1.12m in additional gross profit in the long term, resulting in a ROMI of 5:1. In this hugely mature category, the judges admired the courageousness of the repositioning of such a well-known brand against a new occasion and the positive ROI achieved in the face of significant competitor investment.

Introduction

Who are people who come second? They're the first people to lose.

On this the business books are agreed. Second sucks. If you're not number one in a market, you need to find the market you CAN be number one in.[1] Or become one of the also-rans.

This paper shows an alternative route out of this second cul-de-sac for a small brand with tiny budgets but huge ambitions: not finding a niche market to dominate, but grabbing a tiny slice of an enormous one.

It shows how Ovaltine moved from a poor second (of two) in the malted sleep aide market (dominated by Horlicks who outspent Ovaltine 13:1) to grab over 1% of the enormous £1.65bn daytime hot drink market.

It shows how, by finding a unique take on that market, and using media to 'act big', the brand brought in new consumers, established itself in a different occasion and grew rapidly as a consequence.

The result: a £225k investment will generate up to £1.12m in additional gross profit in the long term – a return on marketing investment of 5:1.

Small budget, huge rewards.

The problem

It was 2008, and the Ovaltine brand was in anything but rude health. As a malted pre-bedtime drink, it was a distant number two brand in a market that was declining fast, based on a disappearing occasion and drunk by an ageing audience.

The dominant brand leader – Horlicks – was consistently and regularly supporting the idea of the category as an aide to sleep (Figure 1).

Figure 1: Horlicks's consistent sleep messages

As a result, that was how the category was viewed and used in the UK – the complete opposite of the case in mainland Europe, where the same products were used as energy drinks (Figure 2). The power of marketing, eh?

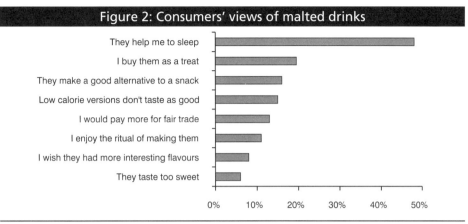

Figure 2: Consumers' views of malted drinks

Source: Mintel 'Hot Chocolate and Malted Drinks Report', March 2010. Data is from 2009

Its drinkers were heavily skewed towards older groups: as a result, Ovaltine was heavily dependent on the over-65s for sales (Figure 3).

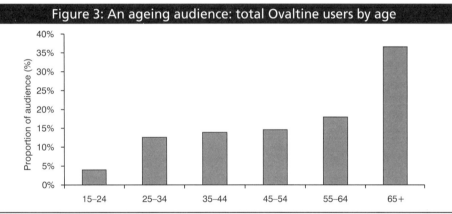

Figure 3: An ageing audience: total Ovaltine users by age

Source: TGI Jan–Dec 2009

The combination of this ageing audience and a lack of relevance of milky sleep aides for younger groups (many of whom would rather sink a couple of glasses of Pinot or a chamomile tea before bed than warm up the milk pan) meant that the market in which Ovaltine operated was declining fast, and projected to decline further (Figure 4).

Not only was the market declining, but Ovaltine was being comprehensively out-gunned by the leading player. Horlicks was double the size of its smaller rival, with own label barely registering as a competitor (Figure 5). This declining market was very much a two-horse race, with one horse half way down the track at the time of the starting gun.

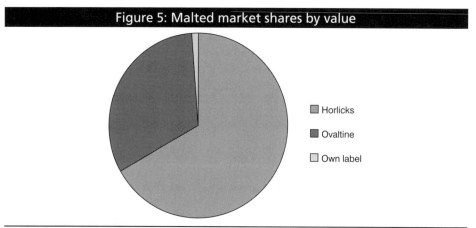

Figure 4: Malted drink market actual and projected decline, 2004–2014

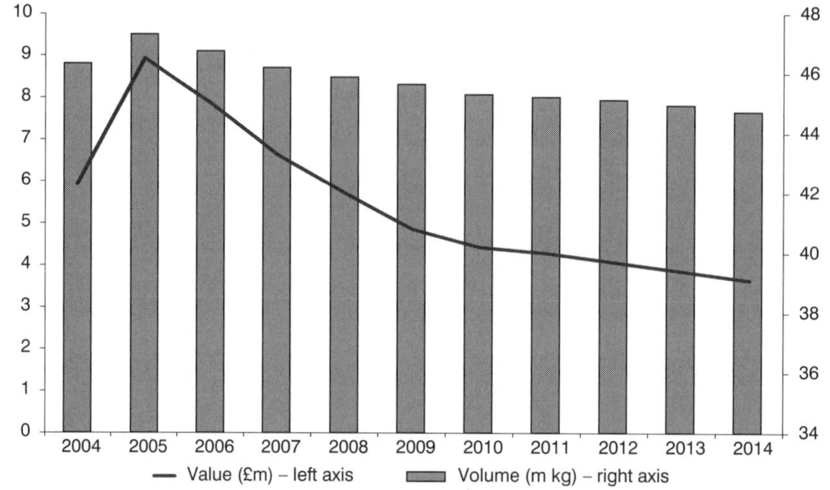

— Value (£m) – left axis   Volume (m kg) – right axis

Source: Mintel 'Hot Chocolate and Malted Drinks Report', March 2010

Figure 5: Malted market shares by value

Horlicks

Ovaltine

Own label

Source: Mintel 'Hot Chocolate and Malted Drinks Report', March 2010

And Horlicks was clearly keen to keep it that way. Whilst Ovaltine barely communicated at all outside the supermarket, Horlicks spend an average of £1.4m a year every year on advertising alone (as well as promoting much more heavily) (Figure 6).

Without the spend to challenge Horlicks's pre-eminence in this market, the chances of Ovaltine growing significantly as a milky sleep aide were slim.

Ovaltine needed to carve out a distinctive territory for itself to step out from its larger rival's shadow.

The brand needed a different strategy that took it to a different place to seek out the growth its ambitions demanded.

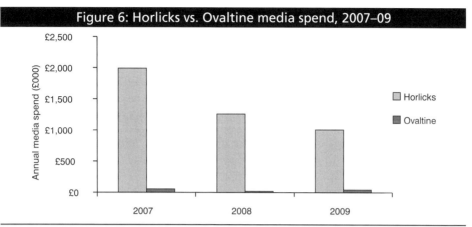

Figure 6: Horlicks vs. Ovaltine media spend, 2007–09

Source: Nielsen Ad Dynamix – AC Nielsen's Advertising and Media tracking tool

The strategy: smaller slice, bigger pie

So if remaining the solid number two in the milky sleep aide malted drink market was a recipe for sure, slow decline, what was the alternative?

The temptation with a small brand and a similarly small budget is to think niche. Find a profitable need no-one else is exploiting. Grow by small increments with discrete audiences. 'Find the thing you can be best in the world at' ('Good To Great'). Find your 'Blue Ocean'.[2]

The team accepted this idea – up to a point. The brand needed a new market space for growth.

But by the end of the strategic development process, the opportunity that was identified wasn't a uniquely ownable niche, but one of the most fiercely contested sectors of food and drink category (albeit with a uniquely Ovaltine spin): the daytime 'have a break' hot drink market.

There were four strategic shifts that got the brand to that place.

1. Shift in audience

To ensure the long-term success of the brand, it was clear Ovaltine needed to recruit younger drinkers.

Qualitative research revealed that a core audience of younger consumers who still remembered Ovaltine from their childhood were the most receptive to hearing from the brand again (Figure 7).

2. Shift in occasion

To appeal to this audience, Ovaltine clearly needed to be something other than a nice milky drink before bedtime – not least because Horlicks had that well sewn-up.

Ovaltine needed to be a daytime drink, not a pre-bed drink: that was the second strategic shift.

Figure 7: Younger core audience's perceptions of Ovaltine

• Imagery wholly anchored in nostalgic days of childhood, but well and truly entrenched with bedtime or illness
• When prompted to consider brand without any challenge, immediate barriers are raised – do I like it? Would I drink it during the day? Would I ever bother?
• BUT assume Ovaltine will be more filling, satisfying and wholesome

CONCLUSION: Despite lack of current relevance for non users, consistent beliefs about the brand reveal very relevant, inherent credentials.

Source: DCRM Research, 2008/9

3. Shift in market

Following the logic of the first two shifts meant changing the very market in which Ovaltine competed in. Not the £44m milky sleep aide market (Horlicks, Ovaltine… and that's it), but the £1.65bn daytime break market (tea, coffee, hot chocolate).

So the challenge was set: not growing beyond the 1/3 share of the market we were in, but grabbing an extra 0.1% share of the £1.65bn daytime hot drink market – another £1.5m in annual sales (Figure 8).

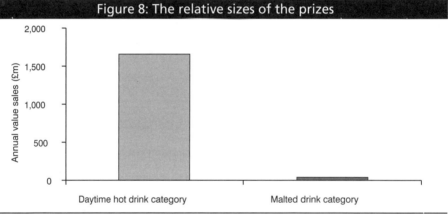

Figure 8: The relative sizes of the prizes

Source: Mintel 'Hot Chocolate and Malted Drinks Report', March 2010

4. Shift in message

Moving from a market that was spending £1.4m a year on advertising to one that's spending £42m a year made it all the more vital that a distinctive and ownable Ovaltine take on the daytime break was uncovered and communicated.[3]

It was here that Ovaltine's substance on the one hand, and its heritage as a sleep aide on the other, perversely came to the rescue.

You can't rush an Ovaltine. Go on – try it. It takes time to prepare, and time to drink. You can't drink it on the run.

Combine this with our heritage in pre-sleep relaxation, and you have a different kind of break that Ovaltine provides: a proper, truly relaxing one that is impossible to rush.

Tea might quench your thirst.

Coffee can give you a kick.

Hot chocolate will give you a sweet treat.

But that's nothing compared to the proper break that a substantial, comforting mug of Ovaltine can provide.

A combination of marketing team insight and research had uncovered Ovaltine's unique take on the daytime hot drink market: *a proper break*. Effectively the same benefit associated with the category all along, but in a condensed, daytime, form.

The new core audience loved it in research (Figure 9).

Figure 9: An Ovaltine 'proper break' – research feedback

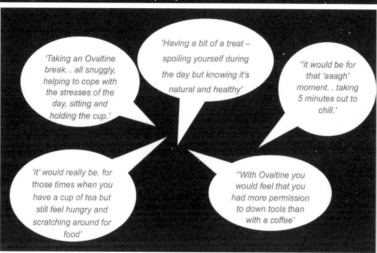

In terms of precise daytime occasion, it seemed that afternoon was the most plausible territory. Firstly from a consumer need point of view – late afternoon being the moment in the day when you most need a break after chasing your tail for hours. But secondly from a consumer acceptance point of view – talking about a morning breakfast boost, for example, would be a story too far for consumers used to associating the brand with sleep.

Our strategy was set: we now needed a smart, absurdly hard-working media and creative vehicle to bring it to our audience outside of the artificial environment of the research studio (Figure 10).

Figure 10: The strategic shift

	From	To
Audience	Over-65s	Younger
Occasion	Pre-bed	Daytime drink
Market	Malted sleep aides	Daytime hot drinks
Message	Have a good night's sleep	Take a *proper* break

Bringing the strategy to life: creative and media execution

With a total budget of £225k for media and production, we needed to act big, but spend small.

We needed to do one thing well, and it needed to punch above its weight. Like the small kid in the fight who draws himself up to his full height, we needed a vehicle that could do the same, in the most broadcast way possible.

A vehicle that could focus on the core target audience.

A vehicle that would associate Ovaltine directly with daytime drinking.

A vehicle which would allow us to talk frequently enough to the audience to get over the 'but it's for bedtime!' barrier.

The answer was an innovative 6-month sponsorship of ITV3 daytime between January and June 2010. Its schedule of well-loved British dramas provided exactly the kind of proper break we hoped Ovaltine would accompany. It also perfectly reflected the warm, comforting values of Ovaltine as a product (Figure 11).

More importantly, by sponsoring the slot rather than the programme, we could reach huge numbers of our audience (53%) and talk to them a lot (44 OTS).

Figure 11: The media campaign

- 6 months continuous on-air from 1 January–31 June 2010
  - 2–7pm every day
  - Approximately 80″ of air time every hour
  - Cost = £195k
- Delivery against target audience
  - 2310 TVRs
  - 53% reach of core target
  - 43.7 OTS
  - 85m total impacts
  - Individual idents
  - 1 × 15″
  - 6 × 10″
  - 1 × 5″

Source: ZenithOptimedia

Secondly, we needed to execute the new positioning creatively with enough idents to keep people's interest despite this high exposure – and all on a tight production budget.

The idents needed to do a number of things.

They needed to create the association between daytime and Ovaltine, and demonstrate the 'proper break' that an Ovaltine provided.

They needed to create a campaign tone of voice that reflected the calm goodness that an Ovaltine break would provide.

They needed to show more modern ways of making Ovaltine (with a kettle rather than the milk pan of yore).

And they needed to do all of this within the strict confines of broadcast sponsorship rules.

The creative solution: animated mugs which, when stirred, would charmingly demonstrate the shift from hectic to calm that an Ovaltine break provided. Without us having to say a single word.

Eight sets of break bumpers were created: in each, a different part of the Ovaltine making process – pouring in the water, stirring the mug – caused a flurry of activity, then calm, and finally satisfaction in the Ovaltine mugs. All simply summed up in the phrase, 'an Ovaltine break' (Figure 12).

Figure 12: The 'Ovaltine break' idents

Communications results

The idents ran for six months from January to June 2010. A full tracking study or econometric model would cost more than the activity itself, but dips were conducted pre and post, and we have analysed Kantar data throughout to isolate the sales (and ultimately profit) effects of the activity.

Here's how the campaign worked.

Total communications awareness more than tripled pre and post the campaign for the core target audience, and almost doubled more generally (Figure 13).

Figure 13: The rise in total communications awareness

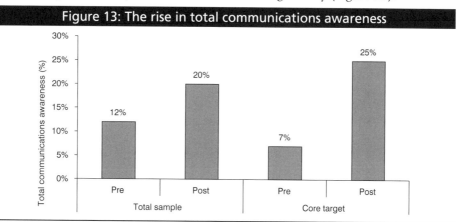

Source: Base: total sample (301), core target (102). Both increases significant at 99% level

Recognition of the idents was more than double the norm (Figure 14).

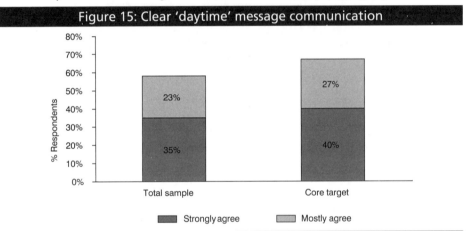

Figure 14: Ident recognition double the norm

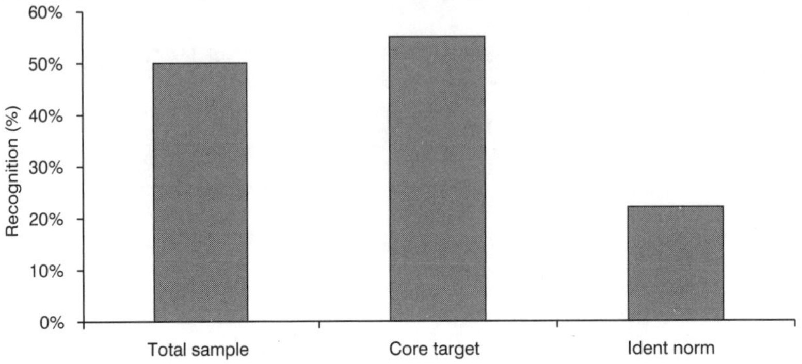

Source: Millward Brown Tea Tracker

The 'daytime break' message was communicated clearly (Figure 15).

Figure 15: Clear 'daytime' message communication

Source: Q: 'Ovaltine means a proper break'. Base: total sample (200), core target (58). Target audience is significantly above the TV norm of 58% (at 90% level)

Perceptions of Ovaltine as a daytime product shifted – those aware of the campaign were significantly more likely to agree that Ovaltine can be drunk during the daytime and 'means it's time for a break' (Figure 16).

This led to significant brand reappraisal – greater than the ident norm, particularly amongst our core target audience (Figure 17).

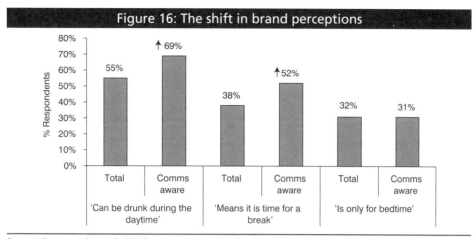

Figure 16: The shift in brand perceptions

Source: Base: total sample (301), comms aware (151) = statistically significant increase at 95% level

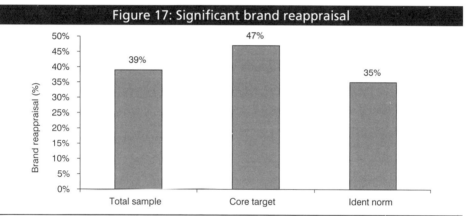

Figure 17: Significant brand reappraisal

Source: Base: total sample (301), core target (102). Target audience is significantly above the ident norm (at 95% level)

As a result, consideration amongst the core target audience increased (Figure 18).

Sales results

So the right people clicked the right buttons on the online questionnaire. But how did that translate through into actual sales?

We have used Horlicks as a point of comparison throughout this section. Not because we saw them as direct competition, but because they provided a control for what might have happened if we had remained in the pre-bedtime world.

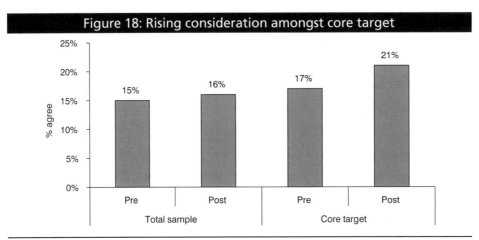

Figure 18: Rising consideration amongst core target

Source: Base: total sample (301), core target (102). Q: 'It would be my first choice'

If anything, it's worth pointing out that this is a harsh comparison simply because in the year in question Horlicks upped their spend to £2.4m, so effectively we were outspent 13:1 in communications terms by them over the period of the campaign (Figure 19).

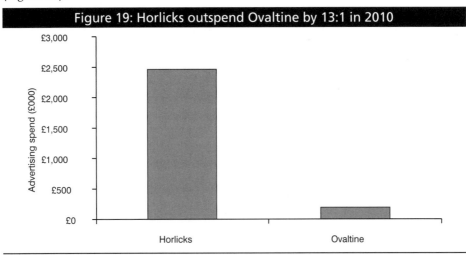

Figure 19: Horlicks outspend Ovaltine by 13:1 in 2010

Source: Nielsen Ad Dynamix

Despite being so comprehensively outspent, Ovaltine volume sales rose strongly over the 6-month period of the sponsorship.

Whilst one would expect sales to be high in the January–March period (as a warming, wintry product), an MAT analysis controls for that natural skew and still the uplift against the previous year was strong – around 15%. More than that, it was sustained after the campaign went off-air (Figure 20).

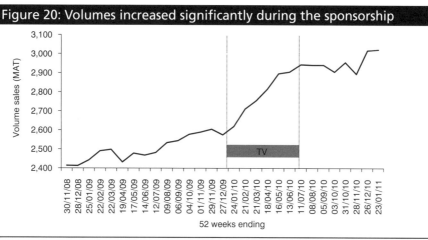

Figure 20: Volumes increased significantly during the sponsorship

Source: Kantar Worldpanel, market research company

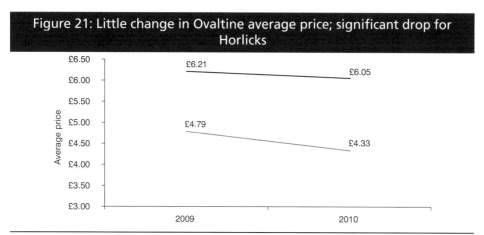

Figure 21: Little change in Ovaltine average price; significant drop for Horlicks

Source: Kantar Worldpanel

This increase was achieved with no significant reduction to the average price (−3%), unlike Horlicks who promoted much more heavily over the year (−9%) (Figure 21).

Ovaltine continued its rise in relative price rise compared to Horlicks – a compelling argument to Ovaltine's retail customers for continued – or indeed improved – distribution (Figure 22).

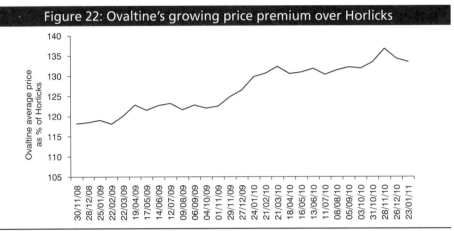

Figure 22: Ovaltine's growing price premium over Horlicks

Source: Kantar Worldpanel

As a result, value sales increased by 25% – £1.816m – of the period of the sponsorship, more than double the rate of Horlicks on one-thirteenth of the spend. The £1.5m annual target had been achieved in six months (Figure 23).

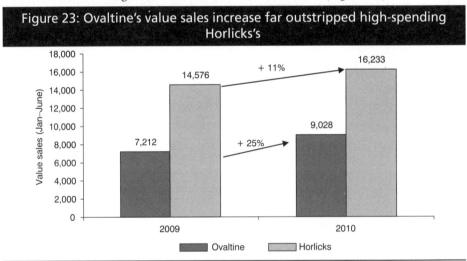

Figure 23: Ovaltine's value sales increase far outstripped high-spending Horlicks's

Source: Kantar Worldpanel

This increase in sales was overwhelmingly a function of bringing new users into the malted drink category, rather than switching between brands (Figure 24).

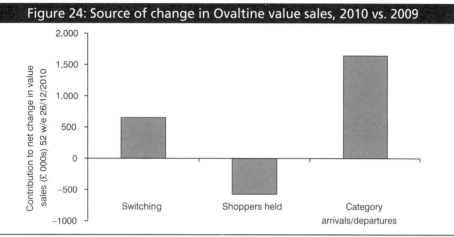

Figure 24: Source of change in Ovaltine value sales, 2010 vs. 2009

Source: Kantar Worldpanel

An analysis of the change composition of Ovaltine buyers over that period suggests that these new entrants were likely to have come from our target audience.

Household data analysis shows that over 2010, Ovaltine households became more likely to have at least three members and have children (Figure 25).

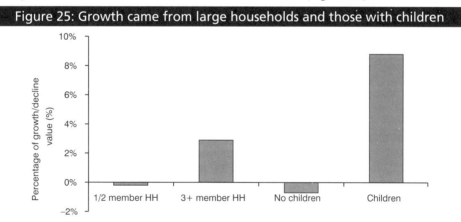

Figure 25: Growth came from large households and those with children

Source: Kantar Worldpanel

This suggests that the new users were certainly not in the one or two person households typically lived in by the over-65s, but rather a much younger target.

Other factors contributing to sales growth

Whilst communications activities weren't the sole generator of these sales uplifts, we believe that the ITV3 sponsorship was by far the most important one. Here's the due diligence...

Product

There were no changes to the product in 2010. The last significant innovations – more convenient 'just add water' variants – had been added some years previously.

Promotions

As in all FMCG categories, promotions are a fact of life for Ovaltine. However, average price in 2010 was broadly stable compared to the previous year, and significantly higher than 2008 (see Figure 21). This was against a backdrop of aggressive price discounting from Horlicks, so effectively Ovaltine's relative price increased.

Distribution

This remained broadly constant over the period of the activity compared to previous years. Good (Figure 26).

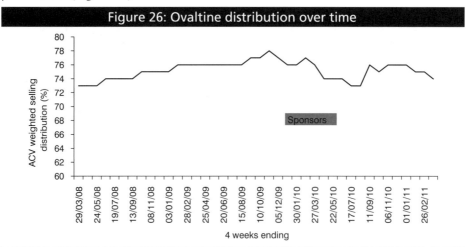

Figure 26: Ovaltine distribution over time

Source: Nielsen

Other Ovaltine activity

Ovaltine has not undertaken any above the line activity in a number of years. However, for some time it has undertaken a tightly-targeted pregnant mum strand of activity through Bounty packs (fortification with Folic Acid makes it an excellent pregnancy supplement). However, as neither the birth rate nor the nature of the activity has changed significantly over the years, we can strip this out as a constant.

Weather and seasonality

You'd expect Ovaltine sales to go up when the temperature drops, and that is indeed what happens (Figure 27).

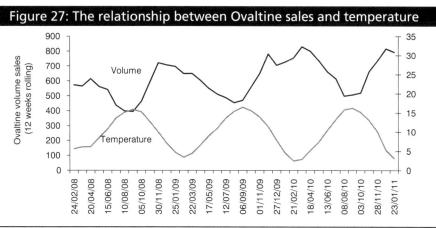

Figure 27: The relationship between Ovaltine sales and temperature

Source: Kantar Worldpanel; Met Office

However, by looking at MAT data we have controlled for seasonality within the data.

Those with good memories who feel the cold will recall that winter 2010 was especially nippy. As a result, the average temperature for the period of the sponsorship was a one degree Celsius colder than average.

Regression analysis (Figure 28) shows that a one degree reduction in average temperature naturally increases volumes by 6,700 in a 4-week period. This would account for 41,000kg of the volume increase during the six months of the campaign, or 3% of the 25% value sales uplift reported earlier.

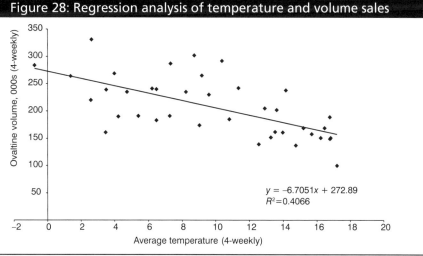

Figure 28: Regression analysis of temperature and volume sales

$y = -6.7051x + 272.89$
$R^2 = 0.4066$

Source: Kantar Worldpanel and Agency econometric analysis

Competitor activity

Direct competitor activity (from Horlicks) was significant both before and during the campaign, outspending Ovaltine by a factor of 13. In the broader 'daytime break' drink market (tea, coffee and hot chocolate), spend remained both large and sustained over the period (Table 1).

Table 1: Competitor media activity	
Year	Spend
2006	£35.8m
2007	£37.4m
2008	£29.8m
2009	£41.9m
2010	£42.3m

Source: Nielsen Ad Dynamix

Return on marketing investment

Incremental sales of £1.816m were generated over the six months of the Ovaltine sponsorship. This was achieved with no increase in distribution, and a very slight decrease in average price (3%).

Stripping out the 3% increase in value sales attributable to the colder weather brings incremental sales generated by the sponsorship to £1.567m.

Understandably, Associated British Foods will not disclose the gross profit margin on any specific brand. However, across the portfolio their gross profit margin was 29.7% in 2010.[4] As this includes agricultural commodities with historically low margins, this is likely to be a conservative estimate.

So this gives a short-term additional gross profit of at least £539,000 from the incremental sales. Taking away the cost of the sponsorship gives a short-term return on marketing investment of 1.39:1.

However, we believe that there is likely to be a long-term as well as short-term effect of the sponsorship on sales.

In many ways the sponsorship acted like advertising: messages were communicated; perceptions shifted; sales responded during and were sustained after the sponsorship (Figure 20).

For this reason, we believe it's not inappropriate to assume a multiplier effect of the sponsorship similar to that of advertising.

Academic analysis suggests a 'rule of thumb' multiplier of 2.5 for the incremental sales directly driven by advertising.[5] Taking this multiplier effect on board would produce extra revenue of £4.54m and gross profit (with marketing costs subtracted) of £1.12m.

Thus the long-term payback of the campaign could be up to £5 for every £1 spent (Table 2).

Table 2: Return on marketing investment	
Description	**Value**
Incremental value sales, Jan–June 2010	£1.816m
Incremental temperature-related sales	£252,000
Sponsorship-related incremental sales	£1.567m
Gross profit margin	29.7%
Gross profit from sponsorship-related sales less marketing costs	£314,000
Short-term ROMI	**1.39:1**
Long-term incremental value sales	£4.54m
Long-term gross profit from sponsorship-related sales less marketing costs	£1.12m
Long-term ROMI	**5:1**

Source: Kantar Worldpanel; Nielsen Homescan; Associated British Foods Annual Report; Bloomberg Analysis (see note 4)

Conclusions

In the 2010 Associated British Foods Annual Report, a document that covers seven industry sectors across 44 countries, there was only one brand that was specifically singled out for its growth performance over the year, and that was Ovaltine.

We believe that Ovaltine's strategic shift of market, communicated through the 'Ovaltine break' campaign, was crucial in helping deliver that growth.

Too often in marketing small budgets are an excuse for small thinking, and small returns.

This paper shows how, if you do it right, big ambitions matched by big thinking can really deliver for a brand.

Notes

1   For example, Jim Collins (2001) *Good to Great: Why Some Companies Make the Leap and Others Don't*, London: Random House; W. Chan Kim and Renée Mauborgne (2005) *Blue Ocean Strategy: How to Create Uncontested Market Space and Make the Competition Irrelevant*, Boston: Harvard Business School Press.
2   Ibid.
3   Nielsen Ad Dynamix – 2010 combined advertising spend of tea, coffee and hot chocolate.
4   Source: Bloomberg/Saxo Bank Equity, research analysis of gross margins of leading global grocery businesses, February 2011.
5   Tim Broadbent, 'How advertising pays back', *Admap*, 422, November 2001.

SECTION 4

Silver winners

Chapter 11

Aquafresh Kids

Helping mum win the Bedtime Battle

By Andrew Niven, Claire Taylor and Chris Binns, MediaCom and Gary Pope, Kids Industries
Credited companies: Advertising and Media Consultancy: Turner; Client: GSK

Editor's summary

Sales for the Aquafresh Kids range have increased by 144% in the past four years. This success came through an understanding that for mums, getting their kids to brush their teeth and go to bed is a nightmare. Communications aimed to help mum win the Bedtime Battle. So the Nurdles, three lovable characters who helped make brushing fun, were created. Through songs, books, virtual worlds and instore events, Aquafresh permeated kids' culture. The campaign has driven incremental sales of £3.5m with a payback of £1.41, and is now the blueprint for Aquafresh Kids worldwide. The judges particularly admired how the child audience was split into three development phases, and the multi-channel approach applied across the different age groups.

Introduction

This is a story of how non-traditional communications vehicles can grow an entire market, turn around a brand's fortunes and create significant monetary value.

This is a story of songs, books, virtual worlds and instore events.

It is a story about how three unknown characters (the Nurdles) took on a market of movie franchise tie-ins, and the massive Colgate and won.

It is a story of injecting impetus into a stagnant market, brand growth of 143%, and payback of £1.41.[1]

It is a story about the value created in executing communications against human rather than brand insights.

Most significantly it is a story about parenting.

Background

We begin this story in 2006.

In the UK 25% of homes have children under ten.[2] Yet kids' oral health products represented just 3.5% of the total market.[3] Even worse, the market was in 4% MAT value sales decline.[4] There was clearly a huge gap between market potential and market reality.

At the same time GSK's once dominant Maclean's *Milk Teeth* had lost significant share to Colgate (Figure 1).

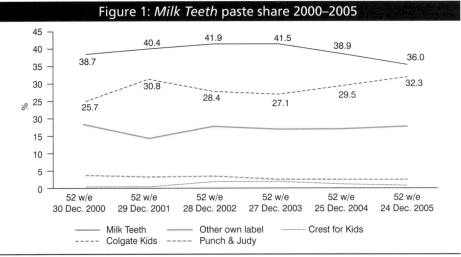

Figure 1: *Milk Teeth* paste share 2000–2005

Source: IRI

Colgate Kids had focused their attention for the period on promotional movie tie-ins borrowing appeal from cultural icons such as Shrek and Donkey and the strategy appeared to be working.

Compounding the market and brand issues, parents started using adult toothpastes for their kids as soon as their children were two or three.[5] Adult toothpastes actually contain too much fluoride for children but it was symptomatic of the lack of category engagement that parents were reverting to a 'one size fits all' solution as soon as possible.

Objectives

Our first objective was to return the poor-performing *Milk Teeth* SKU to growth.

Secondly, we were tasked with successfully launching two new pastes, *Little Teeth*, for 3-6 year olds and *Big Teeth*, (6+), under the Aquafresh brand, rather than Macleans (Figure 2).

Our final challenge was to reinvigorate Kids Oral Care and create category value. An ambitious set of tasks given that we had an original A&P budget of just £600k per annum.

Figure 2: Aquafresh Kids paste range

Source: GSK

The strategic solution

Consumer insight: the Bedtime Battle

The category had spent years telling mums that children needed their own toothpaste to best care for their teeth; simple, rational, educational messaging (Figure 3).

Figure 3: *Milk Teeth* campaign 2004

Source: GSK

This approach was driven by insight from focus groups that if mums simply knew the facts they would act, because all mums want the best for their kids.

Except what you say in focus groups often bears little relation to real life.

Ethnographic research[6] told us that tooth brushing wasn't the most harmonious time of the day. According to parents it's a bit like a battleground.

When you've just got in from work and the children are tired but don't want to go to bed it's not a great time to shove a great big plastic stick in their mouths. The children hate it, mums hate it and this needs to go on for two minutes; every single day.

It's no wonder that even the best parents let the little terrors get away with not brushing sometimes. But the world can see clearly whether children's teeth are looked after or stained yellow and parents see the judgement as a slight on their parenting skills:

The state of their teeth is the most obvious reflection of my parenting to other mothers.[7]

Ultimately, mums didn't care about our product claims and didn't like us telling them what to do. They just wanted their kids to brush their teeth; willingly!

Communications insight: one size does not fit all

The relationship between parents and kids changes enormously over the first seven years from one of total dependence to gradual development of independence. This is no different in oral care.

For the first couple of years mum is heavily engaged to the point of having to brush her child's teeth and will seek out advice as her baby goes through teething and begins brushing.

As the child gets older they begin brushing their own teeth. At three years old the Bedtime Battle reaches its nadir as mum tries to supervise and her child tries to assert independence.

With three different pastes to communicate, we effectively had three audiences: mum (*Milk*), mum and child together (*Little*), and more independent child (*Big*) (Figure 4).

Figure 4: Engagement with child's oral health by age

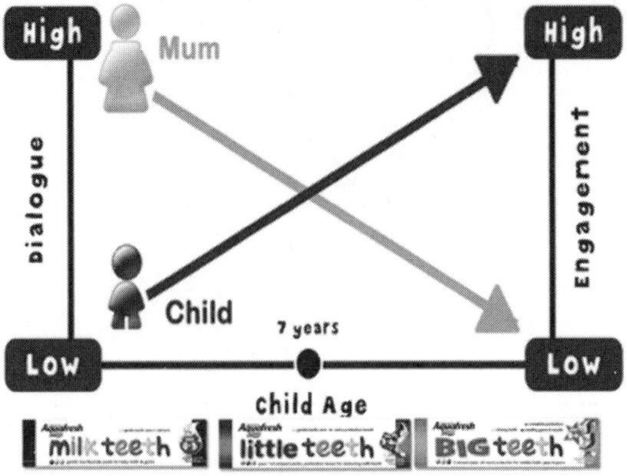

Source: Kids Industries

The communications task

It was clear from our ethnographic work that we firstly needed to offer mums greater understanding of how to look after their children's teeth and why it is important.

Crucially, we also had to get kids engaged with brushing their teeth and with the Aquafresh Kids range. If we could get them on side the chances were that mum would buy.

Our overall task was to make brushing a positive experience for mums and kids. We'd be a family friend for life and make the Bedtime Battle a thing of the past.

The campaign idea: Learn, Brush, Grow

We translated these insights into a connections platform:

Learn Together, Brush Together, Grow Together

- **Learn Together:** We needed to educate and empathise with mum while helping children learn the importance of oral care.
- **Brush Together:** We needed to make the evening brushing experience a fun time for everybody rather than the difficult time it had always been.
- **Grow Together:** We needed to allow children to assert their own independence whilst the family and Aquafresh remained a helping hand in the background.

The creative idea: The Nurdles

Today, a child makes sense of the world by exploring the experiences of well-loved characters and stories and drawing comparisons to their own experiences.

To drive engagement with kids we created characters that were rich, cute and ownable by Aquafresh. Using the brand icon of the Nurdle of toothpaste we invented the Nurdles (Figure 5).

We built specific identification patterns into our characters that would mean recall and request.

- **Milky** (0–3) has a nurturing identification pattern; the children want to look after him.
- **Lilly** (3–6) has emulatory and reflective identification patterns; the younger ones want to be her and the older ones to see something of themselves in her.
- **Billy** (6+) is emulatory for the younger end to drive progression and reflective at the older end, so the children feel comfortable following his lead in oral care.

Mum was able to use the characters as leverage to win the bathroom battle.

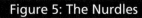

Figure 5: The Nurdles

Source: Kids Industries

The activity

1. Learn together – educating mum

First steps for new mums

We first talked to mums at the moment of birth through a Bounty pack which they receive when they leave hospital. It includes a leaflet about oral development and a *Milk Teeth* sample.

We also created a series of advertorials which ran in *Parenting Press* to help mum with some of the trickier aspects of children's oral care, such as teething (Figure 6).

Figure 6: Aquafresh magazine advertorial

Source: *Parenting Press*, IPC

Creating a knowledge bank for mums

Aquafresh.co.uk is designed as a place for mum to find information and discover the techniques to help her ensure a healthy mouth for her child (Figure 7).

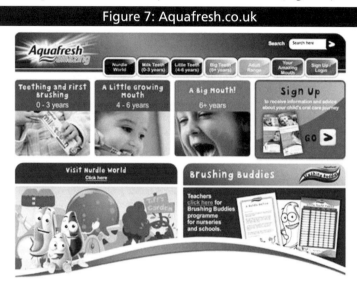

Figure 7: Aquafresh.co.uk

Source: www.aquafresh.co.uk

Creating dialogue with mum

We developed an eCRM campaign that delivers emails to mum during the life of the child's use of the brand. By mapping the oral development of children we are able to send timely advice and information to mum when it is relevant and useful, with topics such as:

- how to deal with teething;
- how to brush a mouth full of milk and adult teeth.

To recruit for the eCRM programme we offered mums the chance to receive a free Nurdles storybook, perfect for bedtimes (Figure 8).

2. Brush Together – making brushtime fun

The Nurdle Schmurdle

The centrepiece of our campaign to win the Battle of Bedtime was **The Nurdle Schmurdle**, a 90 second song, which runs on Cartoonito and Boomerang every night at 6.55pm, just before bedtime (Figure 9).

Aimed at the under 5s audience of mums and kids brushing together, the Schmurdle teaches kids how to brush their teeth and makes brushing fun.

Figure 8: eCRM communication

Source: GSK

Figure 9: The Nurdle Schmurdle

Source: GSK

Vox Pops

We also created TV advertising to drive awareness of each Aquafresh product. We wanted to use the Nurdles to get mums and kids engaged with brushing. So we created Vox Pops; 20" ads that include live action responses by children to the Nurdles' request to know 'What's your favourite thing about Brushtime?'(Figure 10).

Figure 10: Vox Pops[8]

Source: GSK

The campaign runs across core children's channels and GMTV.

NurdleWorld – play with The Nurdles online

We created NurdleWorld; an immersive and interactive online world for children to learn good oral health habits. It is chock full of brushing related games for each age group; e.g. you can build your own Nurdle house and collect stars to dress your Nurdles (Figure 11).[9]

Figure 11: NurdleWorld

Source: GSK

Making dentist visits less of a pain

The visit to the dentist is a key moment we had to make better for mums and kids. We created Dentists Packs to keep children engaged; games, stickers and even their own Passport to NurdleWorld, which the dentist stamps at every visit (Figure 12).

Figure 12: NurdleWorld Passport

Source: GSK

Making mornings fun too

We didn't forget that mornings can be a battle too. The Vox Pops are upweighted in the morning and we also ran a sponsorship with GMTV and gmtv.com offering help for mums and fun for kids (Figure 13).

3. Grow Together – educating and engaging kids

Brushing Buddies

Brushing Buddies is a multimedia oral health education programme where the children, working with the Nurdles (direct from NurdleWorld) complete a series of tasks at home and in school. The programme targets Nursery, Reception and Year 1 children and has been developed to form part of the Early Years Foundation Stage Curriculum (Figure 14).

Figure 13: GMTV sponsorship

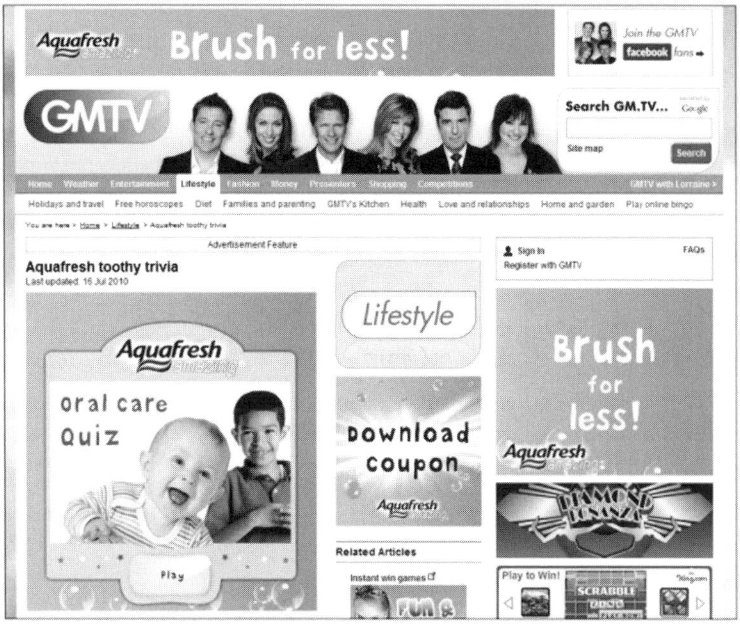

Source: GMTV.co.uk

Figure 14: Brushing Buddies

Source: GSK

Experiential: meet the Nurdles

Meeting the Nurdles is the best way to bring them to life for children. In 2007 we ran a summer competition with London Zoo. Children had to discover all the animals with big teeth and how they brushed them (Figure 15).

The Nurdles have also spent every summer holiday visiting the UK's biggest supermarkets, making shopping educational and fun and driving trial.

Figure 15: Experiential activity

Source: GSK

The campaign plan can be seen in Figure 16 below.

Figure 16: Overall schematic

		2007	2008	2009	2010
		O N D	J F M A M J J A S O N D	J F M A M J J A S O N D	J F M A M J J A S O N D
Learn Together	Bounty Partnership				
	Magazine advertorial				
	Online				
	www.aquafresh.co.uk				
	eCRM programme				
Brush Together	The Nurdle Schmurdle				
	Vox Pops (TV)				
	www.nurdleworld.co.uk				
	Dentists				
	GMTV Sponsorship				
Grow Together	Brushing Buddies schools partnership				
	Experiential: Meet the Nurdles				

Source: MediaCom

Results – media value, increased brand equity and 143% sales growth

Media value: appointment to view advertising

The Schmurdle was one of the most popular 'programmes'[10] in the bedtime slot (see Table 1).

Table 1: TVRs for bedtime hour shows

	Channel group	Programme title	TVR (max)
1	Boomerang	What's New Scooby-Doo?	1.1
2	Cartoonito	Cartoonito Karaoke	1.1
3	Boomerang	Nurdle Schmurdle	1.1
4	Cartoonito	Nurdle Schmurdle	0.9
5	Boomerang	The Garfield Show	0.8
6	Boomerang	Tom and Jerry Tales	0.8
7	Cartoonito	Strawberry Shortcakes Berry Bitty	0.8
8	Boomerang	Bugs Bunny	0.7
9	Boomerang	Tom and Jerry	0.7
10	Cartoonito	Frances	0.7

Source: DDS

An award winning campaign

Aquafresh Kids is a multiple award winner, with two Gold awards at the 2008 *MediaWeek* Awards, for '*Media Idea; Medium*' and '*Sales Pitch of the Year*' and the award for '*Best Campaign: Fashion, Beauty and Healthcare*' at the 2008 *Campaign* Awards (Figure 17).

Figure 17: *MediaWeek* award coverage

Source: Brandrepublic.com

Which was all very gratifying but what did it mean for the brand?

Brand equity: the nation's favourite for kids' teeth

Brand equity has grown consistently during the course of the campaign.
Firstly, awareness has grown significantly (see Figure 18):

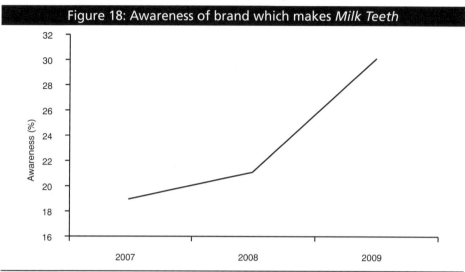

Figure 18: Awareness of brand which makes *Milk Teeth*

Source: Millward Brown

First choice consideration has jumped 20% (see Figure 19).

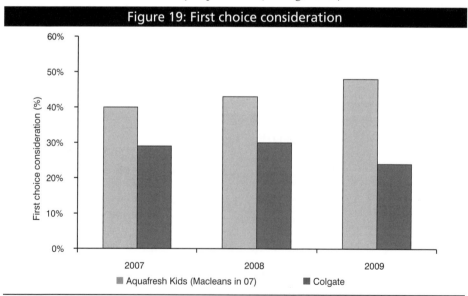

Figure 19: First choice consideration

Source: Millward Brown

Being fun and helping mums has meant we are now seen as the expert in kids' oral care (see Figure 20).

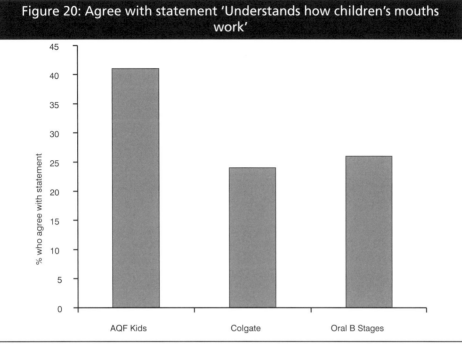

Figure 20: Agree with statement 'Understands how children's mouths work'

Source: Millward Brown

Millward Brown analysis shows why equity has grown. The Schmurdle scored very well on the key metrics of making brushing fun and educating kids, creating strong buzz (Figure 21).

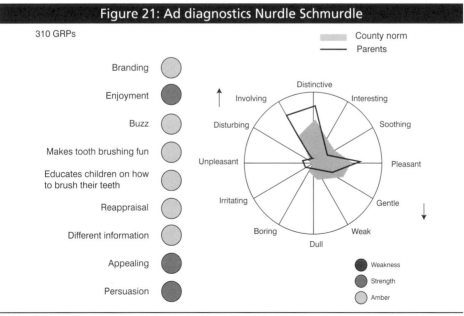

Figure 21: Ad diagnostics Nurdle Schmurdle

Source: Millward Brown

Increased sales: more buyers

Penetration has increased by 50% since Q4 2007 (Figure 22).

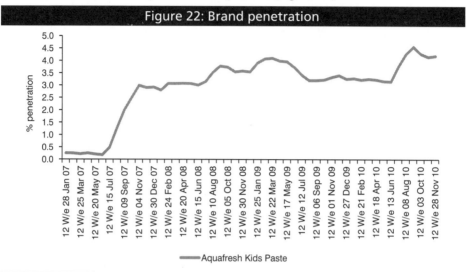

Figure 22: Brand penetration

Source: Kantar

144% sales growth

Between January 2007 and December 2010 Aquafresh Kids sales have increased by
£6.6m; a phenomenal 144% increase (see Figure 23).

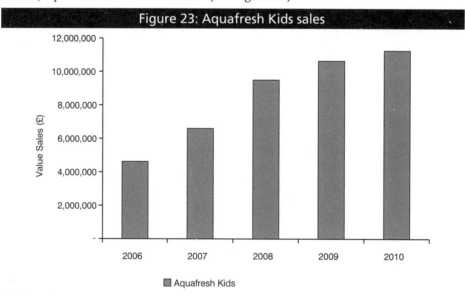

Figure 23: Aquafresh Kids sales

Source: AC Nielsen

Aquafresh has increased total category share from below 30% to 33% (Figure 24).

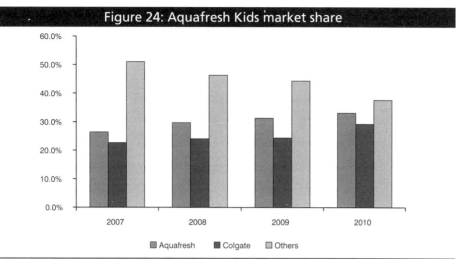

Figure 24: Aquafresh Kids market share

Source: AC Nielsen

In paste, where we had fallen to 36% share, we are now at a record 51%! (Figure 25).

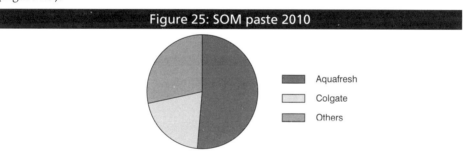

Figure 25: SOM paste 2010

Source: AC Nielsen

And finally, we have driven category growth (Figure 26).

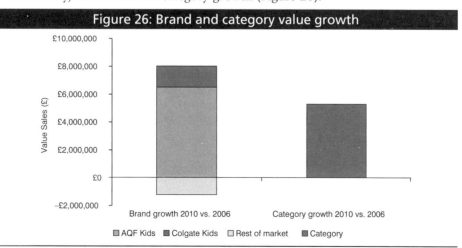

Figure 26: Brand and category value growth

Source: AC Nielsen

A global success story

Spurred on by the UK's success, the Nurdles are now a global phenomenon and the UK strategy is now the global blueprint for campaigns across the USA, South Africa and South America (Figure 27).

Figure 27: Aquafresh.com USA website[11]

Source: www.aquafresh.com

As a result of the campaign's success the A&P budget has also increased substantially. We invested £1.4m in 2010 (up from £600k) and in 2011 we are developing new content and new media partnerships.

Proving the effectiveness of advertising

Econometric models for Aquafresh Kids were set up in 2005 to evaluate the effectiveness of the overall Aquafresh communications strategy. This analysis has been crucial in driving accountability, confidence in the communication strategy and helping to optimise the plan going forward.

It has proved that spending on the Aquafresh Kids range delivers one of the best ROI's not only amongst the Aquafresh portfolio but across the mouthcare category and indeed across FMCG benchmarks.

Before moving on to the payback, let's show how we have been able to isolate all other potential drivers of sales, using econometric analysis:

NPD: *Little Teeth* and *Big Teeth* launched in 2007. Within the models we have stripped this impact out. These launches added an incremental 11% to sales since 2007 (Figure 28).

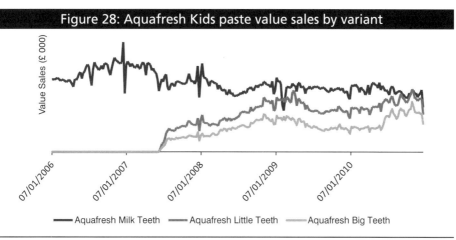

Figure 28: Aquafresh Kids paste value sales by variant

Source: AC Nielsen

Distribution

Distribution has remained stable for *Milk Teeth* and therefore has not contributed to growth. Both *Big* and *Little Teeth* have launched over this period and thus have seen growth in this measure but this has been stripped out within the models, as quantified in Point 1 (Figure 29).

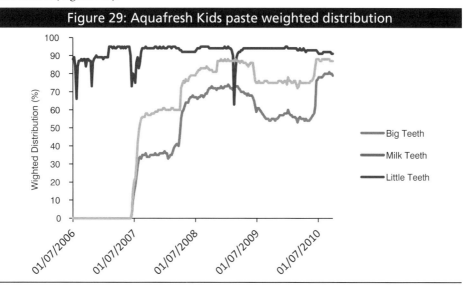

Figure 29: Aquafresh Kids paste weighted distribution

Source: AC Nielsen

Price

There has not been any advantageous change in price. In 2007, price actually increased by 28% vs. 2006, and was sustained over the whole period which would lead to deflationary impacts on overall sales. We have quantified that price and promotions contributed 25% of sales in 2006 vs. an average of 11% in 2007–2010 (Figure 30).

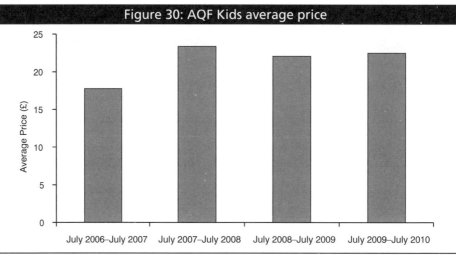

Figure 30: AQF Kids average price

Source: AC Nielsen

Market dynamics

Aquafresh has grown over 140% since 2006. The category and Colgate have only grown by 18% over the same period and thus the increase seen is not due to any market factors (Figure 31).

Figure 31: Brand vs. category growth

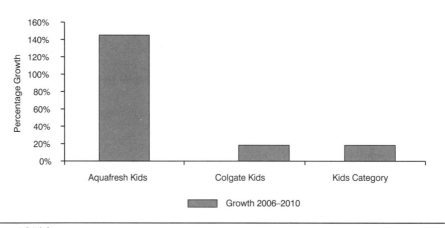

Source: AC Nielsen

Other factors accounted for or tested within the models are competitor pricing, advertising, NPD and distribution and seasonality.

In Figure 32 you can see the output from our econometric model, stripping out all key drivers of sales and showing the short-term impact from communications:

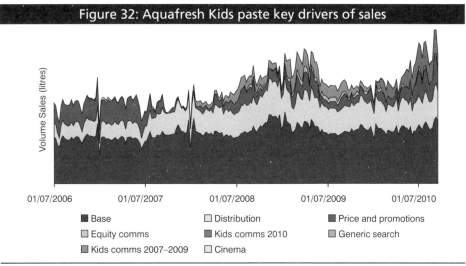

Figure 32: Aquafresh Kids paste key drivers of sales

Source: MediaCom Economiser

As you can see from this model, the base has also been increasing since the advertising started in 2007. Thus we have built a separate base model which isolates the fact that communications has been the key driver of this step change (Figure 33). This is the medium-term impact of the communications activity:

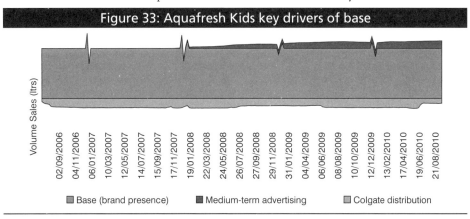

Figure 33: Aquafresh Kids key drivers of base

In addition, we have measured an incremental halo impact onto brush.

Quantifying the impact

Taking into account the short and medium term impact from the models, communications for Aquafresh Kids has delivered incremental sales of £3.5m since the campaign launched[12] also taking into account the advertising adstock. Given a spend of just over £2m, this is an impressive return of £1.64. Efficiency has also grown exponentially year-on-year (Figure 34):

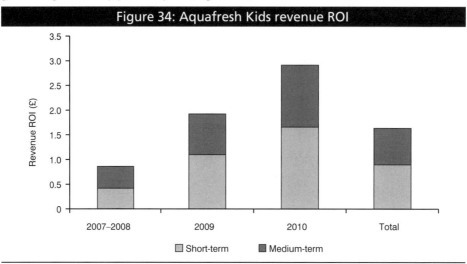

Figure 34: Aquafresh Kids revenue ROI

Source: MediaCom Economiser

Building in the total marketing budget including production costs as well as the retailer margin and cost of goods, we have delivered a profitable return as well as a sales return (see Table 2):

Table 2: ROI and ROMI

	Short–medium term
ROI	£1.64
ROMI	£1.12

Source: MediaCom Economiser

Although we have taken account of the impact of advertising in causing a step change in the base, this still only accounts for the medium-term impact of the communications as the impact is subject to a normal advertising adstock. We believe, however, that this base step change will continue over time. We can see this to be true given the increase in penetration that we have observed over the period.

However, we can't assume that this base will be maintained indefinitely, but that it will decay over time. In order to establish what this level is we have calculated the persistence we see in the base from our econometric model and applied the same factor, thus assuming that each week the base will decay by 1%.

Thus, we have calculated that the additional long-term impact will contribute additional £1.3m sales, which gives an outstanding ROI of over £2 and a ROMI payback of £1.41 (Figure 35).

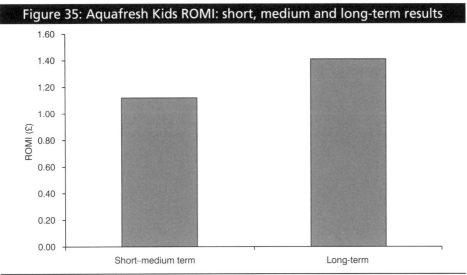

Figure 35: Aquafresh Kids ROMI: short, medium and long-term results

Source: MediaCom Economiser

Conclusion

This is the story of how a very human insight led to a campaign which transgressed our traditional silos of media, advertising, events and instore. This is the story of an idea that has permeated kids' culture. An idea that has created strong financial value for GSK, but also an idea that has created massive value for parents and kids in the UK, and will start to do the same the world over as the Bedtime Battle becomes a thing of the past.

Notes

1 Long-term ROMI calculated by MediaCom.
2 Source: TGI.
3 Source: AC Nielsen.
4 Source: AC Nielsen.
5 Source: TNS 2008.
6 Source: Kids Industries/MediaCom Enthographic Research March 2007 conducted over one week with 10 families.
7 Source: Kids Industries/MediaCom Enthographic Research 2007.
8 Produced by Turner Broadcasting.
9 http://www.aquafresh.co.uk/index.cfm?event=NurdleWorld&intCentralContentID=6444.
10 Source: DDS.
11 Source: www.aquafresh.com/nurdleworld/default.aspx.
12 Modelled period Nov 2007–Sept 2010.

Chapter 12

first direct

first direct live

**By Arvind Kapavarapu and Don Larotonda,
Mindshare**
Credited companies: Creative Agencies: JWT and JWT Cheetam Bell; Digital
Agency: MadeByPi; Client: first direct

Editor's summary

By 2009, first direct faced a long-term decline in brand awareness and
consideration, and their position as most recommended bank was under
threat. The solution was to make prospective customers understand its
services in a truthful and transparent way. first direct became the first
brand to find out what its customers were saying online and broadcast it
live and unedited through advertising. The campaign's success has driven a
100% uplift in consideration, 55% uplift in share of new current accounts
as well as a profit ROMI of £1.54. The judges thought this to be a very
strong paper with a bold and inventive real-time communications solution
at its heart that delivered results, all within a sector that continues to face
some real challenges.

Q: How does a bank increase consideration and drive positive word of mouth at a time when people hate banks?

A: Make prospective customers understand the first direct difference through the simple, unvarnished truth.

first direct became the first brand ever to find out what its customers were saying online and broadcast it live through advertising.

The results were prolific, driving 100% uplift in consideration, 55% uplift in share of new current accounts as well as a profit ROI of £1.54.

In the words of one Financial Services blogger: 'This isn't brave, it's right'.

first direct history

When first direct launched its revolutionary banking service on 1 October 1989, it was the UK's first telephone bank offering customers access 24 hours a day, 7 days a week, 365 days a year. No branches, just overtly friendly people at the end of the phone who could really help.

20 years later the first direct phone and internet banking platform had been slavishly copied by much bigger competitors and consequently first direct lost their product differentiation in the market (Figure 1).[1] They maintained their unrivalled reputation for amazing service but this was invisible to non-customers.

By 2009 things went from bad to worse: first direct were losing the battle to acquire new customers, share of switchers was down (Figure 2),[2] brand awareness was in long-term decline (Figure 3),[3] consideration was in steep decline (Figure 4)[4] and even their position of most recommended bank was under threat (Figure 5).[5] Action needed to be taken and fast.

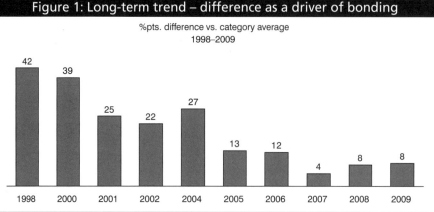

Figure 1: Long-term trend – difference as a driver of bonding

%pts. difference vs. category average
1998–2009

Source: Millward Brown BrandZ. Base: total sample

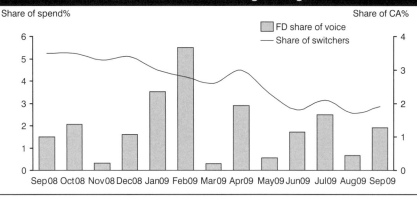

Figure 2: Share of all SWITCHED current accounts opened in last 6 months – 6 month moving average

Share of spend%   Share of CA%

☐ FD share of voice
— Share of switchers

Source: GFK FRS, Nielsen media. Base: all switched current accounts L6M

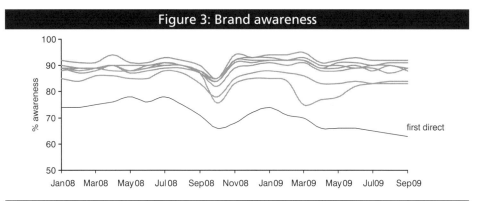

Figure 3: Brand awareness

first direct

Source: Millward Brown, Nielsen media. Base: total sample

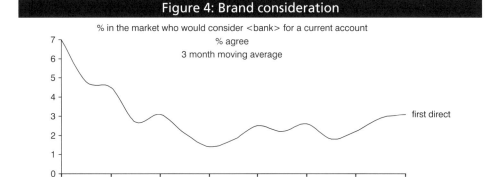

Figure 4: Brand consideration

% in the market who would consider <bank> for a current account
% agree
3 month moving average

first direct

Source: GFK FRS. Base: all likely to take out/switch current accounts England & Wales

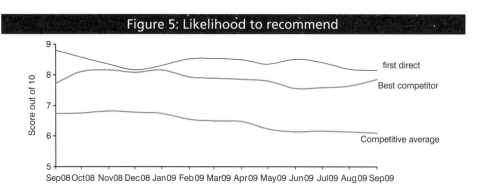

Figure 5: Likelihood to recommend

Source: Millward Brown, Nielsen media. Base: all holders of current account at <bank>; Competitor average = average reported for Barclays, Lloyds TSB, NatWest, Halifax, HSBC, Nationwide, Santander

To make matters worse all these new business challenges were unraveling amidst one of the worst global recessions in history. The media onslaught and trust in banks had hit an all-time low (Table 1).[6] It was therefore the worst possible time for first direct to be lumped in with all other banks.

Table 1: Trust in institutions	
	Net trust increase %
Discount supermarkets	21
Local independent shops	4
Your local supermarket	−1
Your mobile phone provider	−9
The media	−49
Utility companies	−56
The government	−64
Banks	−69

Source: The Futures Company, 2009

The market

The banking sector is characterised by extreme inertia. Although banking customers may perceive that the level of service they receive is not fantastic, it is adjudged to be just 'normal banking service'. Staying with a current provider is perceived to be easier than switching. Thus only 5% of current account customers switch in any given month.[7] These market conditions are compounded as first direct is a small player within the category, seeking only higher value customers.

The competition

first direct operates in a market dominated by banking giants with huge marketing budgets and large branch networks (Figure 6).[8] first direct accounts for only 2% of the advertising expenditure within the competitive set (Figure 7)[9] and with no branches, continually fights against consumer desire for 'branch convenience'[10] when choosing a new bank.

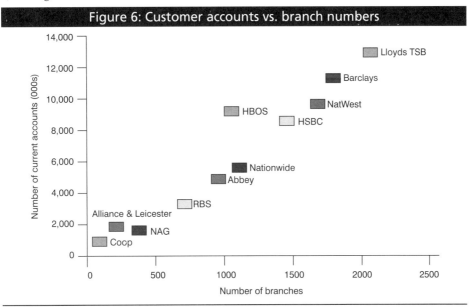

Figure 6: Customer accounts vs. branch numbers

Source: Datamonitor

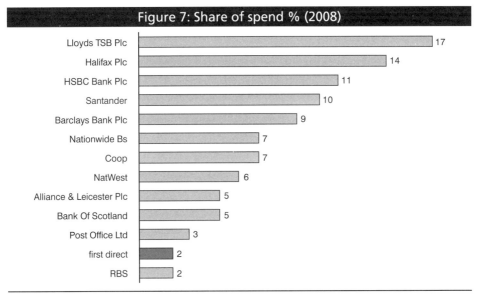

Figure 7: Share of spend % (2008)

Source: Nielsen media

Summary of challenges:

- underinvestment in the brand had caused brand metrics to be eroded;
- their position of most recommended bank was under threat;
- brand consideration was in steep decline;
- limited budgets;
- as an online/telephone bank, they could not leverage a large branch network to acquire customers;
- all of this in the midst of one of the worst recessions in history.

The communication challenge

first direct needed a communications platform which would help distance it from the mass of unpopular and untrusted banks and dial into first direct's core brand ethos – its amazing customer service.

However, with low budgets and the negative effect of the economic crisis we couldn't just tell people 'first direct has amazing service'. The idea needed to be new, innovative, challenging and uniquely first direct. It had to force reappraisal of first direct and drive comparison with people's own experience of their banking service.

Our strategic solution

The customer research we did with the marketing team at first direct always brought us back to the same problem: first direct offers amazing service, but we couldn't just tell people because in the economic climate no one believed what any bank had to say.

We looked in depth at our audience's media habits and their attitude to service in general. We found they demanded a clear value exchange in everything they engaged with, be that a bank or a restaurant. They are passionate about their beliefs in service and act as real brand advocates or outright rejecters. Through the use of web tools they are happy to make themselves heard, be that through their own blogs, review sites, forums, social platforms or face to face.

This insight gave rise to a simple experiment: to see what people were saying about first direct on Twitter. We found that while first direct customers were posting both negative and positive comments about first direct, positive posts were largely dominant. This experiment turned into the eureka moment that gave rise to our strategy. From this point forward we knew that whatever we did had to:

1. involve our own customers;
2. be totally transparent.

The communication brief

- Get: Our target audience (Service Challengers).
- To: Challenge their perception of their current bank.
- By: Projecting what first direct customers had to say about theirs.

The communication idea

Most advertisers use social media to talk to their audience. We realised our customers were already doing the talking for us. All we had to do was further amplify their voices. This changed the way we thought about social media and put it at the centre of our communications strategy.

Our idea was something no other brand had ever done and something no other bank would or could dare consider – to broadcast live the views and opinions of its customers.

Thus first direct 'live' was born, it would harness the latest data visualisation techniques, social and participation marketing concepts to express first direct customers' views on its service ethos, and project that to the world. By mining and collating data from forums, blogs, comment threads and social networks and visualising both negative and positive sentiment, first direct moved away from presenting their chosen message to the world – to an unedited customer community message.

While Mindshare conceived and executed the concept of 'live', our colleagues at JWT London, JWT Cheetham Bell and MadeByPi were responsible for the creative delivery of the idea.

The media strategy

Our strategy was to challenge people's perceptions of their own bank by projecting what first direct customers had to say about first direct. We wanted to do this as close as possible to the moment of interaction with people's own bank, be that branch or online.

Out of home

We looked at existing digital infrastructure much of which is in and around the London Underground network. Through a mapping exercise we identified the footprint of digital 48, 6 sheets and escalator panels all in close proximity to high traffic branches in central London. Our core audience of high value banking customers also use London Underground on their daily commute.

The use of more traditional media (tube car panels) on the trains helped build the story and further build coverage of the campaign outside the central London area. Additional digital 6 sheets and the Centre Spectacular at Westfield shopping centre extended the reach of the campaign (Figure 8).

The use of overground stations helped reach high value commuters from outside London.

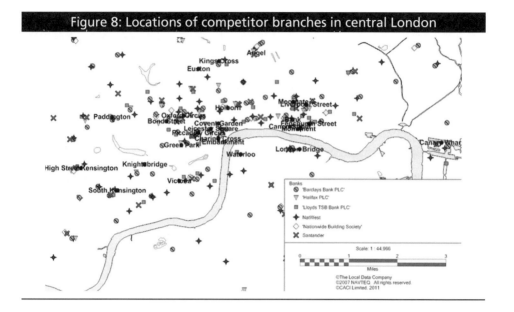

Figure 8: Locations of competitor branches in central London

Online

The online component further increased the coverage of the campaign outside central London and served as the main driver to the campaign microsite. Online activity specifically targeted high value online banking customers, through a series of network, financial and lifestyle vertical buys.

This was supplemented with product specific activity for current accounts and mortgages.

Press

Direct press for both current accounts and mortgages drove a clear call to action and was strategically integrated with the rest of the campaign.

Online display

The online ads pulled data feeds from 20,000 online news sources, in excess of 8 million blogs and over 100,000 message boards, forums, Usenet news groups[11] and the first direct 'live' microsite. This data was then visualised and updated live to all online ad units. The online ads clicked through to www.firstdirect.com/live (Figures 9 and 10).

Full list of ad units: Leaderboards, MPUs and Skyscrapers.

Out of home

The digital outdoor utilised the same data mining, collating and visualisation techniques and updated copy was supplied daily for escalator panels, 6 sheets and centre spectaculars (Figures 11–13).

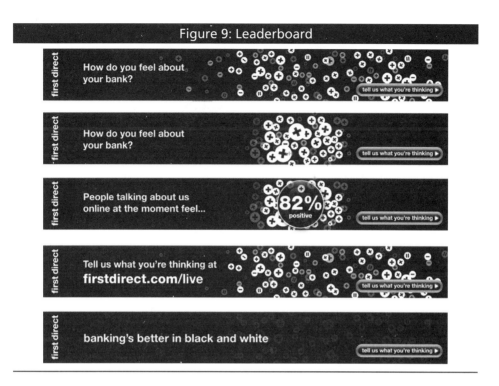

Figure 9: Leaderboard

Figure 10: MPU

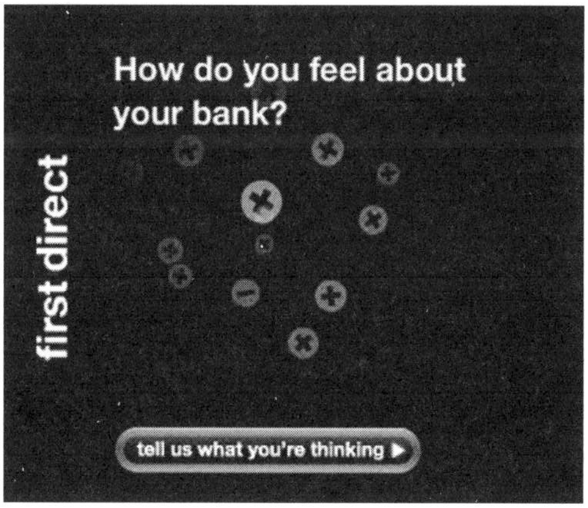

Figure 11: Escalator panels

Figure 12: 6 Sheets

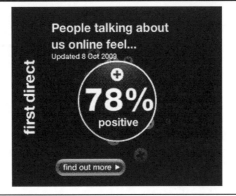

Figure 13: Centre spectaculars

Quotes were taken from Talking Point and projected on 48 sheets, uploaded to digital 48 sheets in mainline stations and printed onto tube car panels (Figures 14–16).

Figure 14: 48 sheets

Figure 15: Transvision

Figure 16: Tube car panel

Microsite

first direct homepage

Actions taken:

A live banner which dominated the first direct homepage projected positive and negative sentiment and invited customers to get involved (Figure 17).

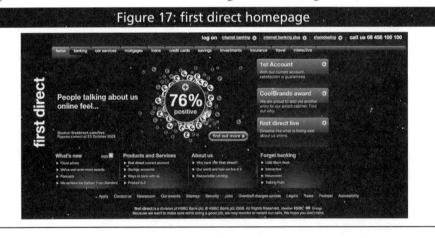

Figure 17: first direct homepage

Microsite landing page

Actions taken:

Once clicking through from the homepage, or arriving directly from the online ads.

Visitors to the microsite had the option to provide live comments, positive and negative on Talking Point, showing how people were 'feeling' about first direct and what words were most prominent in what people were saying (Figures 18–21).

Figure 18: Microsite landing page

Figure 19: Talking Point page

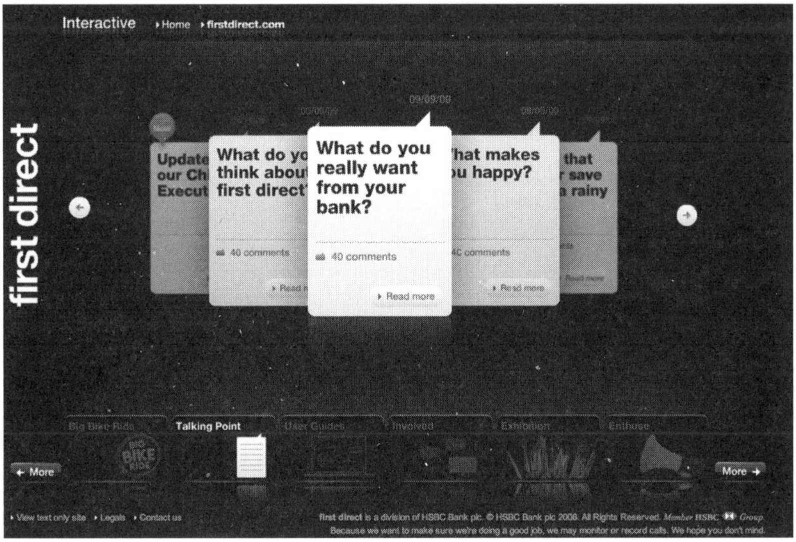

Figure 20: Visualisation of feeling

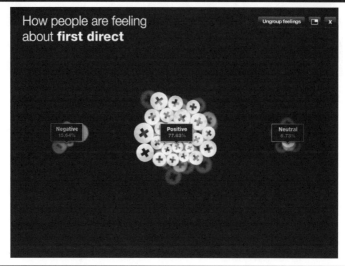

Figure 21: Visualisation of dominant words

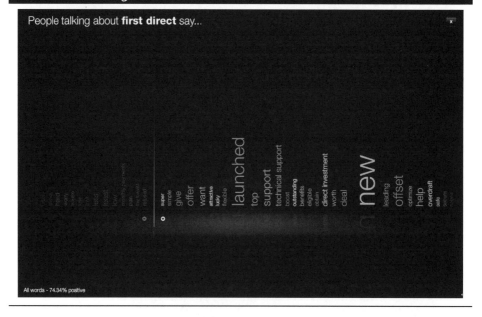

The campaign activity

Brand campaign

See Table 2.

		Total budget inc VAT	September				October				November					December			
			7	14	21	28	5	12	19	26	2	9	16	23	30	7	14	21	28
Outdoor	Transvision Commuter Pack	£455,130																	
	XTP Commuter Interchange Pack																		
	TCPs																		
	LCDs Morning Commuter Interchange Pack																		
	DEPs Commuter																		
	Westfield Spectacular (FOC)																		
	Westfield LCD Network (FOC)																		
Online	Traffic Driving	£341,287																	
	Brand – News																		
	Brand – Lifestyle																		
	Product Display																		
	Optimisation																		
Press	National Press	£327,708																	
	Direct Press Titles																		
Search	Affiliates	£198,275																	
	PPC																		
PR and fees		£463,726																	
Total net media inc VAT exc prod		£1,786,126																	

Table 2: Brand campaign

The results

So what did we achieve?

1. In a category where brand awareness is stagnant we shifted the metric with a tiny share of spend.
2. We reversed the decline in positive media coverage and recommendations and re-established our lead position in the market.
3. Service and innovation scores all improved by a third. As a result we were able to clearly differentiate ourselves and pull away from the pack.
4. Brand consideration amongst those taking out a new current account or switching doubled.
5. Our share of people who were switching or opening new accounts substantially increased.
6. From satisfaction scores that were already in the nineties we pulled away even further from competing banks.

7. We drove customer acquisitions in both current accounts and mortgages and showed a net incremental profit ROI of 1.54.
8. Current account closures decreased by 15% year-on-year.

In order to evaluate success for brand metrics and show the impact of this campaign we made comparisons against market and competitor averages to eliminate market forces. The best competitor is defined as the strongest performer (other than first direct) on each measure.

We also used econometric analysis on applications data to isolate the impact of this campaign from other factors and quantify commercial returns.

Over the period of the campaign (Oct–Nov) we compared performance against the average level in the preceding six months and to the immediate pre-level in September to eliminate any time specific bias. December gives post campaign levels.

Brand awareness

Despite our low share of voice and against the run of play, we increased brand awareness by 4% from the pre-campaign level (Figure 22).[12] But this was only the beginning of the story.

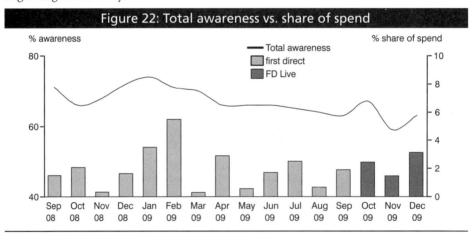

Figure 22: Total awareness vs. share of spend

Source: Millward Brown, Nielsen Media. Base: total sample

Favourable media coverage and word of mouth

The campaign successfully increased the proportion of people who saw or heard favourable media coverage about first direct by 14% compared to the six month pre-campaign level.

In comparison positive media coverage was flat during this period for competing brands. As a result we extended our lead from the competitor average. We also extended our lead from our best competitor from 4% to 10% (Figure 23).[13]

From an already strong position of 54% of customers recommending us (six month pre average) we improved this to 60% by the end of the campaign.

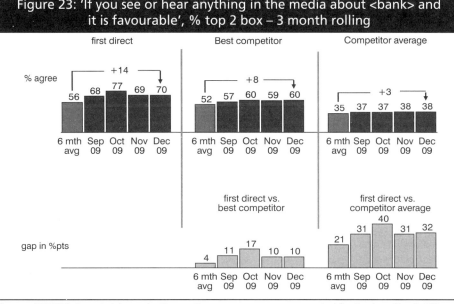

Figure 23: 'If you see or hear anything in the media about <bank> and it is favourable', % top 2 box – 3 month rolling

Source: GFK FRS. Base: total sample. Competitor average = average reported for Barclays, Lloyds TSB, NatWest, Halifax, HSBC, Nationwide, Santander and RBS

Our best competitor had caught up with us on this measure. By the end of the campaign, we had gone from 2% (Sep) behind to 18% ahead (Dec) – a 20% swing[14] (Figure 24).

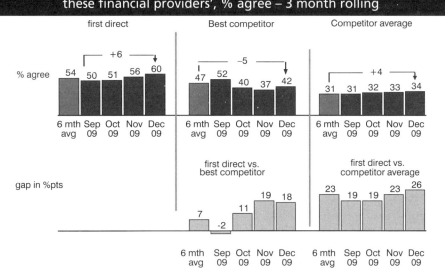

Figure 24: 'In the last 12 months have you actually recommended any of these financial providers', % agree – 3 month rolling

Source: Millward Brown. Base: all holders of current account at <bank>. Competitor average = average reported for Barclays, Lloyds TSB, NatWest, Halifax, HSBC, Nationwide, Santander

As a result of improving recommendations and positive media coverage, more people heard good things about first direct.

Against the six month pre-campaign average of 25%, by the end of the campaign 31% of people agreed that first direct was a bank that they had heard good things about – a 6% increase.[15]

We were therefore able to improve our position from being 3% below competitor average on this measure to being 2% above average during this period. We were also able to close the gap to the best competitor from −13% to −5% (Figure 25).

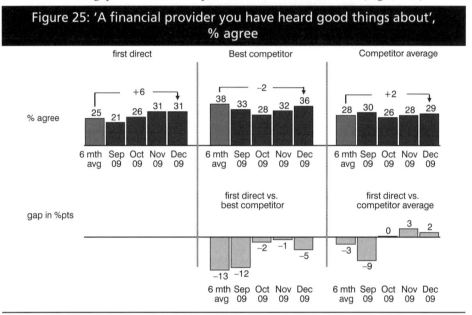

Figure 25: 'A financial provider you have heard good things about', % agree

Source: Millward Brown. Base: total sample. Competitor average = average reported for Halifax, HSBC, Nationwide, Santander. Others not reported

Brand measures

The campaign brought to life first direct's service proposition, as evidenced with a 7% increase in 'first direct is a brand that provides leading standards of service.'[16]

The innovative advertising campaign also helped improve our perception as a bank that 'comes up with fresh ideas' by 7% (Figure 26).

Brand differentiation

We were able to re-establish our lead on differentiation in a market that is notorious for its lack of product differentiation.

Compared to the six month pre-campaign average, we achieved a 23% (8%pts) increase in the number of people agreeing that first direct was a bank that was 'really different'.

This helped us extend the gap to our best competitor by 10%pts during the campaign (Figure 27).[17]

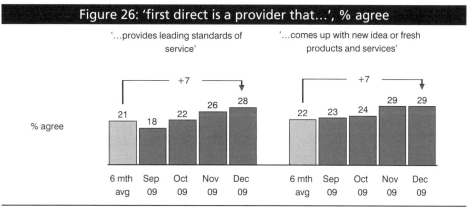

Figure 26: 'first direct is a provider that...', % agree

'...provides leading standards of service'

'...comes up with new idea or fresh products and services'

Source: Millward Brown. Base: total sample

Figure 27: 'first direct is a brand that stands out as really different from other financial institutions', % agree

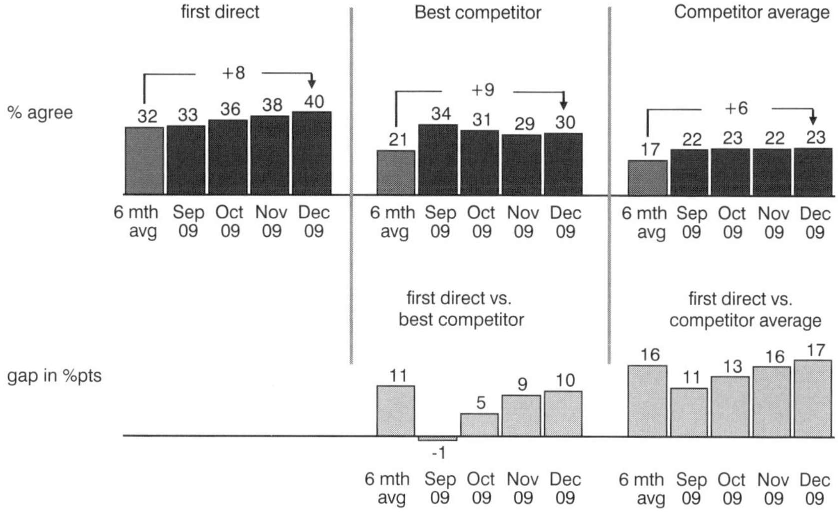

Source: Millward Brown. Base: total sample. Competitor average = average reported for Barclays, Lloyds TSB, NatWest, Halifax, HSBC, Nationwide, Santander

Consideration and acquisition

By improving differentiation scores, we were able to double our brand consideration amongst those considering switching their bank or opening a new account.

This was set against a back-drop of the rest of our competitors where consideration levels were falling – we therefore were able to close the gap to the competitor average by 6%pts (Figure 28).[18]

By improving brand consideration we substantially improved our share of all new current accounts opened during this period from a six month pre-campaign average of 1.35% to 2.1% by December 2009 (Figure 29).[19]

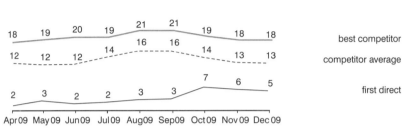

Figure 28: % in the market who would consider <bank> for a current account

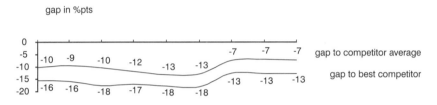

Source: GFK FRS. Base: all likely to take out/switch current accounts England & Wales. Competitor average = average reported for Barclays, Lloyds TSB, NatWest, Halifax, HSBC, Nationwide, Santander, RBS

We also succeeded in increasing our share of switchers from the pre-campaign six month average of 1.96% to 2.8% by December 2009 (Figure 30).[20]

Figure 29: Share of all new current accounts (excluding internal transfers) opened in the last 6 months vs. share of spend

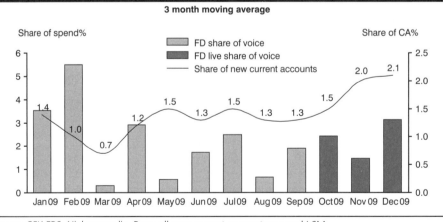

Source: GFK FRS, Nielsen media. Base: all new current accounts opened L6M

As can be seen in the charts above, both these measures are notoriously hard to shift. These are therefore significant achievements for a brand that has no high street presence and a share of spend of 2% in this category.[21]

Figure 30: Share of all new SWITCHED current accounts opened in last 6 months vs. share of spend – 6 month moving average

Share of spend%

Share of CA%

Legend:
- FD share of voice
- FD live share of voice
- Share of switchers

Values on line: 3.0, 2.8, 2.6, 3.0, 2.3, 1.8, 2.1, 1.7, 1.9, 2.2, 2.6, 2.8

X-axis: Jan 09, Feb 09, Mar 09, Apr 09, May 09, Jun 09, Jul 09, Aug 09, Sep 09, Oct 09, Nov 09, Dec 09

Source: GFK FRS, Nielsen media. Base: all switched current accounts L6M

Customer satisfaction

We were able to further improve satisfaction scores levels from an already high level (90%); this was achieved in a world where satisfaction was falling for other banks – as a result, we managed to increase our lead to both the competitor average (by 3%pts) and to our best competitor by (5%pts) (Dec vs. Sep) (Figure 31).[22]

Figure 31: Satisfaction with telephone banking, % extremely/very satisfied – 6 month moving average

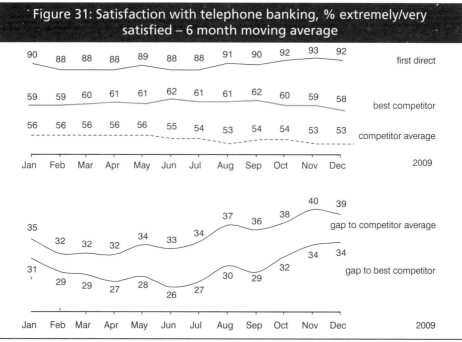

first direct: 90, 88, 88, 88, 89, 88, 88, 91, 90, 92, 93, 92

best competitor: 59, 59, 60, 61, 61, 62, 61, 61, 62, 60, 59, 58

competitor average: 56, 56, 56, 56, 56, 55, 54, 53, 54, 54, 53, 53

Jan Feb Mar Apr May Jun Jul Aug Sep Oct Nov Dec — 2009

gap to competitor average: 35, 32, 32, 32, 34, 33, 34, 37, 36, 38, 40, 39

gap to best competitor: 31, 29, 29, 27, 28, 26, 27, 30, 29, 32, 34, 34

Jan Feb Mar Apr May Jun Jul Aug Sep Oct Nov Dec — 2009

Source: GFK FRS. Base: all current account holders using phone banking in last 3 months (E&W). Competitor average = average reported for Barclays, Lloyds TSB, NatWest, Halifax, HSBC, Nationwide, Santander and RBS

Sales uplift – acquisitions

first direct has been using econometric models to make business decisions and plan marketing campaigns for the past four years. Models have been built for individual sales channels for both current account and mortgages. These models control for factors such as product changes, fees, rates, offers, seasonality.

Based on these econometric models, we estimate that the campaign in total contributed 31% of current account sales and 38% of mortgage sales during the period when it ran (Figure 32).[23]

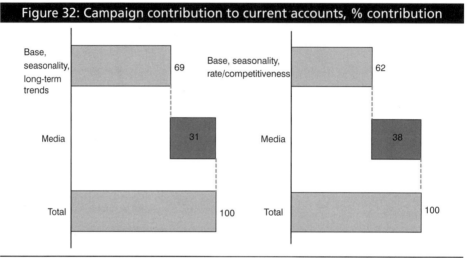

Figure 32: Campaign contribution to current accounts, % contribution

Source: Mindshare econometrics

Retentions

In addition to acquisitions, current account closures were 15% lower than the same quarter in the previous year. In comparison, the number of switchers in the overall market increased by 4% (Figure 33).

ROI

Econometrics was used to quantify the number of incremental applications driven by the campaign. Applying conversion rates to sales and using product lifetime economic profits (LEP) this campaign generated £4.5m of profit (gross). Taking out the marketing investment of £1.8m we arrive at a NET profit ROI of £1.54.

This is an underestimate to which we can add the potential value of retained customers as well as the cross sell potential of current account customers.[24]

Figure 33: first direct current account closures vs. GFK number of switchers in 6 months to Dec 2009

first direct current
account closures
(index)

GFK– Switchers in last 6
months (000s)

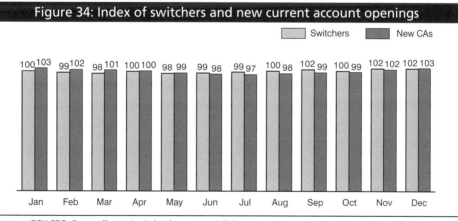

Switchers in total
market increased by 4%

Account closures for
current accounts
decreased by 15%

Source: first direct; GFK FRS. Base: all switched accounts L6M

Controlling for other factors

Seasonality

Looking at GFK data on current account openings, the current account market is seasonally flat. Econometrics on first direct suggests seasonal gain in Jan/Feb but no increase during the campaign period. Seasonality therefore could not have had a strong impact on any of our KPIs.

More short-term seasonality such as holidays has been controlled for in our econometric models (Figure 34).

Figure 34: Index of switchers and new current account openings

Switchers ☐ New CAs ☐

	Jan	Feb	Mar	Apr	May	Jun	Jul	Aug	Sep	Oct	Nov	Dec
Switchers	100	99	98	100	98	99	99	100	102	100	102	102
New CAs	103	102	101	100	99	98	97	98	99	99	102	103

Source: GFK FRS. Base: all new/switched accounts L6M

How about product changes?

Between 2008 and 2009, there was no change in the current account product:

- current accounts were free as long as £1,500 was deposited in the account every month;
- if this was not the case, a fee of £10 per month would be charged.

Product changes could not have been a factor in driving the observed changes.

first direct also offered consumers an incentive to switch. first direct offered £100 to all those who switched current accounts to them and another £100 if they were not satisfied – this however was in force both before, during and after the campaign.

Given that there was no change in this offer, it cannot be an explanation for any of the changes in our KPIs during this campaign.

For mortgages, interest rates have an impact on product sales; this has been controlled for in our econometric models.[25]

In conclusion

first direct 'live' was not only a brave and innovative campaign that delivered against the business challenges first direct faced, it worked in the midst of one of the worst recessions in history where consumer trust for banks was at its lowest. It did all this without the budgets available to larger banks.

What we learnt from the campaign:

Consumer experience is more important than brand rhetoric: In today's connected world where trust in peer recommendation counts more than what a brand says, the importance of transparency in product and service performance is paramount for future brand health.

Listen to your customers and encourage conversation: A brand's customers are their most important asset. A brand should seek to involve and stimulate their conversations and, through the use of social media, amplify and facilitate these conversations (good and bad) with their peers.

Embrace convergence: Advertising, media and content are all converging; first direct 'live' is a great example of how these three are intrinsically linked and are incredibly powerful when combined to full effect.

Client quote

'live' has changed the way that we view social media as a business, helping us to embrace it as a key marketing and customer service channel. It's a powerful and innovative idea – one that we knew was totally on brand and relevant to the target audience the minute that Mindshare presented it to us.
Natalie Cowen – Head of Brand and Communications.

Notes

1 BrandZ 2010.
2 GFK FRS 2010.
3 Millward Brown 2010.
4 GFK FRS 2010.
5 Millward Brown 2010.
6 The Futures Company, 2009.
7 GFK FRS 2010.
8 Datamonitor 2010.
9 Nielsen 2010.
10 GFK FRS 2010.
11 Millward Brown Precis.
12 Millward Brown 2010.
13 GFK FRS 2010.
14 GFK FRS 2010.
15 Millward Brown 2010.
16 Millward Brown 2010.
17 Millward Brown 2010.
18 GFK FRS 2010.
19 GFK FRS 2010.
20 GFK FRS 2010/Nielsen 2010.
21 GFK FRS 2010/Nielsen 2010.
22 GFK FRS 2010.
23 Mindshare Econometrics.
24 first direct and Mindshare Econometrics.
25 first direct.

Chapter 13

Jungle Formula

From repellent to compelling or how Jungle Formula took the sting out of summer

By Andrew Perkins, VCCP
Contributing authors: Amy Whittaker, VCCP and Elspeth Fisher, Total Media
Credited companies: Media Agency: Total Media; Partnership Agency: VCCP Health; Client: Omega Pharma

Editor's summary

Jungle Formula operated in a category with no major investment in communication for two decades, relying instead on the summer season to drive growth year-on-year. However, the credit crunch of 2009 affected the brand, with the first fall in foreign holidays since the 70s meaning the category declined. To address this, a TV campaign in the summer of 2010 was aimed at broadening the appeal of the brand and building fame in time for the holiday season. Within six months, perceptions of Jungle Formula were changed. Most importantly, despite the lack of historical data, they demonstrated a short-term ROMI of just over 1:1.03, securing funding for new marketing investment for the following year. This is a neat paper delivered in a very engaging tone, describing how communications has protected the brand and increased distribution.

Introduction

This paper is, unapologetically, a work in progress.

Or, to slip into the more fashionable jargon, it's real-time.

A quick read through some of the most successful 'Odd Year' IPA Effectiveness Awards shows that, very often, it's organisations with a bigger marketing infrastructure that are best able to prove their case – whether that's an isolated campaign of an otherwise big-spending brand, a brand that has maintained a 7-figure marketing spend year in year out, or public sector communications.

Having written this paper, we can see why this should be so. Without the luxury of ongoing brand tracking, adstock models, category norms or case studies, and all the other paraphernalia that come with consistent category spend, the challenges facing marketers are arguably greater, the questions tougher.

Should we spend at all in this category? And if the whole category is worth under £20m, can we justify ATL spend? How quickly should we see results? What will success look like?

Life for brands in this world is inevitably a more seat-of-the-pants experience, and defined by a classic Catch 22: they will need to fight harder to justify to their Finance Director any significant investment in advertising, but without the investment in long-term research needed to make that very justification.

And so we present Jungle Formula in real time. In a category with a total value of around £16.8m, and no significant advertising investment in two decades, Jungle Formula ran a TV campaign in the summer of 2010. We now have to justify the business value of that activity to secure this year's funding.

In an ideal world, this would mean econometric modelling, and historical data applied to long-term forecasting.

In the real world, we have the paper you are about to read.

Jungle Formula: the repellent truth

Jungle Formula is the number one insect repellent brand in the UK. Owned by Omega Pharma, it has been around for over 20 years and is trusted by far-travelling consumers and trade alike.

As far as we have been able to ascertain, there has never been significant ATL advertising in this category, and Jungle Formula had been able to do without major investment in communications for two decades, relying on the steady year-on-year growth in overseas travel to keep brand value growing. As you'd expect, category and Jungle Formula sales are highly seasonal, with around half of all sales in the three months of summer, and the majority of purchases being for overseas trips.

So the obvious choice was business as normal. Keep investing enough instore to hold off competitor brands such as Autan, and await another bumper summer.

But all was not quite as healthy as it seemed. The credit crunch was about to squeeze the brand in four distinct but interconnected ways.

1. The fall in foreign holidays meant the category was in decline

83% of those who use insect repellent do so abroad,[1] so clearly a decline in overseas travel was a worry for Jungle Formula. Unfortunately, that was exactly what was happening.

In 2009, the number of Britons taking foreign holidays fell 15% year-on-year. This represented 10.4 million overseas visits, and was effectively the first major decline in foreign holidaymaking in four decades, right back to the growth of the package holiday in the 1970s. What's more, provisional figures for the first quarter showed that the decline was continuing, with a further 9% fall.[2]

Looking at more recent trends, provisional figures for the first quarter of 2010 revealed that the downturn in Britons' foreign holidays was continuing – falling by a further 9%.

As a result the category was in decline, and indeed the first half of 2010 looked particularly worrying, with volume sales in the first six months of the year down nearly 8% on 2009.[3]

2. The type of holidays being taken did not favour Jungle Formula

Not only were people taking fewer overseas holidays, but increasing costs of air travel were reducing the distances people were willing to fly, and an unwillingness to risk hard-earned money meant people were retrenching to more tried-and-tested holiday destinations.

This was a serious problem: while Jungle Formula is as effective on a French or Spanish mosquito as it is on its Gambian or Thai cousins, the image of the brand could potentially make it seem like overkill for your average Med beach holiday.

Indeed, our data suggested that while Jungle Formula usage over-indexed on African and Asian holidays, it under-indexed on Europe. For competitor Autan, the opposite held true (Table 1).[4]

Table 1: Usage of insect repellent brands by holiday region			
Which brand of insect repellent did you use on your holiday to ... (Indexed)	Africa	Asia	Europe
Jungle Formula	107	125	89
Autan	92	69	108

Not unreasonably, people saw Jungle Formula as being more appropriate for, well, jungles.

3. We needed to justify our price premium

Jungle Formula is priced at a significant premium, around 26% higher than the average branded product across the entire product range.[5] Naturally, as holidaymakers try and squeeze the maximum value out of their holiday, insect repellent would be an obvious way to save a few pennies.

For those still making long-haul trips, our name and reputation for effectiveness would still be powerful, but for those popping to Spain for a couple of weeks, or even staying in the UK to feed our native midges, the increased cost of Jungle Formula might well feel unnecessary. Our research showed that retail own brand enjoyed a significant advantage in perceived Value For Money (Figure 1).[6]

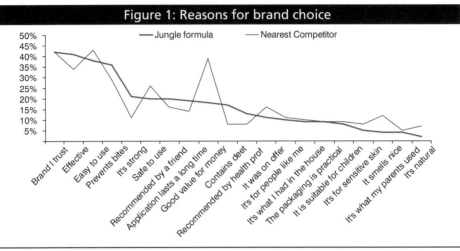

Figure 1: Reasons for brand choice

Source: Jungle Formula Usage and Attitudes Study, The Nursery, 2010

4. Our brand salience was low

A subtler, but still significant side-effect of the economic downturn was the importance of spontaneous brand awareness. While Jungle Formula was the biggest brand in terms of value sales, it still indexed considerably far behind the leading own label in terms of spontaneous brand awareness at just 64.[7]

As long as people were making considered purchases for long-haul destination holidays, our brand strength shone through. But as holidaymakers were increasingly trying to grab last minute bargains they were inevitably making snap decisions about their insect repellent, often at the airport itself. In such situations, the fact that we weren't going into the summer as the brand leader for awareness was a matter of real concern.

Doing nothing is not an option

This analysis in 2009 led to a realisation that Jungle Formula would benefit from a significant investment in the brand in 2010. Indeed, it was clear that without such investment, the brand would risk a seriously poor summer in terms of reduced revenue. And when the sales results from the first half of 2010 came through, this was indeed what we saw. Without fail, Jungle Formula value sales in 2010 were down on 2009 for every single month. And as the summer holiday season approached, the situation was getting worse with value sales 6.5% below the 2009 figure (Figure 2).[8]

If the trend continued through 2010, value sales would be £184,126 down on 2009.

But with our campaign waiting to be unleashed, the picture would be very different.

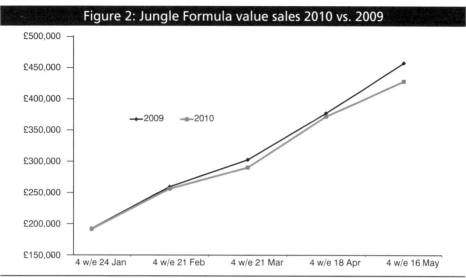

Figure 2: Jungle Formula value sales 2010 vs. 2009

Source: IRI, TNS, EPOS

The strategy

So the decision was taken to invest in the Jungle Formula brand. But what did we need to achieve? We identified three key objectives:

1. Increase brand fame: improve spontaneous brand awareness, and show Jungle Formula as the leading brand.
2. Demonstrate that Jungle Formula is just as much for those going to Spain as Senegal.
3. Justify the price premium, by building on Jungle Formula's reputation for being the most effective.

In other words, we needed to show the power of Jungle Formula to put off the mozzies, without making it seem like an over-the-top response.

The strategy

At the heart of our objectives was a challenge that might at first glance seem a contradiction – we needed to increase brand name awareness, but our name itself risked making us irrelevant: the more we said Jungle, the more we were in danger of missing our key audience of European holidaymakers. Equally, if we downplayed our junglehood, we risked losing sight of the key brand differentiator of better effectiveness.

In addition, we needed to be true to the carefree spirit of the average Med holiday: the danger for Jungle Formula would be in emphasising the misery of mozzies at a time when people are dreaming of their perfect holiday.

So a joyless purchase to mitigate a holiday irritant. How could we turn that into a compelling campaign?

The key was *identification* – showing European holidaymakers that we were a brand for them (Figure 3):

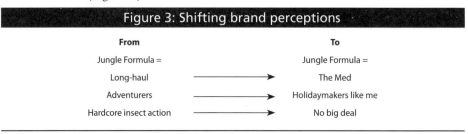

Figure 3: Shifting brand perceptions

From	To
Jungle Formula =	Jungle Formula =
Long-haul	The Med
Adventurers	Holidaymakers like me
Hardcore insect action	No big deal

The campaign

Creative

Our campaign idea was *Jungle Boogie*.

To show that this was a brand for Med holidaymakers, we went to the Med and filmed them taking on the region's finest bloodsuckers – swatting, slapping, or merely running away screaming and flapping their arms.

The humour and location downplayed the seriousness of the brand's tropical heritage, but to ensure brand recognition we needed to get the jungle in there. So we set the whole thing to Jungle Boogie, much-loved and still-cool funk track that has graced many a memorable Med fortnight.

Although we showed the irritating nature of mosquitoes, by playing up our slightly silly over-reactions, we did so in a way that didn't make us seem like party-poopers.

Our message was clear: with Jungle Formula, you won't need to do the Jungle Boogie (Figure 4).

Media

The campaign was supported by a modest budget of £470,000. Despite this, we still felt TV would be our most appropriate channel for creating impact and driving spontaneous brand awareness. Our strategy was to target mainstream holidaymakers on a selection of channels including Channel 4, Five, GMTV, ITV2 and ITV3, More 4 and the Travel Channel. The campaign ran from June 17 to August 1 2010 to build awareness in time for the summer holiday season and to encourage the trade to reorder stock early in the season.

To squeeze the maximum value from the budget, we:

- upweighted peak on terrestrial channels to drive additional 1+ coverage efficiently;
- upweighted Wednesday–Saturday to coincide with key shopping days;
- placed in travel programmes to improve communication;
- deployed week on week off to stretch the campaign and generate higher 1+ coverage;
- ran a 10" to deliver additional weight;
- selective use of ITV due to high World Cup costs.

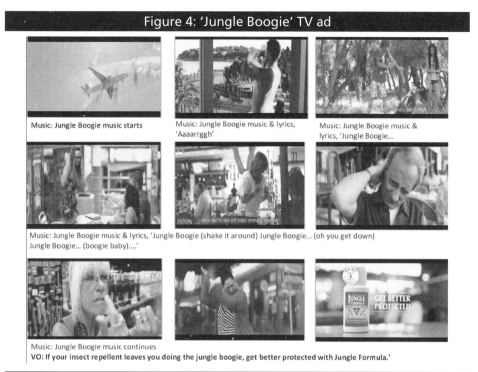

Figure 4: 'Jungle Boogie' TV ad

Music: Jungle Boogie music starts

Music: Jungle Boogie music & lyrics, 'Aaaarrggh'

Music: Jungle Boogie music & lyrics, 'Jungle Boogie...

Music: Jungle Boogie music & lyrics, 'Jungle Boogie (shake it around) Jungle Boogie... (oh you get down) Jungle Boogie... (boogie baby)....'

Music: Jungle Boogie music continues

VO: If your insect repellent leaves you doing the jungle boogie, get better protected with Jungle Formula.'

Real-time activity

As a small spender we also kept a sharp look-out for tactical opportunities.

And they came at the expense of Cheryl Cole, who contracted a nasty dose of malaria while in Tanzania. We quickly picked up that no brand was buying search terms against Cheryl Cole + Malaria, so were able to snap up a search bargain, generating 1,376,658 impressions for just £250 (Figure 5).

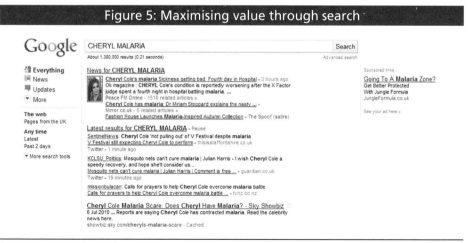

Figure 5: Maximising value through search

Source: www.google.co.uk

169

While the destination was clearly not relevant to our core target audience, the celebrity in question certainly was, and a good reminder that keeping the mosquitoes at bay isn't just about avoiding a minor irritation.

Results

Qualitative research

Qualitative research convinced us that we have successfully tapped into the attitudes of our audience, and created a memorable bit of advertising (Figure 6):[9]

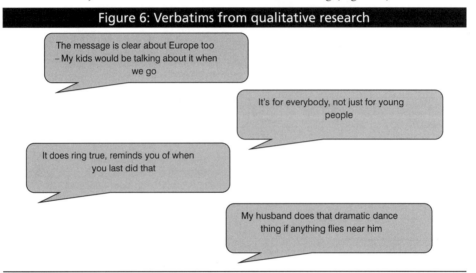

Figure 6: Verbatims from qualitative research

The message is clear about Europe too – My kids would be talking about it when we go

It's for everybody, not just for young people

It does ring true, reminds you of when you last did that

My husband does that dramatic dance thing if anything flies near him

Source: VCCP Qualitative research, 2010

Quantitative research

While we didn't have an ongoing tracking study, a pre and post dip enabled us to see the broad impact of the campaign.

Our primary soft measure was spontaneous brand awareness, the clearest indicator as to whether we had made the brand more famous.

Before the campaign, the leading own label enjoyed a 7% point lead over Jungle Formula. Since the campaign, however, Jungle Formula's spontaneous awareness has risen by over half to become the number one brand in the category (Figure 7).[10]

While we don't have the luxury of being able to measure our campaign against any historical results, our ad diagnostics stack up extremely well to the take-out and purchase intention norms as quantified by the likes of Millward Brown (Table 2):

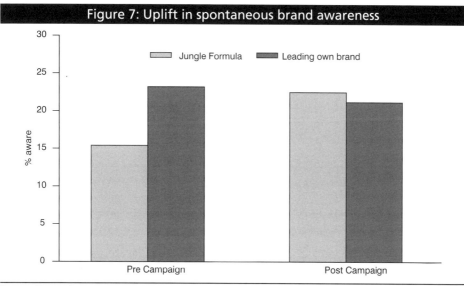

Figure 7: Uplift in spontaneous brand awareness

Source: Research Now

Table 2: Ad diagnostics

The ad ...	% who agree or definitely agree
Tells me Jungle Formula is appropriate for use in Europe	47
Tells me that Jungle Formula is the leading insect repellent brand	48
Tells me that Jungle Formula gives me better protection than other insect repellents	48
Does ad ...	**% who say more likely**
Make you more or less likely to buy Jungle Formula the next time you buy insect repellent	29

Source: Research Now online survey, 2010

Business results

1. Volume sales

After a decline in 2009, Jungle Formula volume sales grew by over 5% in 2010 (Table 3):

Table 3: Uplift in volume sales 2010

EPOS data	Indexed unit sales
2008	100.0
2009	97.9
2010	103.8

What's more, this uplift in 2010 was entirely driven by the second half of the year, once our campaign broke, and in fact was a dramatic recovery from what was a very poor first half of the year (Table 4):

Table 4: Uplift in volume sales H2 2010		
EPOS data	Indexed first half-year sales	Indexed second half-year sales
2008	100	100
2009	100	96
2010	92	115

2. Value sales

With the brand campaign protecting our price premium, value sales growth was even more striking, with a year-on-year leap of 15%, despite a poor first half of the year (Figure 8):

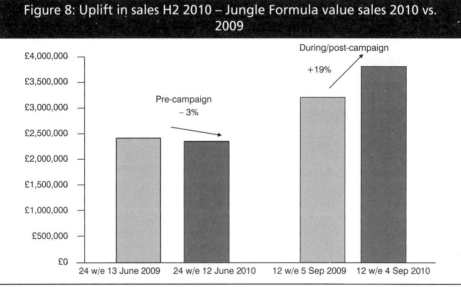

Figure 8: Uplift in sales H2 2010 – Jungle Formula value sales 2010 vs. 2009

Source: IRI, TNS, EPOS

As a result, Jungle Formula's value share grew significantly in the short term after the campaign broke, up by 6% in the 12 weeks since campaign launch (Figure 9):

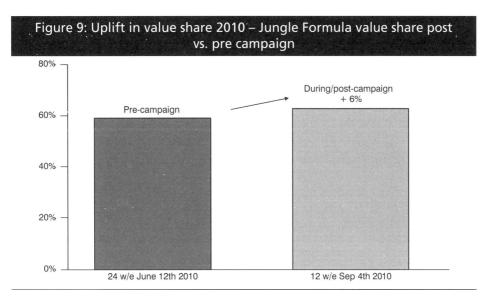

Figure 9: Uplift in value share 2010 – Jungle Formula value share post vs. pre campaign

Source: IRI (excluding Boots)

Indeed, five of the six biggest growing SKUs in 2010 were Jungle Formula products (Figure 10):

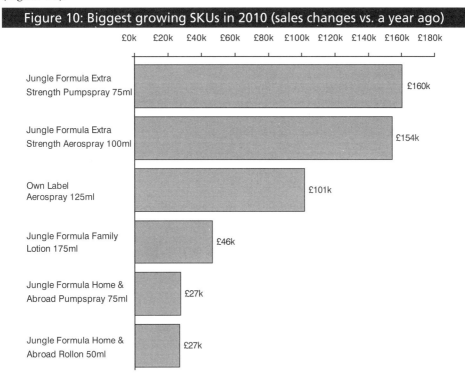

Figure 10: Biggest growing SKUs in 2010 (sales changes vs. a year ago)

Source: IRI HBA Outlets, latest 12 w/e Sept 2010

Eliminating other variables

Price

The sale price of Jungle Formula actually increased slightly in 2010, from an average unit price of £5.65 to £5.87. This meant the brand maintained its substantial price premium over other branded products and own label.[11]

Promotions

Jungle Formula promotions over the period matched closely those of the year before across all retailers.

Product development

There was no new product introduced in 2010.

Other Jungle Formula activity

The only other investment in the brand over the period was in ticket wallets distributed through TUI Travel. The investment on this activity was slightly down on 2009 levels.

Competitor activity

Competitor spend was consistent with 2009 levels.

Payback

By extrapolating from 2009, we can see that our campaign generated significant incremental revenue for the brand (Figure 11 and Table 5).

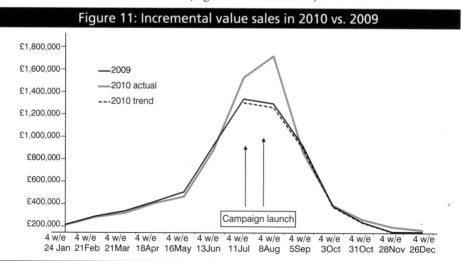

Figure 11: Incremental value sales in 2010 vs. 2009

Source: IRI, TNS, EPOS data

Table 5: Incremental value sales in 2010	
	£
2009 value sales 28 w/e 26 December	4,045,083
2010 value sales 28 w/e 26 December *predicted*	3,393,175
2010 value sales 28 w/e 26 December *actual*	4,741,803
2010 incremental sales value	810,628

The total client investment, including media, production and agency fees, was £638,690. So, incremental value sales more than outstripped the total cost of the investment. But what of the profit return?

For confidentiality reasons, we are not able to give an exact profit margin for Jungle Formula, but we are able to say that this incremental revenue and our marginal contribution means that, already by the end of the year, the campaign had repaid the investment in media, at an ROMI of just over 1:1.03.

Is that it?

We appreciate that, compared to the spectacular ROMI's reported in the history of the IPA Effectiveness Awards, this may not seem like the most powerful story.

But we would strongly argue that this case is compelling, and the reasons for that are threefold:

1. We enter 2011 a stronger brand with consumers

Thanks to the campaign, we have higher spontaneous brand awareness, and a greater understanding and experience that Jungle Formula isn't just for the jungle.

So even if the long-haul travel market doesn't pick up in 2011, we can still expect value growth from Med travellers.

2. We enter 2011 a stronger brand with retailers

In the first place, our value share has grown and continued to stay high over the six months since the campaign launch. We entered the new year with a value share of 60.2%, as compared to 53.5% over the same period for the previous year.[12]

What's more, we believe that our campaign has actually increased the value of the category as a whole, by driving up the average cost per unit as consumers upgraded to us from own label and lower cost brands.

Value sales for the whole category grew by 1.2% versus the previous year for the 12 week period from the start of our campaign, despite the very slow start to 2010.[13] Clearly, in a difficult trading period, this has given the brand valuable kudos with retailers. A leading retailer said:

Insect Repellents was our best performing category from a year-on-year perspective, and I credit Jungle Formula with driving that.

As a result, our distribution has benefited significantly. We go into the new season with 73 distribution points compared to 59 for the previous year.

3. We enter 2011 a stronger brand with the FD

And perhaps most importantly of all, the above results have been convincing to the Finance Director at Omega Pharma that the media investment has washed its face (in the parlance) within just 24 weeks.

Without the luxury of adstock models, we can't yet make a credible case for the long-term business value of the campaign, but as the above suggests, the indicators are very positive, and we would expect 2011 to start the forthcoming peak season in better shape than it entered 2010.

We think the case we have made is compelling enough to justify investment again in 2011, and recently that has proved to be the case, as new product launches and marketing support have just been given the go-ahead.

Real-time effectiveness

As we made clear at the start, this is still work in progress.

In fact, we seriously considered delaying entering this paper for another two years, until the long-term effectiveness had become fully apparent.

But then we wondered whether entering now wasn't more in the spirit of brands that work with smaller budgets, where payback isn't something that can be laboriously calculated while the marketing budget continues to be provided. Instead, brand owners must make pragmatic calls based on the best evidence they have to hand.

What we hope we have demonstrated is that, for brands operating with a smaller marketing infrastructure, real-time measuring can still be robust enough to prove genuine effectiveness.

Notes

1 Source: Nursery Jungle Formula U&A Development Research 2010.
2 Source: ONS, http://www.guardian.co.uk/travel/2010/jul/13/fewer-britons-take-overseas-breaks.
3 Source: EPOS data across the 8 biggest insect repellent retailers in the UK.
4 Source: Nursery Jungle Formula U&A Development Research 2010.
5 Source: IRI data 2009.
6 Source: Nursery Jungle Formula U&A Development Research 2010.
7 Source: Nursery Jungle Formula U&A Development Research 2010.
8 Source: IRI, TNS, EPOS Data 2009–10.
9 Source: Opinion Leader Qualitative Research.
10 Source: Now Research Quantitative dips: September 2009, August 2010.
11 Source: IRI data.
12 Source: IRI data (excluding Boots) average over 24 w/e.
13 Source: IRI, TNS, EPOS data.

Chapter 14

Organ Donor Register

When it is better to receive than to give

By Ila De Mello Kamath, AMV BBDO
Contributing author: Bridget Angear, AMV BBDO
Credited companies: Media Agency: Manning Gottlieb OMD; PR Agency: Munro Forster;
Client: NHS Blood and Transplant

Editor's summary

The task was to launch the first ever UK campaign to increase the number of registrations on the Organ Donor Register (ODR) from 16 million to 25 million in three years, specifically generating 37,600 registrations in the first five weeks. Insight reframed the problem: organ donation was not about altruistic giving, but about reciprocation, people will give because they want to receive. The campaign put people in the mindset of the recipient, and in doing so was able to generate sufficient empathy as well as self-interest to encourage them to register. The results were impressive. The campaign exceeded the previous year's registrations by 400%; is likely to have helped save five lives, which at a financial cost of a life saved in a society of nearly £1m, gave a ROMI of 4:1. This campaign's central insight work drew comment from the judges, who noted the significant impact and ROI achieved in a relatively short space of time.

Executive summary

Our task was to increase the number of registrations on the Organ Donor Register (ODR) from 16 million to 25 million by 2013, in three years. Specifically, to generate 37,600 registrations in the first five weeks.[1] An extremely tough challenge, because not only did our campaign have to be eight times more effective than other health campaigns,[2] but we had to get people to confront the idea of death and challenge deep-set beliefs about mortality. On our journey we discovered that organ donation is not about donation but reciprocation; that we will give because we want to receive. We learnt from vampire bats (Figure 2) that we had been looking at our problem the wrong way around, which led us to ask the right question about organ donation: not 'would you be willing to give an organ?' but 'would you be willing to receive an organ?'. Reciprocal altruism gave us a powerful insight that motivated people to register by finding a balance between self-interest and empathy and delivered results that will save lives.

And it worked

In the first five weeks our campaign generated 128,218 completed registrations, four times more registrations than the same period the previous year, exceeding our estimated target for that period of 37,600 registrations by over 400%. Importantly, the intention of the campaign was to save lives, and the additional uplift in registrations is likely to have helped save five lives: a cost saving to society of £4.7m,[3] which covers the campaign cost of £1.2m, and gives an ROI of 4:1.

Introduction

The UK has one of the lowest rates of organ donation in Europe. As a result there are 8,000 people registered for a transplant who are in the heart-breaking situation of having to wait for an organ. Shockingly, 1,000 people die every year whilst waiting for a donor organ to become available. As such the government had set NHS Blood and Transplant (NHSBT) a target to increase the number of people registered on the Organ Donor Register from 16 million to 25 million by 2013, an extra 9 million registrations in three years from the campaign launch. To achieve this, our campaign needed to increase awareness and support of organ donation as an issue and convert this support into registrations. Specifically, it needed to achieve 37,600 registrations in the first five weeks.[4] To put into context the scale of our task, this was the first ever advertising campaign in the UK about organ donation and it needed to be eight times more effective than the average health advertising campaign.[5]

The challenge

A simple task, or so we thought

Despite the daunting nature of the challenge, and that this was the first UK advertising campaign for organ donation, we felt our task should be relatively simple. 90% of people in the UK say they are 'in favour of organ donation'[6] and although only 27% have registered on the ODR,[7] quantitative research highlighted the main barriers to registration were largely rational: 'I don't know how to', 'I hadn't thought about it', 'I didn't know about the ODR'.[8] Surely all we needed to do was to remind the 63% of adults 'in favour but not on the register' to register. As one man pointed out in groups, 'You don't wake up every morning thinking "I must register to be an organ donor today"'.[9] So, we set respondents in groups a simple task: to write down how they felt when we said 'I just want you to register to donate your organs, *today*.' We thought the added sense of urgency would be enough to push them over the line. But to our surprise their response was not quite what we were hoping for. Instead of saying 'Of course, what a good idea' they were horrified.

This simple question had left them feeling surprisingly pressured (Figure 1).

Figure 1: Qualitative research group response maps

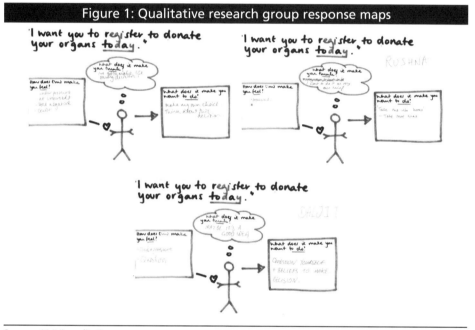

Source: AMVi qualitative groups

When asking them about their reaction, we realised that organ donation was not as simple a decision as we had expected. This question had unlocked deeper emotional barriers, namely 'I don't want to think about death' and 'I don't want to tempt fate'. By asking people to register we were actually asking them to confront the idea of death.

Our journey

In search for a more persuasive approach

Our new hypothesis was that we needed to give people a compelling reason *why* they should donate their organs. So we recruited some more groups representative of the British public to explore possible approaches. The first, and we thought most powerful approach, was to confront people with the seriousness of the problem by reminding them that three people were dying every day. While this shocked people and struck a chord with them about the importance of organ donation, it unlocked a 'bad guilt' which left people feeling angry that we were unfairly blaming them for people dying. Afterall, organ donation is not like giving blood where your donation can help save lives straight away. With organ donation you need to die before your organs can be used, so it's unlikely your registration will help people today. Guilt was a powerful emotion, but we needed to generate the right sort of guilt: guilt about not being on the register.

We tried a different tack. What about making people feel good about saving lives and leaving a legacy? What better gift to leave than the gift of life? Whilst this resonated with people, it only put organ donation on the 'list of things to do before I die'. It lacked any sense of urgency.

As we delved deeper into what people thought, we started coming up against deep-rooted superstitions. Seemingly rational people would say things like, 'Well, I want to be buried whole, not walking around in heaven with my organs missing'. We tried confronting these superstitions head-on, pointing out that they would be dead, and therefore didn't really need their organs. Although people agreed they were being irrational, these beliefs were so deep-set that it was simply not something we could convince them about overnight, so didn't get them any closer to the idea of registering. It seemed we had hit a dead end.

The insight

Bats and a breakthrough

Quantitative research had told us that 90% of people were 'in favour of organ donation',[10] so why were people so reluctant to register to donate their organs? Was the data wrong or were we missing something? We went back to the numbers and the data was definitely right. So we decided to speak to a psychologist to try to understand what was happening. He told us a fascinating story, a story about vampire bats that went like this (Figure 2):

Figure 2: Vampire bats

Vampire bats need to feed on blood every two days or they will die. They get blood from other bats who regurgitate it for them. Because access to blood is vital, it seems vampire bats have decided it is in their interest to feed any bat in the colony, not just family members, even though that bat may not feed them in return. However, by feeding any bat, they are actually widening the pool of potential feeder bats, improving their chance of getting fed in return. This is known as reciprocal altruism.

The solution

Reframing the problem

With this in mind we looked again at our problem. When people had said they were 'in favour of organ donation' we had assumed they were in favour of donating, but in fact could it be that what people were 'in favour' of was not giving an organ but receiving one? Maybe the question we should have been asking was not 'would you be willing to donate' but 'would you be willing to receive'?

So we put our theory to the test. This time we asked people one simple question 'If you needed an organ would you be prepared to take one?' The response was as surprising as it was uncomfortable to watch. Not only did people say 'yes, of course they would take one' but as they answered the question they started to squirm, quite literally, and giggle nervously as the hypocrisy of their answer dawned on them. As soon as they realised what was in it for them, their conscience got the better of them. After all, if they were prepared to receive an organ, shouldn't they be prepared to donate one? After all, it is only fair. By putting them in the mindset of being a recipient we had not only created a shortcut to empathy but ensured that people could see the clear self-interest in registering. Organ donation is not like charity where giving makes you feel good, it's about reciprocity. You give because you hope that when the time comes, you will receive. We quantified our insight to check our group was not an anomaly and found that 96% of people agreed that 'if they needed an organ they would take one'.[11]

By flipping how we asked the question, we generated the sort of guilt we had been searching for: guilt about not being on the register, coupled with a benefit to oneself for registering, which prompted people to say they'd act.

The creative idea

Our campaign dramatised the simple oxymoron that we'd all take an organ if we or a loved one needed one, yet most of us make excuses to put off registering. The campaign line 'If you believe in organ donation, prove it' posed a challenge to the viewer, because the moment you answer 'yes' it is very hard to argue against registering. This strategy gave us a new PR angle to exploit. The PR campaign exposed the statistics behind the hypocrisy, that 96% of us are willing to take an organ yet only 27% are registered (Figures 3 and 4). This created a ripple-effect across media channels, generating discussions about whether people would accept an organ or not and whether this reflected the attitudes of our society.

Figure 3: Print executions

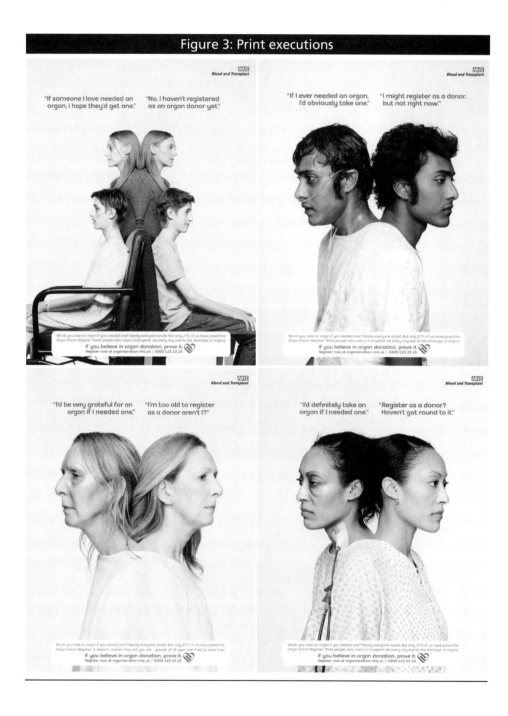

Figure 4: Stills of the TV execution

Three people who need
a transplant die every day

organdonation.nhs.uk

0300 123 23 23

The media approach

Converting awareness into registrations

We developed a 3-pronged media strategy to generate action: Accelerate, Connect, Act (see Figure 5).

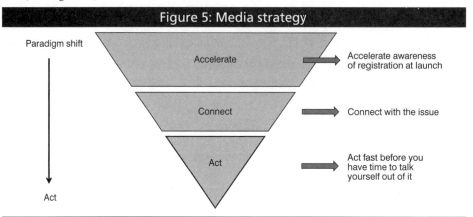

Figure 5: Media strategy

Source: Manning Gottlieb OMD

Accelerate

This was designed to accelerate awareness of the registration issue at launch. PR utilised influential advocates (MPs, transplant surgeons, organ recipients and celebrities) to engage the media with organ donation. This generated over 300 articles, 56 regional TV and radio interviews and an equivalent circulation of 328,324,422 (Figure 6).[12]

Figure 6: Example PR coverage

Source: Munro Forster

Connect

A key part of securing registrations was to give people time to connect with the subject, to talk about it with family and friends, before getting them to 'Act' by registering. Media analysis revealed people were most likely to 'connect' with emotional messages when 'relaxing in front of the TV with family and friends'. Therefore 30sec TV ads were deployed at weekends when families view together and during programmes with strong audience connections and talkability (e.g. The X Factor, I'm a Celebrity, Emmerdale, ITV news). Full-page press ads in tabloids and weekend broadsheets were used to provoke people when they were in the 'mood to chat'.

Act

Having connected with the subject we had to get people to then 'Act' as quickly as possible before they had time to think about it for too long and talk themselves out of registering. Day-part media analysis identified when people were most likely and able to respond: the hypothesis being people were most responsive when alert (black curve) and most able when relaxed taking care of household admin (Figure 7).

Figure 7: Day-part media analysis

The most influential apertures

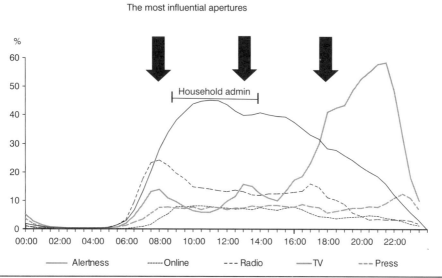

Source: Manning Gottlieb OMD

Overlaying this with media channels suggested up-weighting 'Act' media early-morning and at lunchtime, converted intention into registrations on the most responsive days (Monday to Wednesday), identified radio and online as strong channels as well as utilising online banners, pre-rolls, small-space press with text-response and 10-sec reminder TV and VOD spots to prompt action. Radio was used to increase message frequency and was deployed in Newslink, maximising most alert day-parts. The website was also streamlined and simplified to ensure registration could be completed in just two pages. The analysis also showed the importance of evening TV to create an emotional connection before prompting response.

The results

An incredible uplift in registrations

In the first five weeks of the campaign launching we achieved a total 187,820 responses, which converted into 128,218 completed registrations. This was four times more registrations than the same period the previous year. We exceeded our estimated target of 37,590 registrations by over 400% (see Figure 8).

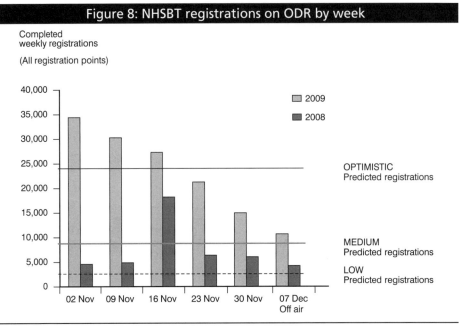

Figure 8: NHSBT registrations on ODR by week

Source: Continental research, 2010 tracking debrief

A highly effective TV strategy to drive registrations

We found a clear correlation between the TV laydown and registrations (Figure 9).

This proved that our strategy of using TV to 'Connect' people to the issue first, then 'Act', worked extremely well. Based on the correlation between TVRs and registrations over this burst of activity, we can predict that had we continued advertising we could have met our target of an additional 9 million registrations in 17 months, instead of the allotted 36 months.[13]

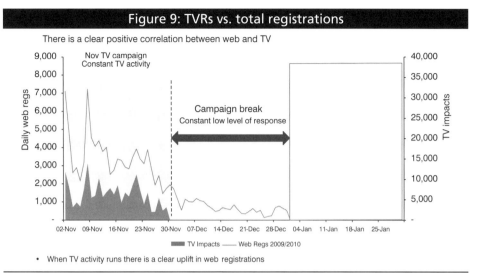

Figure 9: TVRs vs. total registrations

There is a clear positive correlation between web and TV

- When TV activity runs there is a clear uplift in web registrations

Source: Manning Gottlieb OMD

A shift in support of organ donation

Support for organ donation amongst those who had seen the campaign increased significantly by 18% from 36% to 54%; whilst apathy towards organ donation declined by 8% amongst people who 'neither supported nor opposed organ donation'. This positive shift in support is extremely important as there was always a danger that this campaign could turn people off the idea of donating, but instead we managed to engage people with a difficult issue, in a way that resonated with them (Figure 10).

A shift in attitudes to registering

In addition to actual registrations, we also achieved a significant 4% increase in claimed intention amongst those 'very likely to sign-up' having seen the campaign (Figure 11). That intention could convert into a potential 1.9 million future registrations.[14] By including the 16% who are 'definitely planning to register' we have made an additional 7.8 million potential registrations more likely. Conversion of these would nearly meet the 2013 target of 9 million registrations.[15]

Figure 10: Support for organ donation

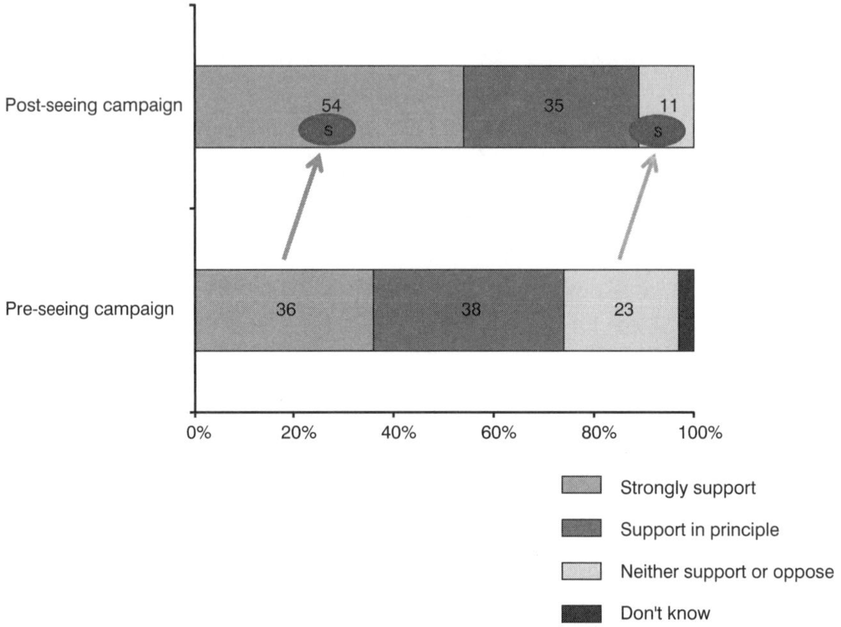

Post-seeing campaign
54 s | 35 | 11 s

Pre-seeing campaign
36 | 38 | 23

0%   20%   40%   60%   80%   100%

Strongly support

Support in principle

Neither support or oppose

Don't know

Source: Continental research, tracking debrief, 2010

Figure 11: Intention to register

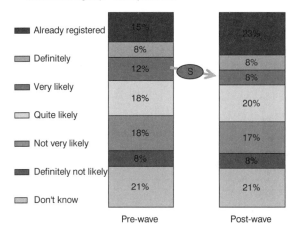

Intention to sign up – all respondents

- Already registered
- Definitely
- Very likely
- Quite likely
- Not very likely
- Definitely not likely
- Don't know

Pre-wave

15%
8%
12%
18%
18%
8%
21%

Post-wave

23%
8%
8%
20%
17%
8%
21%

Q8 How likely are you to put your name on the NHS Organ Donor Register in the near future?

Q9 When do you think you will put your name on the register?

Source: Continental research, 2010 tracking debrief

A well-recognised campaign

The campaign achieved 60% awareness amongst adults, comparable to the successful 2008 Blood campaign with similar media spend and media mix (see Figure 12).

Two-thirds of people saw more than one media channel (see Figure 13). Tracking showed that being exposed to multiple media made them more aware of the ODR, more aware of registering online, more likely to recall the message and more likely to talk about organ donation.[16]

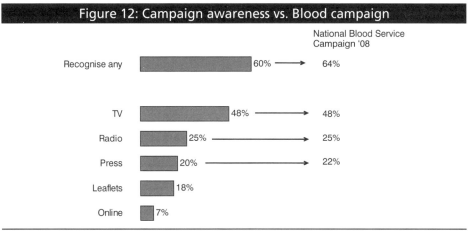

Figure 12: Campaign awareness vs. Blood campaign

Source: Continental research, 2010 tracking debrief

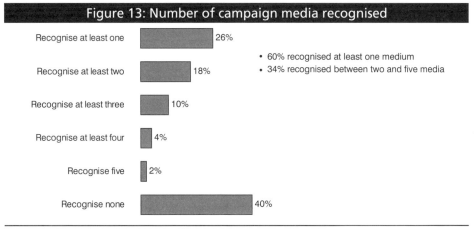

Figure 13: Number of campaign media recognised

Source: Continental research, 2010 tracking debrief

An above average message recall

The campaign had extremely high message recall with people thinking they should register and join the DOR, as well as finding the advertising memorable and aimed at them. The campaign performed significantly above COI norms (see Figure 14).

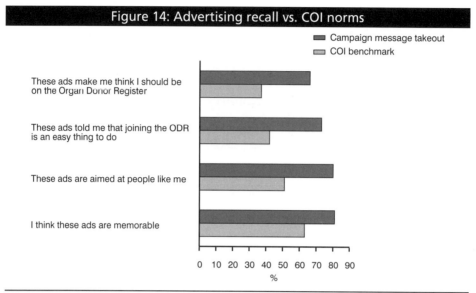

Figure 14: Advertising recall vs. COI norms

Source: Continental research, 2010 tracking debrief

A campaign that generated a lot of talkability

The PR from the campaign generated an additional 110,851,094 OTS, and the total coverage on the issue generated a total of 326,940,322 OTS. Using Metrica insight analysis, the campaign value so far is £301,607. It will have been seen by 4.2 million UK adults with an opportunity to see coverage of 2.2 times.[17]

Eliminating other factors

Can 2009 registration uplifts vs. 2008 be attributed to previous communications?

There have not been any above-the-line advertising campaigns about organ donation in the UK previously so an uplift in registrations is not attributable to residual awareness. The last marketing activity that ran was a Welsh door-to-door leaflet campaign in 2007 distributed to only 280k households in Wales.

Were there any changes in partnerships that could have affected the uplift in registrations?

There are a number of partnerships that NHSBT has to encourage registrations. These are through GP registrations, DVLA, DVLA NI, Boots Advantage, Passport Office, EHIC. All these partnerships have been running for years so will not have affected uplifts in registrations over the campaign period.

Does seasonality play any part in recruitment to the ODR?

Previous analysis of the new recruits to the ODR between April 2005 and September 2009 (prior to the launch of our campaign) shows a steady recruitment across the year driven largely by NHSBT's partnerships. Therefore seasonality will not have affected uplifts in registrations (Figure 15).

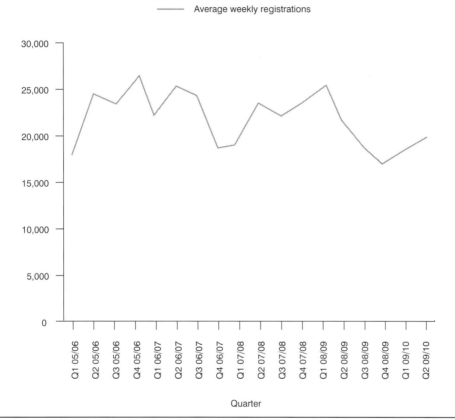

Figure 15: Average weekly registrations Apr 2005–Sep 2009

Source: NHSBT data

Did any TV programmes run at the time that could have affected registrations?

The only programme covering organ donation was *Life Givers* that ran on BBC Daytime in April 2009 for six weeks (Figure 16). This was seven months before our campaign went live so is not relevant to registrations. Interestingly, even though the programme covered the issue in detail, it did not generate any significant uplift in registrations. The rational approach to the issue created empathy but did not generate the self-interest necessary to drive registrations, which further evidences the success of our insight and the advertising.

Figure 16: BBC Daytime, Life Givers, 13–17 April 2009 at 9.15am

New learning

At a basic level, this paper is a reminder that getting the insight right is the most important part of creating effective advertising: advertising that can overcome complex emotional barriers, change deep-set beliefs, and do good. At the heart of this insight we unearthed a new reason to 'give' that taps into our sense of fairness, and whilst we'd like to think we'd do the right thing for altruistic reasons, self-interest wins the day, as long as everyone does well by it. At a more philosophical level this paper questions whether you can attach a value to a life. Is it worth spending £1.2m to save five lives? What we hope to have shown is that there is a financial cost attached to life that is far greater than we might have expected, so the simple answer is that financially it is worth it. The factor you cannot attach a financial value to is the emotional cost of saving the life of a loved one. That is invaluable.

Notes

1 Target from Data Science predictions of response estimates based on media spend.
2 Source: COI Artemis analysis: average CPR for health campaigns is £12; we needed a CPR of £1.62.
3 Based on Department of Transport, 2005 *Valuation of the Benefits of Prevention of Road Accidents and Casualties Highways,* Economic Note No 1.
4 Target from Data Science predictions of response estimates based on media spend.
5 Source: COI Artemis analysis: average CPR for health campaigns is £12; we needed a CPR of £1.62.
6 Source: Market research on barriers to organ donation (2003) – undertaken for UK Transplant.
7 Source: NHSBT ODR.
8 Source: Market research on barriers to organ donation (2003) – undertaken for UK Transplant.
9 Source: AMVi qualitative groups (2009).
10 Source: Market research on barriers to organ donation (2003) – undertaken for UK Transplant.
11 Source: AMV/YouGov quantitative research, base 1975 adults.
12 Munro Forster PR analysis.
13 Based on reaching 9 million additional registrations within 36 months at a registration rate of 128,218 in five weeks. NB this includes the base rate of registrations via partnerships and does not take into account decay of advertising copy.
14 Based on adult population of 49.1 million and 4% shift in intention.
15 However claimed intention is only proof of future effect not actual registrations.
16 Continental research, 2010 tracking debrief.
17 Source: Munro Forster PR analysis.

Chapter 15

Promote Iceland

Inspired by Iceland

By Matt Springate, The Brooklyn Brothers
Contributing authors: George Bryant and Matt Bamford-Bowes, The Brooklyn Brothers; Gurdeep Puri and Janey Bullivant, The Effectiveness Partnership
Credited companies: Creative Agency: Islenska; Media Agency: M2M; PR Agency: Golden Goose; Client: Promote Iceland

---

Editor's summary

When the Eyjafjallajökull volcano erupted in April 2010, tourism to Iceland plummeted; negative stories spread online and the country was left with a projected £180m shortfall in revenue. 'Inspired by Iceland' was the campaign created to harness the power of people as media. Icelanders were encouraged to share their inspiring stories through social tools, including Facebook, Twitter and Vimeo, in order to persuade tourists back to Iceland. This activity changed both attitudes and behaviours in key global markets, bringing an extra £165m to the Icelandic economy with a ROMI of 61:1. The judges were very taken by the uncoventional communications strategy developed here: a strategy that reframed tourism advertising into an issue that galvanised the citizens of Iceland, with a remarkable one third of the whole nation participating within a day of launch.

Introduction

When the Eyjafjallajökull volcano erupted on 14 April 2010, it brought European air traffic to a standstill and threatened to serve a further deathblow to the Icelandic economy. After the 2008 financial meltdown, tourism had become the biggest sector in this small country's economy and in the aftermath of the volcanic disruption tourism numbers were projected to fall by 22% over the busiest months of the year.[1] This decline would leave another disastrous hole in the country's income.

This paper is about how a country of only 318,000 people, with a budget of only £2.24m,[2] created a new type of tourism campaign that used people power rather than a traditional communications approach to rapidly change the perceptions of tourists globally and added £138.7m[3] to the Icelandic economy.

The aim of the paper

To demonstrate how people power can turn negative opinion into positive action

This paper will show the true power of social media; that when harnessed in the right way it can rapidly and sustainably change attitudes and behaviour. We will show how we created a new model for travel communications and challenged a key principle of social media thinking championed by social media theorists,[4] suggesting that social media movements are created by a small number of influencers. But in this paper we will show that the opposite can be true – that starting with a model of *unity* rather than *influence* can create a new level of social participation giving thousands of people a voice and uniting a mass movement behind a common purpose.

The scale of task

The stunning collapse of Iceland

The country of Iceland had transformed itself from one of Europe's poorest countries to one of its wealthiest in the space of a generation.[5]

But fast-forward to September 2008 and the country emerged as the biggest casualty of the global financial crisis.[6] As Prime Minister Geir Haarde explained:

> *There is a very real danger, fellow citizens, that the Icelandic economy could be sucked into the whirlpool, and the result could be national bankruptcy.*[7]

Iceland's future looked bleak (Figure 1).

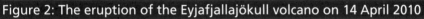

Figure 1: Icelandic demonstrations in Reykjavik after the banking collapse, Oct 2008

From bad to worse: when Europe stopped

On a seemingly ordinary weekday evening back in April 2010, the dormant volcanic glacier, Eyjafjallajökull, unexpectedly erupted and sent plumes of ash into the Icelandic air (Figure 2).

Figure 2: The eruption of the Eyjafjallajökull volcano on 14 April 2010

Black ash clouds engulfed the skies and world air travel was thrown into turmoil.[8]

The ash aftermath

As the cloud spread, so did the negative publicity and Iceland was on the verge of a very real disaster.

Stories from trusted global news sources[9] spread online (Figure 3) and National Geographic issued a health warning, prompting people to think that Iceland was a dangerous place to visit.[10]

Figure 3: Some of the negative news coverage on the eruption

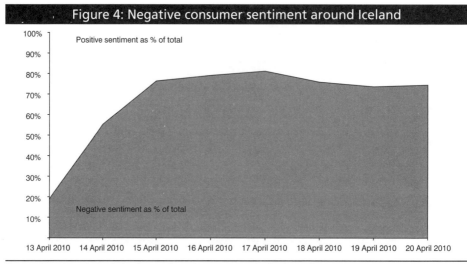

Source: www.bbc.co.uk

A climate of negative stories and sentiment[11] around Iceland was increasingly turning potential tourists off and creating a cycle of negativity around the embattled country (Figures 4 and 5).

Figure 4: Negative consumer sentiment around Iceland

Positive sentiment as % of total

Negative sentiment as % of total

| 13 April 2010 | 14 April 2010 | 15 April 2010 | 16 April 2010 | 17 April 2010 | 18 April 2010 | 19 April 2010 | 20 April 2010 |

Source: Brandwatch Analytics (manual sentiment categorisation), April 2010

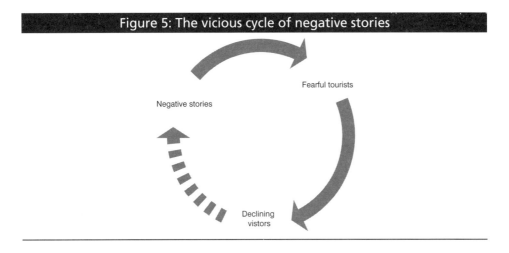

Figure 5: The vicious cycle of negative stories

Attitude surveys in Iceland's key markets[12] showed that interest in the country as a tourist destination had nose-dived.[13]

The effect of the volcano was felt immediately with tourism numbers plummeting 30% in the two remaining weeks of April, a decline that continued on into the start of May.[14]

The Icelandic government had to reset their forecasts for the year based on a 22% decline in visitor numbers from May–September.[15] This was particularly damaging, as these are the busiest months of the year, accounting for 55% of all tourists.[16]

The challenge

The need for a united response

Due to the scale and urgent nature of the challenge it was critical to have an immediate response.

The government of Iceland partnered with the City of Reykjavik, Icelandair, Iceland Express, Promote Iceland and another 80 tourism companies to take positive action against the ash cloud. There were two main objectives:

1. Business objective: rapidly increase tourism to Iceland

Specifically, on a budget of £2.24m, to increase visitor figures above the forecast by 10% between May and September.[17]

2. Communications objective: turn the tide of negative opinion

Hundreds of negative, and uninformed, stories had been written about Iceland in the weeks following the ash cloud.[18] The campaign needed to prove that Iceland wasn't a dangerous travel destination and inspire people to visit it again.

The need for a new model

In our post-recession world, where mistrust in institutions is at an all time high,[19] who would believe a traditional tourism campaign from an embattled country's government? A conventional broadcast-led tourist campaign was at risk of feeling like propaganda rather than genuinely persuasive communication.

Our opportunity

Harnessing the power of people as media

We had to find a radical alternative to the traditional model of tourism communication that would help Iceland bounce back rapidly (Figure 6).

Figure 6: The conventions of travel communications

One thing Iceland had going for it was the latent advocacy amongst previous visitors to the country. A visit to Iceland is not like going to Paris or Barcelona for a weekend. It is another world just two hours away and when people return home they have a huge propensity to share their stories (Figure 7).[20]

We wanted to use social media to harness the power of visitor stories. But these weren't the only people we could use to spread positive stories – we knew the stories should start from within.

Figure 7: Percentage of people who have visited Iceland and would recommend it

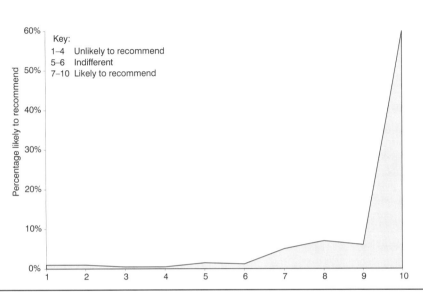

Key:
1–4   Unlikely to recommend
5–6   Indifferent
7–10   Likely to recommend

Source: OMD Copenhagen, Quantitative Survey, 2006

'Inspired by Iceland'

Our campaign idea

'Inspired by Iceland' was the campaign created to harness the power of people as media. Rather than target tourists, we wanted to stimulate Icelanders to share their inspiring stories with the world.

We wanted to turn the cycle of negativity on its head and create a virtual social movement of our own. We called it the *Social Participation Loop*.

Figure 8: The shift from a cycle of negativity to a new model of social participation

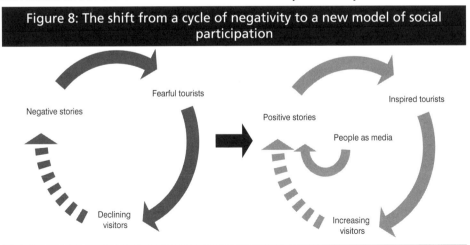

This was the basis of a new model of travel communications that challenged the long-held global conventions within the category (Figure 9).

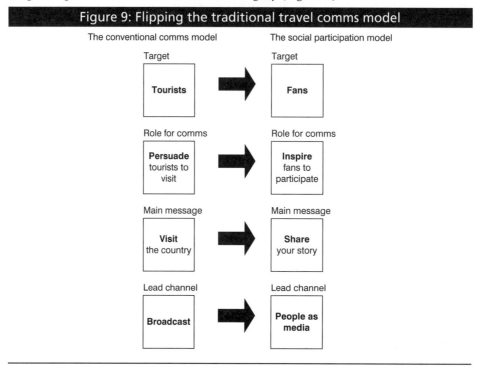

Figure 9: Flipping the traditional travel comms model

Our media strategy

We created a social media-led plan that unfolded over three stages (Figure 10):

- Stage one was to unify and galvanise Icelanders to participate.
- Stage two was to provide Icelanders with the social tools to share their inspiring stories.
- Stage three was to increase momentum of the campaign by publicly rewarding those who had contributed.

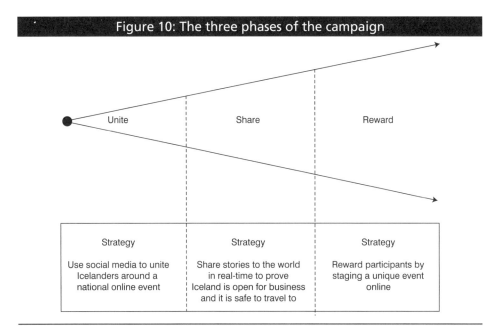

Figure 10: The three phases of the campaign

Unite	Share	Reward
Strategy	Strategy	Strategy
Use social media to unite Icelanders around a national online event	Share stories to the world in real-time to prove Iceland is open for business and it is safe to travel to	Reward participants by staging a unique event online

The total cost of the campaign, including agency fees and production was £2.24m (Figure 11).[21]

Figure 11: The global media plan for the 'Inspired by Iceland' campaign

	May	June	July	August
Social outreach				
Live 6 sheets (3 x cities)				
Newspaper and radio (6 x markets)				
Online search and display				

Source: M2M 2010, campaign launched 14 May 2010

The campaign rollout

Stage one: Unite

In June 2010, in a world first, the entire country of Iceland gathered online to show that their nation was open for business.

We created 'Iceland Hour' where we stopped the country for an hour and got Icelanders to go online en masse and tell the world how much they love their country, why people should visit and how they can also be 'Inspired by Iceland'.

The Prime Minister of Iceland made a live address on TV and we simulcast the whole hour online to the world (Figure 12).[22]

Figure 12: The Prime Minister launching 'Iceland Hour'

Stage two: Share

We created an army of fans that spread news and positive messages across Facebook, Twitter and Vimeo. Friends of Iceland were filmed and their stories posted on the 'Inspired by Iceland' website. This sparked people around the world to get involved and post their own stories. By the end of the first day, 1.5 million people had downloaded different videos from the website[23] and nearly a third of the nation (27%) had sent a video from the website to someone abroad (Figures 13 and 14).[24]

Figure 13: The home of 'Inspired by Iceland'

Figure 14: 'Inspired by Iceland' website where people can share their personal stories

We set up live webcams across the country so people could see the country wasn't covered in ash (Figure 15).

Figure 15: Live Webcam feeds that were set up around Iceland

In cities across the world we also created innovative 'real-time posters' with feeds from the webcams, proving that Iceland was open for business (Figures 16 and 17).

Stage three: Reward

To keep growing the momentum of the campaign, we wanted to reward contributors with a truly public 'thank you'. We held a live web cast concert for the people of Iceland and our supporters worldwide. The event provided a fitting climax to the campaign with acts like Spiritualized and Damien Rice (Figure 18).

Figure 16: 'Real-time' posters in cities

Figure 17: UK Print Ad

Figure 18: Spiritualized playing at the 'Iceland Inspires' concert with PR coverage

The results

We have split our results into five key sections to demonstrate the success of the 'Inspired by Iceland' campaign:

1. The business results;
2. The way the campaign worked;
3. Elimination of all other factors;
4. Payback and ROMI;
5. Manifold effects.

1: The business results

We rapidly increased tourism to Iceland.

From the launch of the campaign to the end of the year, tourism numbers were up over 27% on forecast (Figure 19).[25]

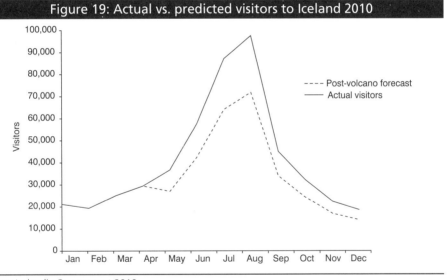

Figure 19: Actual vs. predicted visitors to Iceland 2010

Source: Icelandic Government 2010

The extent of the upturn as compared to the Icelandic government forecast for 2010 is made much clearer when one looks at the difference between the monthly actual and forecast visitor figures. One can see the substantial downturn that took place in April and then the upswing as compared to the forecast from the start of the campaign.

The campaign drove significant increases in visitor numbers in each of the key markets (Table 1).

Table 1: Icelandic visitor numbers for the key markets

Key markets	2010 predicted (000s)	2010 actual (000s)	Actual vs. predicted (% difference)
UK	46.0	60.3	+31.0
Denmark	30.5	38.1	+24.9
Germany	41.0	54.4	+32.7
USA	36.5	51.2	+40.3
Canada	10.8	13.5	+25.0
France	23.9	29.3	+22.6

Source: Icelandic Government 2010

In fact, so significant was the growth of tourism through the campaign period that we actually managed to completely stem the projected decline in 2010 (Figure 20).

Figure 20: Visitors to Iceland 2009 vs. 2010

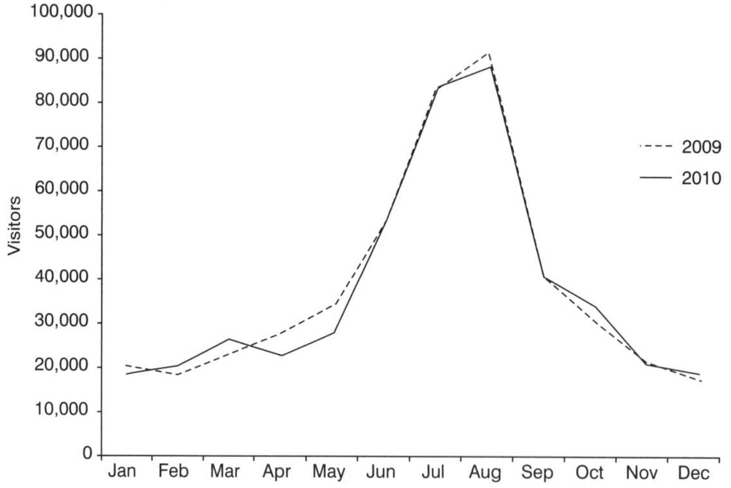

Source: Icelandic Government 2010

We have chosen three key markets from the global campaign to demonstrate the success of 'Inspired by Iceland'. Figure 21 below shows that the United Kingdom saw a sharp decline in visitors to Iceland at the outset of the recession, which was forecast to continue and was halted during the campaign period.

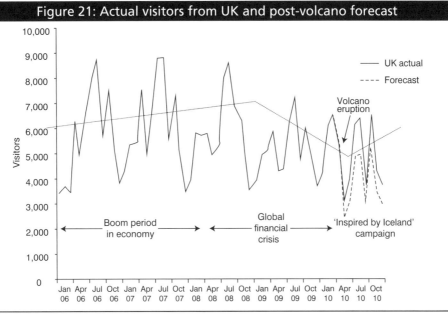

Figure 21: Actual visitors from UK and post-volcano forecast

Source: Icelandic Government 2010

Similarly for the USA and Sweden, the campaign actually reversed the predicted decline from May 2010 onwards (Figures 22 and 23).

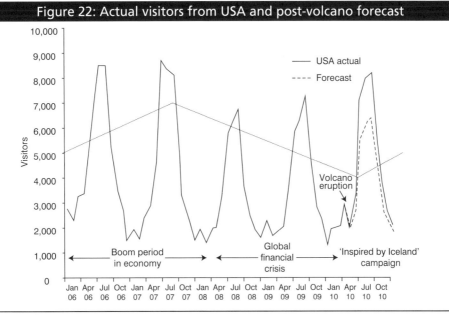

Figure 22: Actual visitors from USA and post-volcano forecast

Source: Icelandic Government 2010

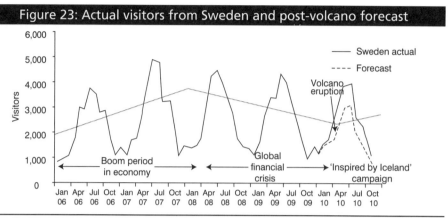

Figure 23: Actual visitors from Sweden and post-volcano forecast

Source: Icelandic Government 2010

2. The way the campaign worked

We have shown how the campaign turned around the actual and predicted decline in tourism to Iceland. We will now demonstrate that the impact of communications was the key driver of this reversal.

Using the *Social Participation Loop* we can evaluate the campaign at each stage of the model.

The Social Participation Loop – Activating People as Media

(see Figure 24).

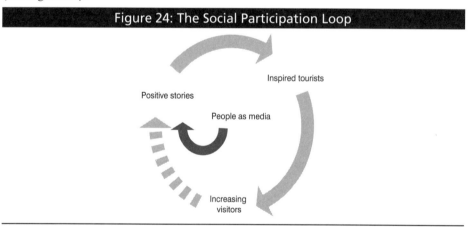

Figure 24: The Social Participation Loop

Within two weeks of the start of 'Inspired by Iceland', over 85% of Icelanders were aware of the campaign (Figure 25).[26]

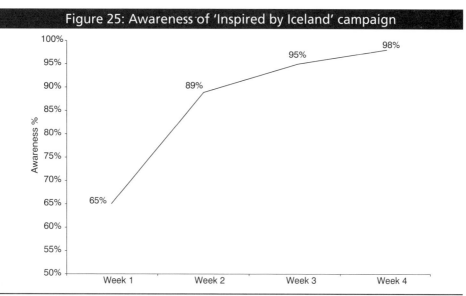

Figure 25: Awareness of 'Inspired by Iceland' campaign

Source: Capacent Gallup Iceland, 4 June 2010

By the end of six weeks, over half of the Icelandic public had contributed stories (Figure 26).[27]

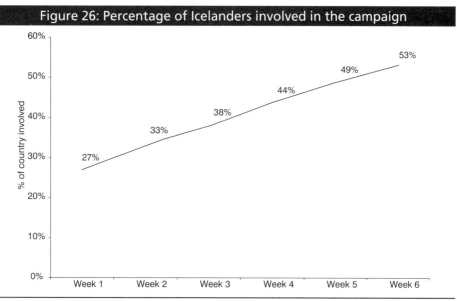

Figure 26: Percentage of Icelanders involved in the campaign

Source: Capacent Gallup Iceland, 4 June 2010

The Social Participation Loop – Using positive stories to turn the tide of Internet sentiment

(see Figure 27).

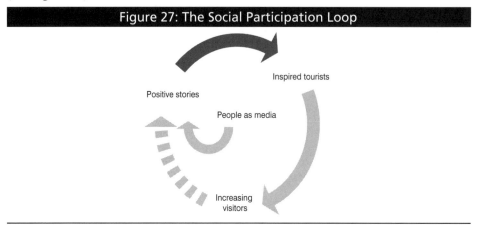

Figure 27: The Social Participation Loop

The number of positive stories contributed to the campaign grew rapidly following launch (Figure 28).

Figure 28: Total number of shared stories over the campaign period

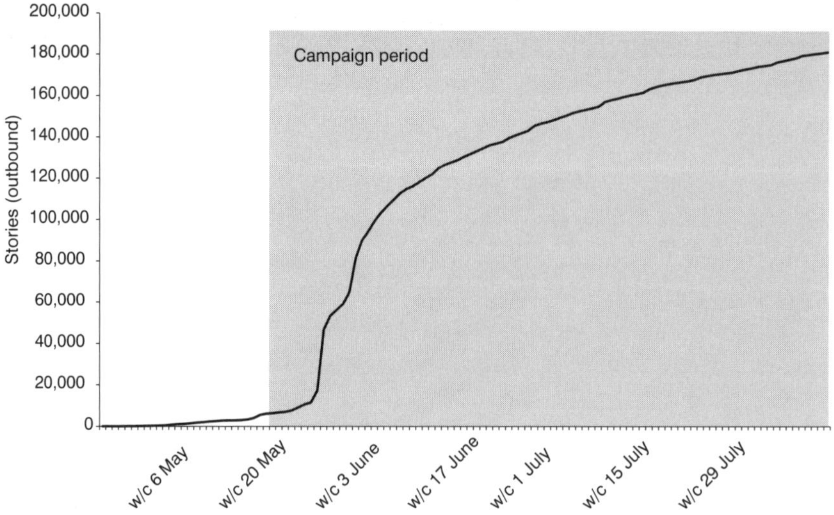

Source: Google Analytics 2010

On Facebook alone we recruited over 45,000 fans and over 2 million stories were seen and sent out by fans via our website, emails and social media channels.[28] Our fans were twice as active as the average Facebook fans. Between June and August the live webcams were viewed 60 million times (Figure 29).[29]

Figure 29: Facebook activity rate of 'Inspired by Iceland' compared to average Facebook activity

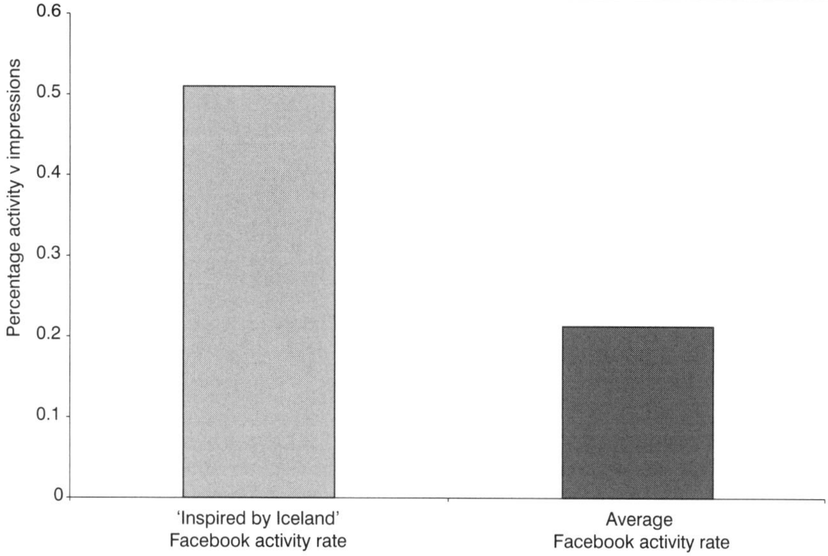

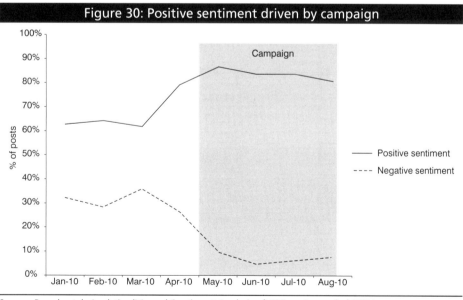

Source: Agency calculations based on Facebook Insights, May–September 2010

The figure below demonstrates that positive stories spread rapidly, creating a sea of change in positive sentiment towards Iceland online (Figure 30).

Figure 30: Positive sentiment driven by campaign

Source: Brandwatch Analytics (Manual Sentiment Analysis of 400 posts per day) 2011

The Social Participation Loop – Inspiring Tourists
(see Figure 31).

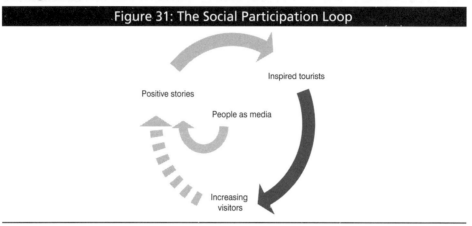

Figure 31: The Social Participation Loop

65% of Icelanders who sent out an inspiring story with our social tools received direct positive feedback from their network abroad (Figure 32).

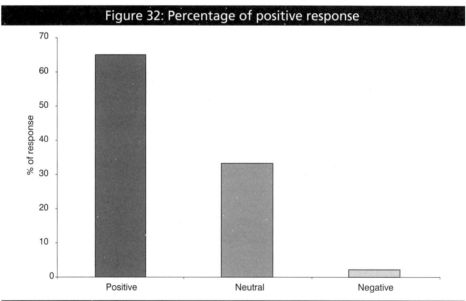

Figure 32: Percentage of positive response

Source: MMR 2010

Through the 10 weeks of the campaign, attitudes towards Iceland as a travel destination increased positively in all key markets (Figure 33).

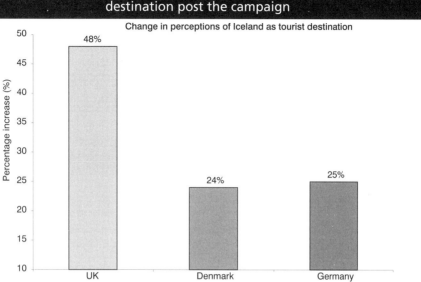

Figure 33: Positive change in perceptions toward Iceland as a travel destination post the campaign

Source: Market and Media Research Ltd 2010, conducted in three key markets of Denmark, UK and Germany. May 2010 (pre-campaign launch) versus August 2010 (post majority of campaign)

In the same period, positive perceptions of Iceland as a safe, danger-free destination increased in all key markets (Figures 34 and 35).

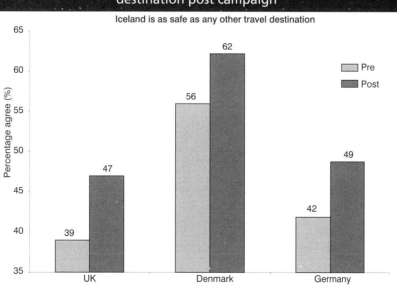

Figure 34: Positive change in perceptions toward Iceland as a safe travel destination post campaign

Source: Market and Media Research Ltd 2010, conducted in three key markets of Denmark, UK and Germany

Figure 35: Positive change in perceptions toward Iceland as a safe travel destination post the campaign

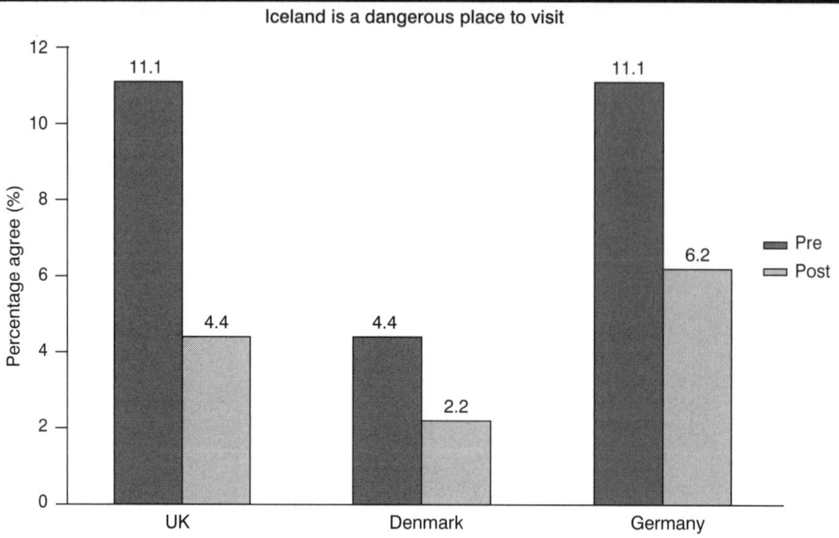

Iceland is a dangerous place to visit

UK: Pre 11.1, Post 4.4
Denmark: Pre 4.4, Post 2.2
Germany: Pre 11.1, Post 6.2

Legend: Pre, Post

Source: Market and Media Research Ltd 2010, conducted in three key markets of Denmark, UK and Germany

The Social Participation Loop – Increasing visitors

(see Figure 36).

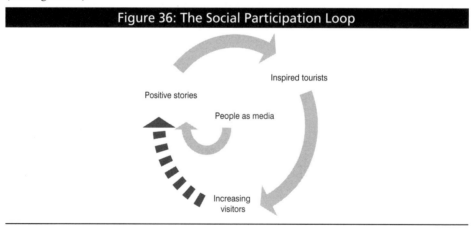

Figure 36: The Social Participation Loop

Inspired tourists

Positive stories

People as media

Increasing visitors

Through the campaign, consideration measures increased significantly in all major markets (Figure 37).

Figure 37: Positive change in perceptions toward consideration of Iceland post the campaign

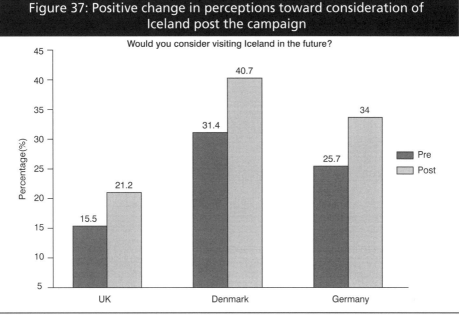

Would you consider visiting Iceland in the future?

Source: Market and Media Research Ltd 2010, conducted in three key markets of Denmark, UK and Germany

There have been many varied attempts to place a ROMI figure on a Facebook fan. Due to the unique closed loop between our Facebook, website and purchase conversion opportunities,[30] we have attempted to demonstrate the conversion value (%) between these different areas (Figures 38 and 39).

Figure 38: Closing the purchase loop

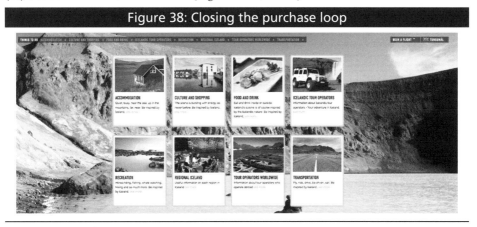

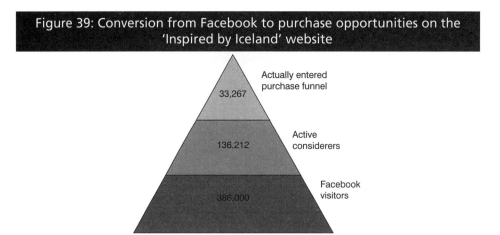

Figure 39: Conversion from Facebook to purchase opportunities on the 'Inspired by Iceland' website

One-seventh of visitors to our Facebook page became fans. The key to understanding performance wasn't looking at these fans but understanding the overall effect of communications within Facebook for the 386,000 who visited.

Overall 9% of visitors to our page were converted to a purchase opportunity demonstrating that it is far more beneficial to understand the overall impact of Facebook communications rather than just attempting to place a value on fans.

3. Elimination of other factors

We will examine variables in two key areas:

1. Iceland
2. The wider market

1. Iceland

Was the Icelandic weather better than expected?

The average temperature and rainfall was no better than average for the period of the campaign.

Was Iceland more affordable?

Iceland did not become more affordable over the period of the campaign with exchange rates remaining constant.

Did the cost of travel to Iceland go down?

There were no reductions in the price of flights for Icelandair and Iceland Express in the period. These two carriers account for 90% of all inbound air traffic and neither dropped prices or offered special deals.[31]

Did the amount of accommodation increase?

The number of registered hotels remained constant through the campaign period.[32]

Were there any incentives for people in Iceland to go online and spread their stories?

There were no financial or promotional incentives.[33]

Were there more festivals and events in Iceland than in previous years?

The number of cultural events was the same.[34]

Was the growth in tourists a natural recovery?

Government estimates suggest that tourism levels typically take in excess of more than three years to recover following a national disaster.[35]

2. Market

Did Iceland's competitors have declining appeal?

None of Iceland's competing markets suffered from any significant national issue in the time period, certainly nothing the size of the Eyjafjallajökull volcano.

Were consumers taking more holidays?

Tourists were actually taking fewer holidays than in previous years.[36]

Did consumers have more to spend on holidays?

Consumers' post-recessionary travel budgets were actually lower than in the previous economic boom years.[37]

4. Payback and ROMI

In total an additional 79,252 tourists visited the country, each tourist contributing on average £1750 in revenue to the country.[38] This is worth an additional £138.7m to Iceland's economy. The total campaign expenditure was £2.24m[39] within this period. This gives a payback figure of £136.46m and a short-term ROMI of 61:1.[40]

Furthermore, it has been estimated that on average just over 21% of visitors return to Iceland at least once.[41] If we apply this percentage to the additional visitors within the period of the campaign, this gives us an additional 16,642 tourists who will revisit Iceland, giving an additional £29m in longer-term revenue.

5. Manifold effects

Social Participation: A new model of travel communications.

Figure 40 clearly demonstrates the commercial success of the 'Inspired by Iceland' campaign as compared to key tourism IPA Effectiveness Awards submissions.

Social Participation: A new model of global communications.

Comparing our ROMI to previous multi-market IPA winners, our campaign delivers a substantially higher ROMI than previous multi-market winning submissions (Table 2). Putting social media at the heart of our approach highlights an alternative model of global communications, demonstrating a radical way of creating international campaigns on a smaller budget.

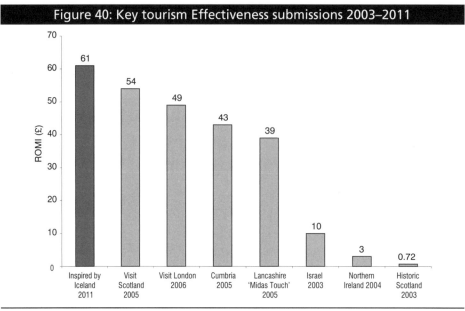

Figure 40: Key tourism Effectiveness submissions 2003–2011

Source: IPA Databank, Warc 2010

Table 2: Multi-market IPA Effectiveness Awards winning papers 2004–2010			
Year	Brand	ROMI	Awarded
2010	Comfort Fabric Conditioner	1.45:1	Silver
2010	HSBC	7.88:1	Silver
2009	LBS	4.5:1	Bronze
2008	Johnnie Walker	3.2:1	Grand Prix
2008	Dove	3.01:1	Silver
2006	Naturella	2.0:1	Gold
2006	Felix	1.38:1	Silver
2006	Nicorette	14.0:1	Silver
2004	Sony Ericsson T610	0.3:1	Bronze
2004	Rainbow Milk	2.8:1	Bronze

Source: IPA Databank, Warc 2010

Social Participation: Sustained effects.

By harnessing people as media we have been able to sustain the momentum beyond the end of the active campaign (Figure 41).

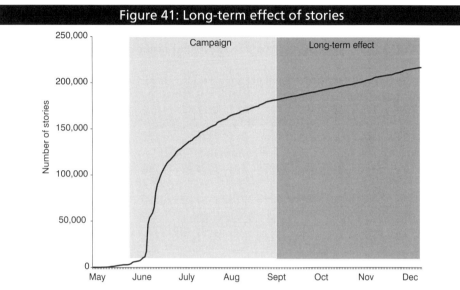

Figure 41: Long-term effect of stories

Source: Google Analytics and Facebook 2010

Q1 2011 has proven to be Iceland's highest first quarter ever (Figure 42).[42]

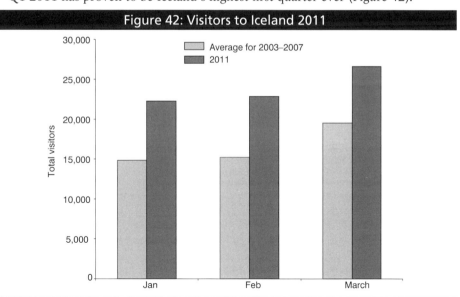

Figure 42: Visitors to Iceland 2011

Source: Icelandic Government 2011

Summary

To see so many people back our campaign has been incredible. We've been able to tell the world that Iceland is a country that can inspire everyone who comes here.

Katrín Júlíusdóttir, Minister of Industry of Iceland

As our learning about social media theory grows, 'Inspired by Iceland' shows how a social-media-led campaign can:

- *rapidly* build mass participation;
- *inspire* a strategy based on unity, not just influence;
- *create* a new model for global communications.

Notes

1   May–September accounts for 55% of all visitors throughout the year. Source: Icelandic Government 2010.
2   Source: M2M 2010.
3   Source: Icelandic Government 2010.
4   That of the 'influencer strategy' e.g. Malcolm Gladwell, 'Law of the Few' from *The Tipping Point*, 2000.
5   Source: *Business Week*, 9 October 2008.
6   Source: *Business Week*, 9 October 2008.
7   Source: Times Online, 9 October 2008.
8   It was the biggest shutdown of airspace since World War II, and affected over 10 million passengers worldwide. Source: International Civil Aviation Organization (ICAO), 14 April 2011.
9   Including the BBC.
10 Source: Market and Media Research Ltd, May 2010.
11 Source: Brandwatch Analytics (manual sentiment categorisation) April 2010.
12 UK, Denmark and Germany.
13 Travel intent in Denmark had declined by 28% and in the UK it was down by 29%. Source: Market and Media Research Ltd, May 2010.
14 Source: Icelandic Government 2010.
15 Source: Icelandic Government 2010.
16 Source: Icelandic Government 2010.
17 Source: Icelandic Government 2010.
18 Source: Brandwatch, May 2010.
19 Source: International Trade & Academic Research Conference 2010.
20 80% of people who have visited Iceland would be likely to recommend it to their friends, family and colleagues. Source: OMD Copenhagen Quantitative Study 2006.
21 Source: M2M 2010.
22 Launched on 3 June 2010.
23 Source: Google Analytics, June 2010.
24 Source: Capacent Gallup Iceland, 4 June 2010.
25 Source: Icelandic Government tourism projections May–December 2010.
26 Source: Capacent Gallup Iceland, 4 June 2010.
27 Source: Capacent Gallup Iceland, 4 June 2010.
28 Source: Brandwatch and Facebook Insight, May–September, 2010.
29 Source: Kakl Analytics, June–August 2010.
30 Our closed loop system tracked visitors to our Facebook on their journey through to the website and onto purchase points (e.g. travel sites, accommodation, tour operators).
31 Source: Icelandic Government 2010.
32 Source: Icelandic Government 2010.
33 Source: Icelandic Government 2010.
34 Source: Icelandic Government 2010.

35   Source: Icelandic Government 2010.
36   Source: The World Travel Trends Report 2009–10.
37   Source: The World Travel Trends Report 2009–10.
38   Source: Icelandic Government 2010.
39   Campaign expenditure includes all agency fees, media costs and production.
40   Source: Icelandic Tourist Board 2010. For every £1 invested in marketing comms, the return is £61.
41   Source: Icelandic Government 2010.
42   Source: Icelandic Government 2010.

SECTION 5

Bronze winners

Chapter 16

East Midlands Trains

How an email CRM programme helped boost the profitability of off-peak services

By Cressida O'Shea, Camilla Patel and Natasha Joslin, LIDA
Contributing author: Marc Turley, East Midlands Trains
Credited companies: Integrated Agency: M&C Saatchi; Database Agency: TBDA; Email Service Provider: E-Circle; Client: East Midlands Trains

Editor's summary

The impact of recession posed a huge threat to East Midlands Trains. Their choice and use of the email channel, and their creative approach, were all designed to minimise cost, minimise waste and maximise effect. Their campaign overcame the barriers to off-peak ticket purchase; increased revenue by 9% amongst customers contacted compared to those who were not; and reduced the off-peak cost per passenger helping to boost the profitability of off-peak services. The judges admired the rigour and professionalism of this paper, which provides a fine example of how to plan the measurement of an email campaign.

Overview

The impact of recession posed a huge threat to East Midlands Trains; if ever a business needed to make efficient use of its marketing budget, this was the time to do so.

Our choice of the email channel, use of that channel and creative approach were all designed to minimise cost, minimise waste and maximise effect.

This paper offers valuable learning about email as a channel – something that is currently missing from the IPA's extensive database.

We will demonstrate how we:

■ Overcame the barriers to encourage leisure customers to buy more off-peak tickets.

■ Increased revenue by 9% amongst customers who were contacted as part of an eCRM programme, compared to those who were not.

■ Reduced the off-peak cost/passenger helping to boost the profitability of off-peak services.

Introduction to East Midlands Trains

East Midlands Trains (EMT) provide the rail equivalent of the M1, operating passenger train services between London, Derby, Sheffield and Nottingham and across country from Liverpool to Norwich.

Formed by Stagecoach Group in 2007, EMT were awarded their train service franchise by the Department for Transport.[1] They run 3,039 trains per week[2] and carry passengers on over 20 million single journeys per year.[3]

During their first year EMT enjoyed exceptional revenue growth, ahead of the market, peaking at 20% in August 2008 (Figure 1).[4]

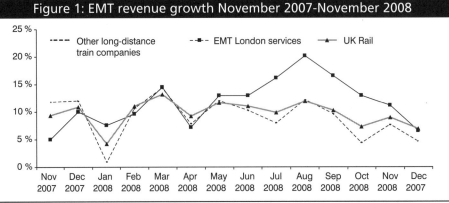

Figure 1: EMT revenue growth November 2007-November 2008

Source: East Midlands Trains Income Reports

But nobody saw this recession coming.

In 2008, the rail industry was hit hard (Figure 2).

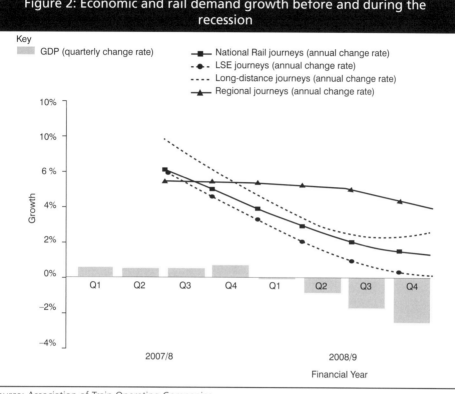

Figure 2: Economic and rail demand growth before and during the recession

Source: Association of Train Operating Companies

EMT's ticket revenue dropped dramatically and at the end of 2008, they were no longer growing ahead of the market. By May 2009 revenue was declining (Figure 3).

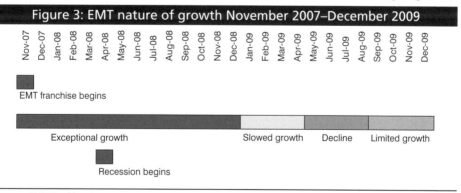

Figure 3: EMT nature of growth November 2007–December 2009

Source: EMT Tracking Report

The dramatic impact of the recession[5] posed a huge threat to EMT, as all the forecasts and projections for their franchise agreement had been based on a period of growth and the terms of their contract were set for seven and a half years.

In fact, conditions for train operating companies were so tough during this period that EMT's East Coast competitor went bust. Less than two years into their seven year agreement, National Express East Coast was brought under Government control (Figure 4).

Figure 4: Press cuttings of conditions for train operating companies

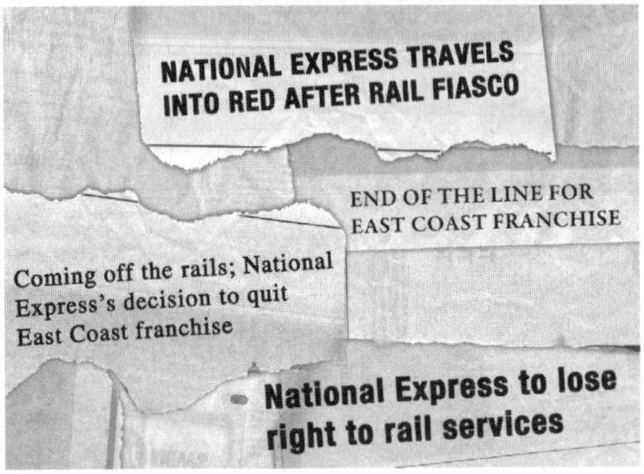

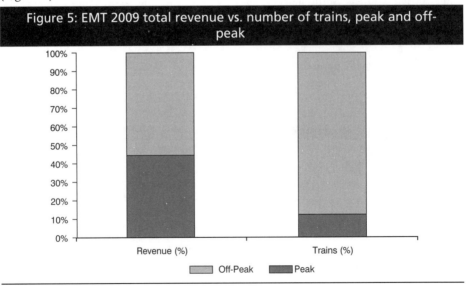

NATIONAL EXPRESS TRAVELS INTO RED AFTER RAIL FIASCO

END OF THE LINE FOR EAST COAST FRANCHISE

Coming off the rails; National Express's decision to quit East Coast franchise

National Express to lose right to rail services

Limited room for manoeuvre

Faced with a bleak economic landscape and bound by the terms of their franchise agreement,[6] EMT had limited room for manoeuvre.

They made most of their revenue from peak ticket sales when demand is high. In fact, only 12% of trains[7] (peak services) generate nearly half of EMT's revenue (Figure 5).

Figure 5: EMT 2009 total revenue vs. number of trains, peak and off-peak

Source: East Midlands Trains

But EMT could not grow peak volumes any further because trains were operating at/near capacity, with an average peak time capacity of 85% (Figure 6).[8]

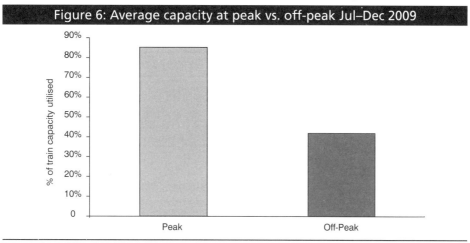

Figure 6: Average capacity at peak vs. off-peak Jul–Dec 2009

Source: East Midlands Trains

Building leisure volume became the key marketing objective

One thing EMT could do was to increase leisure/off-peak volumes as these services typically operate with over half the seats empty (58%, Figure 6).[9]

Since off-peak services are significantly less profitable for EMT (Figure 7), growing off-peak volumes would help boost the profitability of off-peak services.

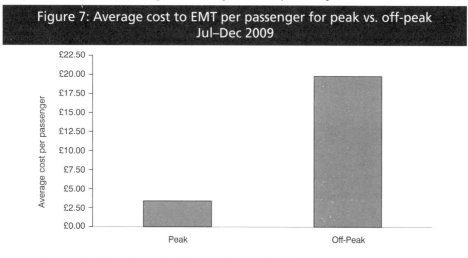

Figure 7: Average cost to EMT per passenger for peak vs. off-peak Jul–Dec 2009

Source: East Midlands Trains

The impact of the recession on the marketing budget

As the recession took hold, the marketing department was dealt a blow when their budget was cut by a third.

Stagecoach Group's mounting pressure on EMT increased their focus on accountability for their reduced marketing budget.

Our strategic principles

Given the scale of our challenge, it was paramount we found a solution that would:

■ be as cost efficient as possible, through improved targeting, channel selection and creative approach;
■ have an immediate impact on volumes;
■ be clearly measurable (given the pressures to use the marketing budget wisely);
■ be flexible and easily adapted to maximise effect.

Understanding the barriers

We looked to the consumer to understand the barriers to off-peak travel, and how to overcome them in the most efficient and cost-effective way possible.

1. Price perceptions are high

Customers think leisure train journeys to cities are expensive:

The train is expensive. Especially if there are a few of you it can be the most significant cost of your trip.[10]

Anecdotes about cheap airline fares do nothing to diminish price perceptions:

It's ridiculous. Train companies fleece you. When you compare the prices with a flight to Spain for £30 it just doesn't stack up!

Nor do newspaper headlines about 'fat cats' and record bonuses (Figure 8). Even though headlines may be about peak prices, they had a general, pervasive effect on perceptions of all ticket prices, including off-peak.

Still, the car does not compete with the train on price as it too is seen as expensive; not just increasing petrol prices, but costs associated with parking and local costs, e.g. London's congestion charge.

We found that there was a disparity between price perception and reality. An Association of Train Operating Companies survey showed that this was typical for train travel, where on average, customers think tickets are **four times** more expensive than they actually are.[11]

2. Low prices are impossible to get

Low fares are advertised, however, cynicism sets in because people don't think these fares are available in sufficient numbers to be able to get one.

Figure 8: Press cuttings of opinions towards train fares

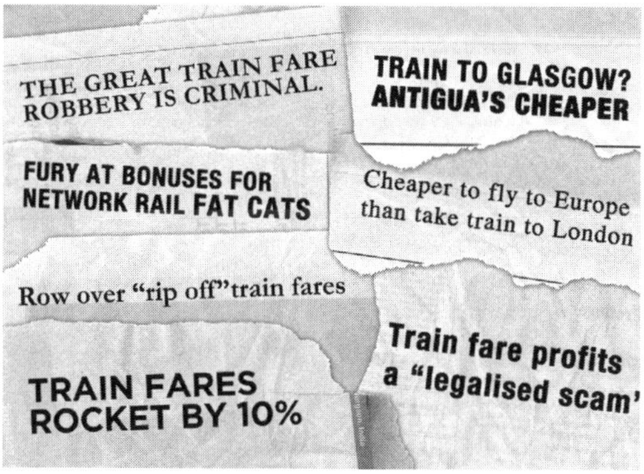

THE GREAT TRAIN FARE ROBBERY IS CRIMINAL.

TRAIN TO GLASGOW? ANTIGUA'S CHEAPER

FURY AT BONUSES FOR NETWORK RAIL FAT CATS

Cheaper to fly to Europe than take train to London

Row over "rip off" train fares

TRAIN FARES ROCKET BY 10%

Train fare profits a "legalised scam'

Source: *Daily Post* (Liverpool) Dec 06; *Sunday Express* Dec 07; *Evening Standard* Aug 08; *London Lite* Nov 08; *Bath Chronicle* Dec 08; *Aberdeen Press & Journal* Dec 08; ITN Jul 09

The first time you see a low fare it's great – but you quickly become disillusioned. You just can't get these fares.[12]

Some even feel hostile towards train operators for deliberately pulling the wool over their eyes.

3. Inertia to taking leisure trips

Habitual travel behaviour is notoriously difficult to change and off-peak train travel is no exception.

For example, London is a universally popular destination and many intend to go more often:

I took my husband there for his birthday. There's loads to do. We should really go more often.

Data suggested there was an opportunity to tap positive intentions[13] to take leisure trips by train, but inertia would make it difficult to convert intentions into action. Especially at a time when people felt they should be cutting back on 'non-essential' leisure trips in times of recession.[14]

Two groups of consumers were of particular interest as they were spending as much as they had as pre-recession, the 'Justifiers' and 'Treaters'.[15] However, they either needed an excuse to 'justify' their expenditure, or a reason to reward themselves with a treat.[16]

So the barriers to off-peak travel were clear; train tickets were seen as expensive, low prices were seen as impossible to get and inertia to taking leisure trips was compounded by recession.

Our solution would have to break through these barriers, even though marketing is a relatively weak force when it comes to changing behaviour.

The spectre of National Express East Coast going bust was ever-present in our minds…

Our solution was direct, accountable and simple

Behavioural economics inspired our approach, in particular a quote from Richard Thaler, the author of *Nudge*:

The best way to change behaviour is to make it easy for people.[17]

This may seem deceptively simple, yet a growing body of research is testament to the insightfulness and effectiveness of this approach to changing behaviour.

So how could we convert intention into action and make it as easy as possible for customers to buy leisure tickets?

The most direct channel

The email channel was the most direct way of smashing through the barrier of inertia.

Email is the channel which makes it easiest for the customer to find the low price tickets they are looking for. They can simply click straight through from the email to the most relevant booking page on the EMT website.[18]

Email also works indirectly, by reminding customers of their intention to purchase, and bumping it up their mental 'to do list'. Some will wait a few days or weeks until they have more time or are doing their 'admin' tasks, and then go to the EMT website via their browser (instead of clicking through directly from the email).

The email channel also offered benefits to EMT in terms of:

- Revenue generation: their website is a lower cost channel than train stations or third party websites.[19]
- Building a customer database[20] and gaining insight based on purchase behaviour.

An accountable solution

The beauty of the email channel is that it is 100% measurable. We can track click-throughs from emails and measure exactly who goes on to make a purchase.

A further level of precision is provided through measurement of offer redemption. By providing individual PIN numbers with each offer, email allows us to track offer take-up by individual.

With eCRM we can test and optimise our strategy, responding quickly to what works and what doesn't. For example, we were able to test which of two incentives was more motivating: £5 off or 10% off.

Simple creative

We deliberately designed the email creative to be very simple so it would work hard to overcome the barriers to purchase (Figure 9).

This was the right solution because simple creative was:

- cheaper;
- easier to adapt and optimise;
- deliberately not flashy marketing;
- able to provide clear prices re-enforced by the message 'tickets cost less than you think';
- create a sense of easy availability with the focus on click-through and to deliver the message that 'there are a large number of low price tickets available';
- able to leverage the EMT brand look and feel.

Figure 9: Example email creative

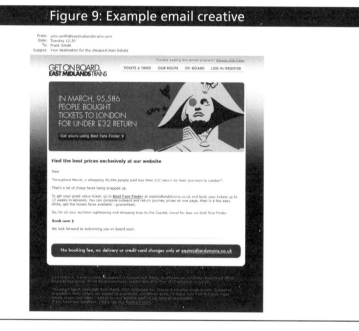

A CRM strategy designed for maximum return

We analysed the customer database and carried out a segmentation based on recency, frequency and value of ticket purchases. The analysis revealed clear insights that enabled us to design discrete tasks and targeted strategies to maximise revenue.

Three key strategies formed part of an overall eCRM programme.

1. Encouraging repeat purchase

Analysis revealed that an unusually high proportion of EMT's customers have only bought tickets from eastmidlandstrains.co.uk once (69%).[21]

Those that had bought a ticket from the website more than once were on average likely to go on to buy four more times.

We found that the 72% of second purchases happened within the first six months and these customers are worth twice as much compared to those that make a second purchase after six months, so a task was defined to encourage customers to make their second purchase from the website within six months.

The solution was a series of emails to establish a relationship, with the critical six month email being a trigger to repurchase. An incentive of money off your next EMT website booking would help 'justify' the purchase.

2. Preventing lapsing

Database analysis revealed that if a customer hasn't bought another ticket within 9–12 months of their last purchase, they fail to purchase again.

A task was defined to prevent lapsing by triggering customers to buy again at 11 months. We reminded customers why booking online is easy and that it provides great value for money. This message was also re-enforced with the offer of 'money off your next online booking'.

3. Rewarding frequency

EMT had assumed that those customers who buy the most expensive (First Class) tickets are the most valuable and should be rewarded accordingly to build loyalty.

Yet analysis of high value customers revealed that this was not the full picture. A surprisingly high proportion of value came from customers who frequently purchased low value tickets.

We were able to recognise and reward these customers with tailored and targeted emails, including third party offers and money off subsequent tickets.

Measurement principles

Measuring and proving success of marketing campaigns in the train industry is notoriously difficult as a huge range of factors can affect usage; e.g. weather, competitor price promotion, advertising and inflation can all affect people's likelihood to travel by train.

However, the email channel offers the opportunity to measure and isolate the effect of communications, due to the ability to create a controlled environment where our communication is the only variable.

To ensure that we obtained significant and robust results our approach would be to not contact a representative control cell of customers who have opted-in[22] to the eCRM programme. This enables true like for like sales comparison and isolates the potential effect of a customer being more predisposed to the brand by opting into the programme.

However, to achieve robust results with this approach would require large volumes of customers to be excluded from the programme.

To ensure that we were optimising volumes for the programme, we created a test (Table 1) to challenge the hypothesis that customers who opt-in to communications are more predisposed to the brand than those who opt-out. The test compared sales of opt-in customers (Control 1)[23] to sales of opt-out customers (Control 2) (see Figure 10).

Table 1: Control test matrix

Customer groups	Communications comparison	Role
Opt-in	Customers who have opted in to the eCRM programme and contacted	To generate incremental revenue
Control 1	Customers who have opted in to the eCRM programme but not contacted	To challenge the hypothesis that if a customer has engaged with an email programme they are more predisposed to purchase from the brand
Control 2	Customers who have not opted in to the eCRM programme and thus not contacted	To provide an ongoing mesurement of incremental sales for the programme

Source: East Midlands Trains

Figure 10: Make up of communications universe

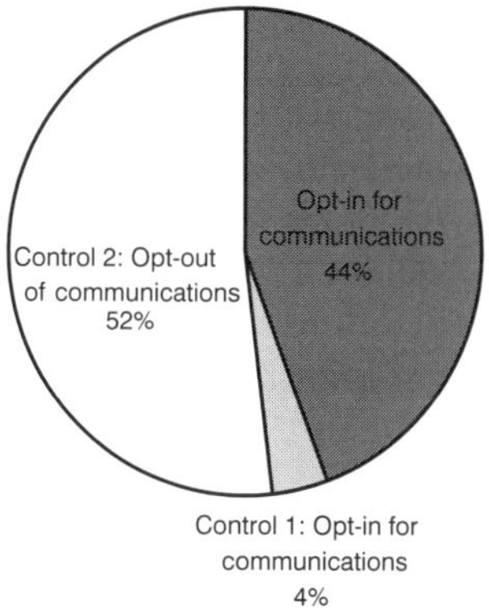

Opt-in for communications 44%

Control 2: Opt-out of communications 52%

Control 1: Opt-in for communications 4%

Source: East Midlands Trains

We compared three months sales activity[24] of Control 1 vs. Control 2 without sending any communications and found no significant difference, which therefore demonstrates that Control 1 is no more pre-disposed to the brand than Control 2 (Figure 11).

Figure 11: Sales rate comparison of Control 1 vs. Control 2 Jan–March 2010

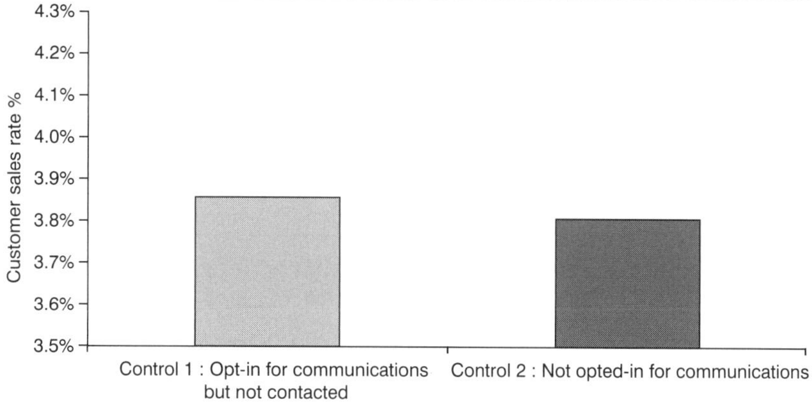

Control 1 : Opt-in for communications but not contacted

Control 2 : Not opted-in for communications

Source: East Midlands Trains

We were therefore confident in using Control 2 as a robust control cell against which we could measure the overall effect of the programme.

Commercial performance

Since launch in January 2010, the group of customers in our eCRM programme have generated over £4.5m incremental sales revenue during the programme period compared to the customers in Control 2. This delivered nearly £4.2m net profit and 12:1 ROMI (Figure 12).

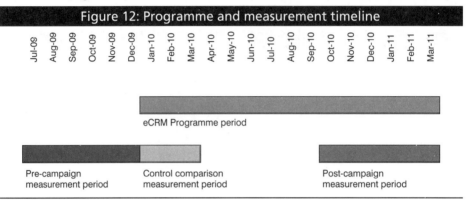

Figure 12: Programme and measurement timeline

Source: East Midlands Trains and LIDA

Over our programme period (Jan 2010–Feb 2011), there was an increase in off-peak volume (Figure 13) resulting in a cost per passenger reduction (Table 2).[25]

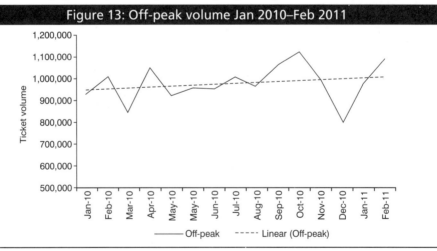

Figure 13: Off-peak volume Jan 2010–Feb 2011

Source: EMT passenger income reports

Table 2: Cost to EMT per off-peak passenger	
Pre-campaign average	£20.30
Post-campaign average	£18.26
Cost reduction	£2.04

Comparing a monthly average volume pre-campaign[26] to a monthly average volume post-campaign, the off-peak volume increased by 102,360 per month (Figure 14).

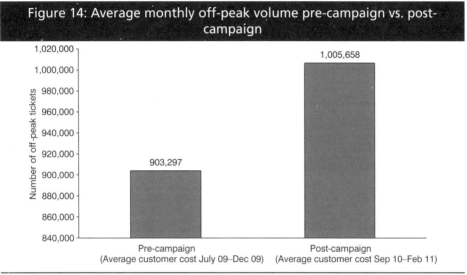

Figure 14: Average monthly off-peak volume pre-campaign vs. post-campaign

Source: East Midlands Trains

The effects of our eCRM programme were threefold

1. Growth in off-peak volume

We knew that some off-peak volume growth was due to business customers changing their travel patterns to cheaper off-peak travel times caused by post-recession budget pressures. However this does not account for all the growth.[27]

Our campaign provided an average of 12,561 incremental passengers per month (Table 3), which equates to 12.3% of the total average monthly volume increase (Figure 15). This was a significant contribution for a single channel and smashed our target of 7%.[28]

Table 3: Average incremental monthly off-peak volume attributable to the eCRM programme

Incremental sales volume calcuations		Explanation
Incremental sales revenue	£4,522,106	Incremental purchases made by customers in our marketing cell compared to Contol 2 for the campaign period
Average price per ticket	£24	Average ticket price of customers transacting on eastmidlandstrains.co.uk
Number of incremental tickets during campaign period (15 months)	188,421	Incremental sales divided by average ticket price
Average number of incremental tickets per month	12,561	No of incremental tickets divided by 15 (months)
Total volume increase per month	102,360	Average monthly difference between pre- and post-campaign averages
Percentage of total monthly increase associated with eCRM	12.3%	Average number of incremental tickets per month/total monthly increase

Figure 15: Average monthly off-peak volume increase apportioned to email

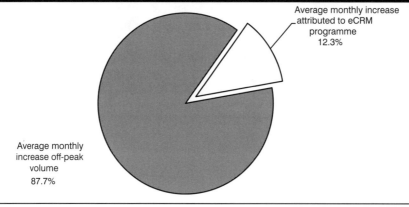

Average monthly increase attributed to eCRM programme 12.3%

Average monthly increase off-peak volume 87.7%

Source: East Midlands Trains

2. Improved price perceptions

The offers provided within the email played their part in giving people a 'reason' to purchase, and this was proven by the sales rate being three times greater than Control 2.[29]

Despite the nature of the offers (money-off and percentage discounts) customers who took up the offers spent on average the same as customers who did not.[30]

We conducted a survey to see if customers on the eCRM programme had improved perceptions of value for money compared to those who were not.

Our benchmark was an ATOC[31] survey which showed that the proportion of EMT passengers satisfied with value for money for the price of the ticket was 57%.

We asked the same question of customers in our eCRM programme and found a considerably higher proportion of eCRM customers were satisfied with value for money from EMT (69%) (Figure 16).[32]

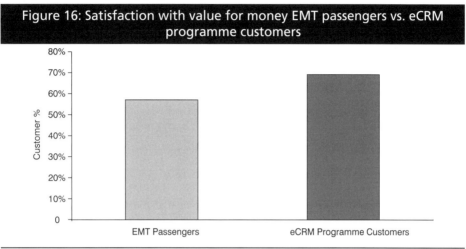

Figure 16: Satisfaction with value for money EMT passengers vs. eCRM programme customers

Source: East Midlands Trains qualitative research April 2011. Sample size 4,403 customers

This demonstrates that the eCRM programme had the desired effect of overcoming the disparity between price perception and reality.

3. Reduction of off-peak cost/passenger and improved profitability of off-peak services

From a marketing budget of £340k we have created £4.18m net profit (Table 4).[33]

Table 4: Profit and ROMI calculations

ROMI calculations		Explanation
Value of incremental sales	£4,522,106	Incremental purchases made by customers in our eCRM programme compared to Control 2 for the campaign period
Value of incremental sales revenue	£4,522,106	The 3% cost of sale via the website has already been accounted for in EMT's sales figures
Marginal contribution to profit	N/A	There is no incremental cost associated with incremental revenue as the cost for running trains is fixed
Campaign costs	£340,311	
Net profit	£4,181,695	Incremental sales revenue minus campaign costs
ROMI	12	Net profit divided by campaign costs x 100%

And we have had a direct impact on reducing the off-peak cost per passenger.

This had dropped during the campaign period by £2.04.[34] Our campaign directly contributed to 12.3%[35] of volume increase during the campaign; therefore it is reasonable to attribute 12.3% of the cost reduction to our activity.

For a marketing spend of £0.03 per passenger we have reduced the cost per passenger by £0.25 (Table 5).

Table 5: Off-peak cost per passenger calculations		
Cost reduction calculations		**Explanation**
Off-peak volume	12,432,293	Total off-peak volume over the campaign period
Marketing budget	£340,000	eCRM marketing campaign budget
Marketing cost per customer	£0.03	Total volume divided by campaign budget
Cost per passenger reduction	£2.04	Average post-campaign compared with average pre-campaign
Per passenger reduction attributable to campaign	£0.25	Cost per passenger reduction x 12.3%

Evaluation

Sales directly attributed to click-throughs

£877,237 of this sales revenue can be directly attributed to click-throughs from emails.[36]

This revenue more than covered the cost of the eCRM programme with a ROMI of £1.58 for every £1 spent.[37]

Overall eCRM programme effectiveness

£4,522,106 incremental sales were generated from customers who were contacted through the programme; this was calculated by comparing the average spend of customers who were in the programme over the 15 month period compared to those who weren't (Control 2).

This contributed a 9% uplift to the total sales revenue that can be attributed to all customers purchasing through eastmidlandstrains.co.uk.

Additional halo effect

However, looking at sales revenue through the website channel alone is not the full picture. Our research with customers[38] in our eCRM programme has shown that 26% of customers also buy at the station and 36% also buy via other train booking websites like thetrainline.com.

Conclusion

The impact of recession posed a huge threat to East Midlands Trains and we have shown how they responded in a responsible and accountable way by making efficient use of a reduced marketing budget.

The solution was direct and simple. Our choice of the email channel, use of that channel and creative approach were all designed to minimise cost, minimise waste and maximise effect.

This campaign has been so successful for EMT that eCRM will now drive the marketing strategy for the final three years of their franchise. The Stagecoach Group also plan to use eCRM as the backbone of their marketing strategy going forward.

Whilst some sectors have developed sophisticated eCRM programmes, many others have yet to leverage their database to deliver targeted email campaigns. We hope this paper will inspire others to make more effective use of eCRM in the future.

Notes

1   Passenger rail services are provided by train operating companies under franchise agreements which generally run for 7–10 years. Responsibility for the operation and condition of the track rests with Network Rail. Strategic decisions on major investment, which also affect service to passengers, are the responsibility of the Department for Transport.
2   Monday to Friday EMT run 474 trains per day; Saturday 452 trains per day; Sunday 217 trains per day.
3   Source: East Midlands Trains Passenger Income Reports.
4   Source: East Midlands Trains Passenger Income Reports.
5   Source: National Statistics/nVision. Six quarters of negative growth starting Q2 2008.
6   The number of trains run peak and off-peak (irrespective of capacity) and the timetable are laid out and agreed as part of the Train Operator's franchise agreement with the Department for Transport.
7   Source: East Midlands Trains.
8   Source: East Midlands Trains.
9   Source: East Midlands Trains Passenger Income Reports.
10 Leisure customer, M&C Saatchi Qualitative Research, July 2008.
11 Association of Train Operating Companies (ATOC) research March 2010 found that a representative selection of adults in Britain believed the average rail fare to be £28.01. The average fare is actually £6.83.
12 Source: M&C Saatchi Qualitative Research, July 2008.
13 EMT Tracking Research Wave 3 Nov–Dec 2008. 45% responders claimed they intended to use the train for leisure purposes in the next 12 months.
14 Source: M&C Saatchi Reacting to Recession quantitative research July 2008. 81% of responders said they are spending more carefully than they used to.
15 Source: M&C Saatchi Reacting to Recession quantitative research July 2008. 'Justifers' and 'Treaters' account for 26.7% of the population. Justifiers' reaction to recession is considered spending. They are unafraid to spend, but during recession they need to find a good excuse to. They're looking for reasons to spend, not just money off. Tightening their belts does not come naturally to Treaters, so they reward themselves for their frugal behaviour with the odd indulgence.
16 84% admit to buying treats to compensate. Justifiers: 87% are prepared to spend, but look for good reasons to justify it.
17 Source: Richard H. Thaler and Prof. Cass R. Sunstein (2008) *Nudge: Improving Decisions About Health, Wealth, and Happiness*, New Haven & London: Yale University Press.
18 eastmidlandstrains.co.uk.
19 The cost to EMT of ticket sales via their stations is 9%, via third party websites (e.g. thetrainline. com) is 5.5% and via their own website eastmidlandstrains.co.uk is 3%.
20 When customers buy tickets direct from EMT's website, we are able to collect and store the transactional data for each website customer. Each one is assigned a unique 'i.d.'; the history and detail of the transactions made by them are attached to this i.d. and stored. In August 2009 the database held 317,442 customer records.
21 Source: East Midlands Trains Recency, Frequency and Value Analysis, Aug 2009.
22 In order to comply with the Data Protection Act 1998 and employ best practice, customers are required to actively tick a box to choose to receive marketing communications from EMT. If a customer does not tick the 'opt in' box they are classified as having 'opted out' of marketing communications. Customers in this group do not receive any emails in our eCRM programme.
23 The control sample size was a significant volume to provide results at a 95% confidence level.
24 See Figure 12 for programme and measurement timeline.
25 Source: EMT Passenger Income Reports.
26 Average for the 6 months prior to campaign activity, see Figure 12.

27   EMT developed a peak time pricing strategy to limit the shift of travel behaviour by its business customers.
28   Target calculated based on incremental sales revenue target of £2,461,265 and an average ticket price of £24.
29   A typical EMT email conversion to sale rate is 1%.
30   Source: East Midlands Trains Closed User Group Offer Analysis. The offers encouraged customers to buy a larger number of tickets or to chose higher priced ticket options.
31   Source: Association of Train Operating Companies National Passenger Survey Autumn 2010.
32   East Midlands Trains Quantitative Research April 2011. Sample size 4,403 customers.
33   The value of incremental sales includes the cost of offers.
34   See Figure 13, Costs to EMT per off-peak passenger.
35   See Figure 15, Average incremental monthly off-peak volume attributable to the eCRM arogramme.
36   Google Analytics.
37   £877,237 (sales revenue) less £340,411 (campaign costs) = £536.862 (net profit). £536.86/£340,411 × 100% = 1.58.
38   East Midlands Trains Quantitative Research April 2011. Sample size 4,403 customers.

Chapter 17

Fiat

Fiat Portal

By Sebastian Kemmler, AKQA
Credited companies: Digital Agency: AKQA; Client: Fiat

Editor's summary

Fiat identified the role of digital as a catalyst to conversion, turning loosely interested people into highly engaged and qualified leads. It did so by breaking with the age-old linear purchase funnel model and applying behavioural economics to nudge users to sale via a set of online tools. Fiat thereby achieved an incremental increase of qualified leads which represents a payback of £5 for every £1 spent. This is an interesting paper which offers some good new learning on the power of web design, providing a strong example of how to discount other variables.

Summary

This paper tells the story of how Fiat reacted most quickly and radically to the revolutionary change in consumer behaviour that the digital age has brought about, and thereby has managed to establish itself as a digital leader in the marketplace over the past three years.

Fiat understood earlier than any other competitor that the true potential of digital did not simply lie in being yet another medium to display advertising, but in directly changing behaviour. It identified the role of digital as a catalyser of conversion, turning slightly interested people into highly engaged and qualified leads.

Fiat broke with the age old linear purchase funnel model, by applying behavioural economics to nudge users to buy via a modular set of online tools that helped users pick and choose what they wanted at any time.

By engaging customers with a best-in-class car configurator, finance calculator, comparison tool and model exploration sections, Fiat managed to push the overall desirability of the brand and triple its conversion rate of users into qualified leads.

Fiat achieved a significant uplift in qualified leads, which represents an additional value of £5,140,543 at an ROI of £5 for every £1 spent.

Background

A new digital playing field

Digital has fundamentally revolutionised the way people buy cars:

- today almost 90% of consumers use the internet to research vehicles – up from 61% in 2005;[1]
- the time it takes to choose a car has reduced from an average of 6 months to 2–4 months;[2]
- 25% of consumers only visit one dealership because they already know exactly what they want;[3]
- 33% of consumers are already prepared to order their new car online – that's a potential 3.3 million transactions;[4]
- car manufacturer websites and car portals are now the single most important source of information in the car purchase process, both in terms of usage and perceived usefulness (see Figure 1).

This change in consumer behaviour posed a historic opportunity for Fiat in the UK marketplace. It opened a completely new playing field for marketing activity, one not driven by media muscle alone, but that allowed a smaller player to compete at eye level with huge volume manufacturers like Ford, Vauxhall and VW.

It created a new arena where size and spend matter less, and cleverness matters more.

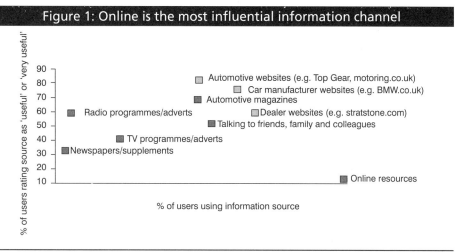

Figure 1: Online is the most influential information channel

Source: ATConsumer Survey, OC&C analysis, 2010. Sources of Consumer Purchase Information and % of users rating them 'useful' or 'very useful', % of respondents, n=154

The challenge

Competing with the big boys

The task Fiat gave us was to use digital to create a long-lasting competitive advantage, which would allow them to compete at eye level with big spending volume manufacturers (Figure 2).

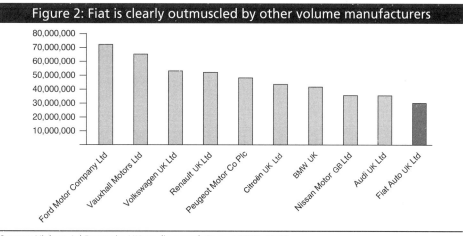

Figure 2: Fiat is clearly outmuscled by other volume manufacturers

Source: Nielsen Ad Dynamix: UK media spend. Report 2009–2010

This lack of media spending power is a huge disadvantage in the volume car segment, where decisions on a car are not based primarily on premium image perception, but largely awareness and price.

The key question we needed to answer was:
How can we use digital to make up the gap?

Our solution

Nudge to convert

Our solution followed a behavioural economic approach. Rather than trying to change attitudes, we tried to change the behavioural choice architecture.

Digital is the perfect medium for this because it allows people not only to communicate, but also gives them something to do.

The longer we manage to keep users on our site and engage in all the key activities of exploring, comparing, configuring and calculating, the less likely they are to look elsewhere.

Similar to the famous 'school canteen' example in the book *Nudge* (where pupils choose fruit instead of chocolate bars simply because they are placed more prominently), users on a car purchase journey build conviction to buy a Fiat simply because we have made it incredibly easy to compare the specs, configure the car, calculate its finances and get a loan.[5]

Rather than investing high budgets in display advertising as key competitors have, Fiat decided to rebuild its digital portal to directly influence the customer journey.

The business rationale behind this approach was simple:

It's cheaper to double conversion than it is to double traffic.

If we could entice twice as many website visitors to take a test drive, we could go head-to-head with competitors with double our media budget.

We knew that once people drive a Fiat, they rarely leave the dealership without a car, due to its great value-for-money proposition and characteristics.

Our objective therefore was to squeeze the most out of every single visitor that comes to the Fiat portal by making sure they did not leave without booking a test drive.

Our business objectives

Catalyser of conversion

We identified the role of the portal as a catalyser for conversion, turning slightly interested people into highly engaged and qualified leads.

On this basis we defined three key objectives:

Engagement

Engage users to ensure they do not need to go elsewhere and that we can dominate their time during the purchase journey.

Desirability

Drive the appeal and desirability of the Fiat brand and models by engaging customers deeply in fun and playful interactions.

Conversion

Nudge users along the journey to drive conviction to purchase and dealership visits.

Consumer insight

People are not robots

To achieve our objectives we needed to gain a deep understanding of the customer purchase journey.

Our key learning: *The linear purchase funnel model is broken.*

In the past, the car-buying journey was relatively opaque. People would educate themselves, discuss different models, compare features and make their decision behind closed doors, at home or among friends.

Car manufacturers could only take a guess at how they had made up their minds.

Marketers could organise focus groups with two dozen potential customers, undertake telephone surveys or ask people for their key car-buying criteria after they bought a car – but they could never truly observe customers in real-time, in their natural habitat, throughout the journey.

This has fundamentally changed with the popularity of digital platforms. Potential car buyers openly share their opinions in social media, analytics can track user behaviour on car portals and automotive websites, and car owners share their personal car ownership experiences in user review sites. For the first time we can acquire a deep understanding of what customers actually do.

The learning is perhaps not surprising: potential car buyers do not follow a linear prescriptive funnel while choosing their car, rather they do so in a highly associative and seemingly chaotic manner. Unlike the assumptions that have been driving auto marketing for decades, customers do not rationally assess the marketplace to build preference, and then emotionally develop desire that converts into consideration and eventually purchase. Some of them fall in love with a certain car first and rationalise their choice afterwards. Others go for a test drive at their favourite dealer first, and research functional features on comparison sites later.

In summary: buying a car is less like a linear funnel and more like a game of snakes and ladders. People are not robots: they buy cars in an associative, not a linear manner.

The key learning is not so much that the world has changed and the linear purchase funnel does not work anymore, but that it did not match reality in the first place.

There were three main consequences for the development of our portal:

- not linear, but associative;
- not pre-defined, but customer-led;
- not attitude-driven, but behaviour-driven.

What we built

The first non-linear digital platform

Digital car platforms before Fiat had been constructed in a linear way, forcing users to choose options in a pre-defined order and to reload the page after each. Modern cars come with up to 500,000 different options to customise – a complexity deemed impossible to manage if users get to pick and choose whichever they like and whenever they like.

The problem with this approach is obvious: people want to pick a specific model, colour and interior, to see how these look together and then go back and tinker with them. And they want an indication of the price of these options right away, to help inform their choice.

Being forced to act in a rigid way was a big barrier to completing the process.

Fiat and AKQA set out to build the first non-linear digital platform, with all options on one page and a fully dynamic finance calculator. We also introduced an integrated e-commerce platform that would sell special edition cars directly online.

This had never been done before. When Fiat had asked another supplier how much it would cost to build such a platform, their answer was: 'This is practically and theoretically impossible.'

Fiat and AKQA set out to prove them wrong.

Elements of the digital platform

Online tools for key user activities

We have developed online tools for the five key activities during the customer journey – exploration, comparison, configuration, calculation and test drive.

These five activities are commonly shared by all car customers. What varies is the sequence, the depth they will go into at each stage and the time they will spend at each stage.

Some customers might start with the comparison to figure out the right car for them, and then go into further exploration and configuration. Others might already have a favourite model and start with the configuration right away before moving onto calculation.

We have developed non-linear online purchasing tools for each of the key activities (Figure 3):

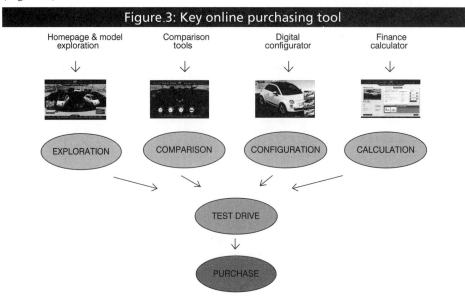

Figure 3: Key online purchasing tool

How the tools perform

A suite of best-in-class tools

According to Psyma (the authority in automotive digital customer research) Fiat has created the best car portal in the segment. Our online purchasing tools have dominated the segment for the past three years (Figure 4).

Figure 4: Best in market online purchasing tools		
Tool	**Description**	**Performance** **% difference to average**
	• Showcases whole range in an appealing and interactive way • Fly-throughs and interactivity, close-ups and hotspots on each model	Best in market: • appealing design +14% • entertainment value +27% • info about new cars +7% • info on features +7% • images of models +11%
	• Best digital car configurator in the world • Non-linear, simple and fun to use: allows all configurations on one page • Directly connected to factory so items can be added or removed with one click	Best in market: • configurator +16% • visualisation of cars in configurator +19% • increase in annual configurations +186% • every third visitor to Fiat portal configures a car
	• Interactive comparison tools that are both helpful and entertaining and allow users to choose by price, performance, economy and storage space	Best in market: • page views generated in 2010: 316,469 • average dwell time within comparison tool: 1:10mins • average page views per visit: 15
	• First fully dynamic finance calculator that updates with each option selected and is directly linked to Fiat finance company, FGA Capital	Best in market: • info about financing and leasing possibilities +19% • presentation of pricing information +13%

Source: UK Automotive Benchmarking Study, Psyma, 9, 2010

How successful were we?

Showcasing the success against key objectives

In the following section we will showcase our success against our three key objectives:

1. Driving engagement
2. Increasing desirability
3. Pushing conversion.

1. Driving engagement

The Fiat portal achieves remarkable engagement and user activity scores: this is particularly true of the car configurator. Since launch, the number of configurations has doubled and customers are saving and sharing their configurations with their friends (Figure 5).

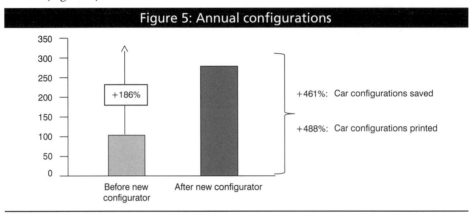

Figure 5: Annual configurations

+461%: Car configurations saved

+488%: Car configurations printed

Source: SMMT Automotive Market Intelligence, 2007–2010; Sophus3 – Fiat website analytics solution, 2007–2010

Every third visitor to the Fiat portal goes on to configure a car: the highest percentage in the marketplace (Figure 6).

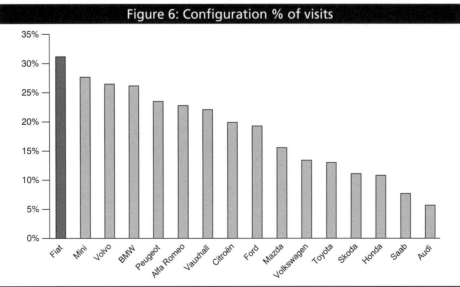

Figure 6: Configuration % of visits

Source: Cross industry benchmarking of website performance, Sophus3 eDataXchange, 01/11

For every £100 spent on media, Fiat achieves three car configurations. Peugeot achieves only one. This is the best conversion of media spend to configurations in the market (see Figure 7).

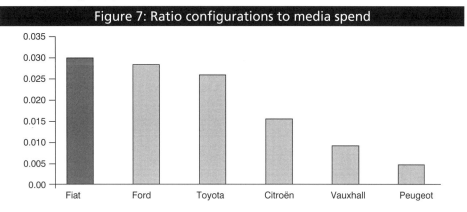

Figure 7: Ratio configurations to media spend

Source: Cross industry benchmarking of website performance, Sophus3 eDataXchange, 2007–2010; Nielsen Ad Dynamix: Report 2007–2010

2. Increasing desirability

High engagement leads to overall appreciation of the Fiat portal, making it the customers' favourite (see Figures 8 and 9).

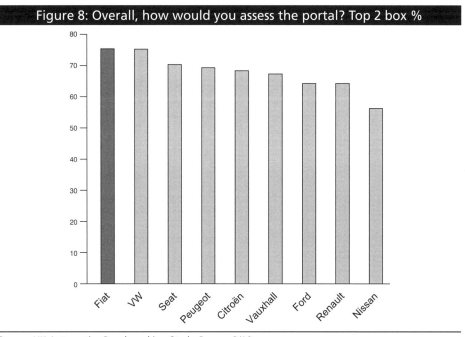

Figure 8: Overall, how would you assess the portal? Top 2 box %

Source: UK Automotive Benchmarking Study, Psyma, 9/10

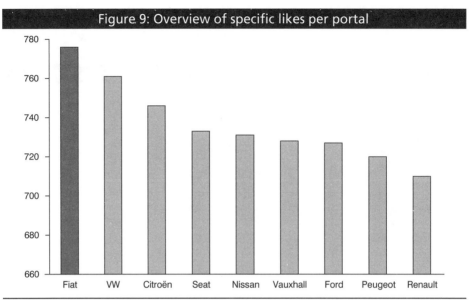

Figure 9: Overview of specific likes per portal

Source: UK Automotive Benchmarking Study, Psyma, 9/10

This in turn positively influences the desirability of the Fiat brand as a whole: 75% of all users feel better about Fiat once they have visited the website (see Figures 10 and 11).

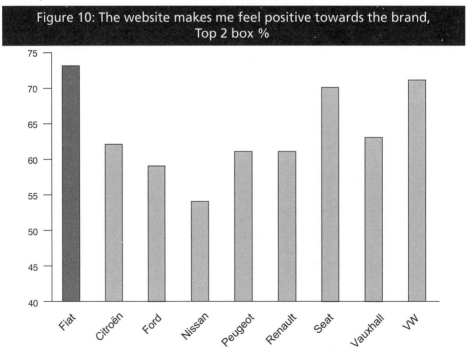

Figure 10: The website makes me feel positive towards the brand, Top 2 box %

Source: UK Automotive Benchmarking Study, Psyma, 9/10

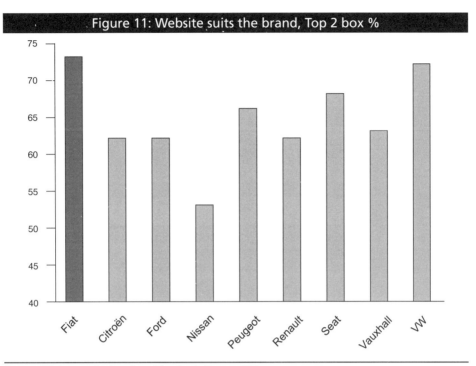

Figure 11: Website suits the brand, Top 2 box %

Source: UK Automotive Benchmarking Study, Psyma, 9/10

The Fiat portal is best-in-class and has been so successful that key competitors are trying to copy it – as Vauxhall, the biggest spender in the marketplace, demonstrates in Figure 12.

3. Pushing conversion

When you compare the Fiat portal today with the portal pre-launch, it's clear to see how much more effective it is at driving leads. Over the past three years the portal has delivered a significant incremental increase in consumer action every single year (see Figures 13 and 14).

Most importantly, the number of qualified leads the portal is generating on average every single year has tripled (Figure 15).

Figure 12: Fiat portal vs. the recently launched new Vauxhall portal

Figure 13: Explosive increase in brochure requests

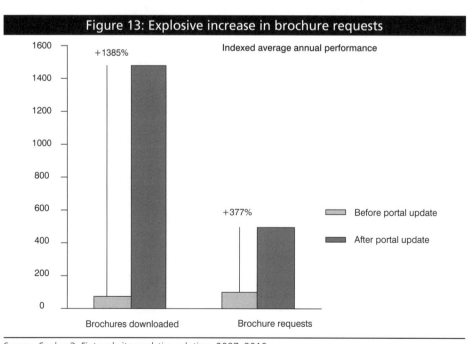

Source: Sophus3, Fiat website analytics solution, 2007–2010

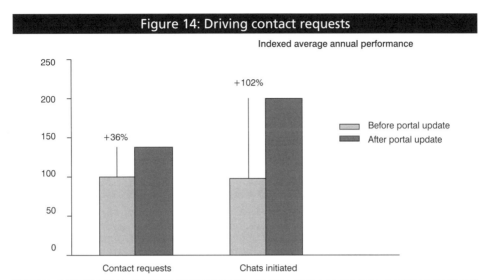

Figure 14: Driving contact requests

Source: Sophus3, Fiat website analytics solution, 2007–2010

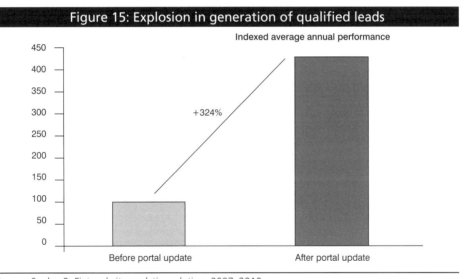

Figure 15: Explosion in generation of qualified leads

Source: Sophus3, Fiat website analytics solution, 2007–2010

Fiat calculates the value of their marketing activity based on the equivalent value of a qualified lead to the business. This calculation is based on long-term modeling of the propensity to purchase a car, and the average profit Fiat makes on this purchase.

Based on this, the incremental value of qualified leads generated every year by the portal is £2.36m.

The configurator has proven to be a particularly powerful catalyser of lead generation.

Demonstrating the contribution of the new portal

Fiat has seen an impressive increase in the generation of leads via the web portal, and there are a few factors that contribute to this.

This section will demonstrate that the update of the portal was fundamental to the success of converting interested customers into qualified leads.

This will be done by discounting other UK market and economic factors.

1. Not just an effect of increased media spend

The first factor to discount is media spend: we need to show that the increased generation of leads is not just a simple effect of greater media investment. To do this, we've plotted the increase in leads against media spend (see Figure 16).

To understand the incremental leads generated via the portal update, we have calculated the conversion rate of media spend to leads in 2007 (before the portal was updated).

We have then plotted the expected generation of leads in the following years, based on this conversion rate and the changing media spend (shown in dark grey).

We then calculated the incremental leads we have generated on top (shown in light grey).

We have created 199% more leads than should have been expected in relation to media spend.

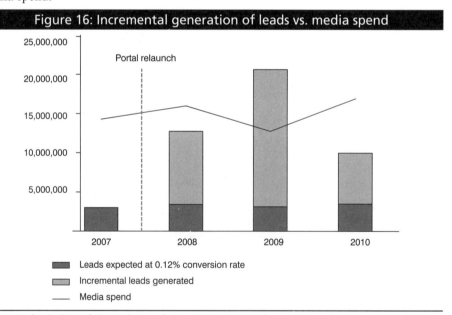

Figure 16: Incremental generation of leads vs. media spend

Source: Sophus3, Fiat website analytics solution, 2007–2010; Nielsen Ad Dynamix: Report 2007–2010

2. Not just an effect of increased traffic

The explosive rise of generated leads could be easily explained if it was simply a result of dramatically higher traffic to the website. What we need to prove is that we've managed to increase the conversion of traffic coming to the portal to qualified leads.

During the past three years there have been two big topics for Fiat that have significantly affected traffic:

- launch of the Fiat 500 has raised significant interest and appealed to a broad audience;
- Fiat has been a great beneficiary of the UK Car Scrappage Scheme.

In Figure 17 we have plotted the changes in traffic and the generation of leads we would have expected from the old portal, which had a 1.21% conversion rate of visits to qualified leads.

The challenge for us is to demonstrate that the updated portal did not just generate an increase in line with overall traffic increase.

Figure 17: Incremental leads generated vs. traffic

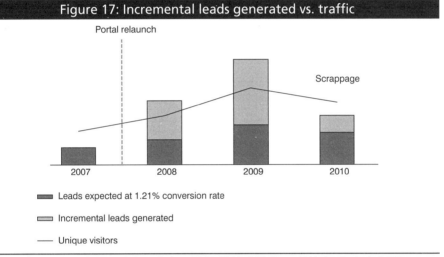

Source: Sophus3, Fiat website analytics solution, 2007–2010, FGA Group Website Analysis, 2010

This overview shows that we have more than achieved on this benchmark. We have increased the conversion rate from 1.21% to an average of 2.7% over the past three years, more than doubling it.

This means that every media £ spent on attracting a visitor to the portal is working twice as hard. Or put another way: Fiat can reduce their investment to attract visitors by half to achieve the same results in leads when compared to the earlier portal.

3. Not just an effect of particularly attractive models or pricing conditions

The third key influence we need to discount is that it might be easier to convert interested users into qualified leads if there is a highly attractive model (such as the Fiat 500) or particularly good financial incentives via the UK Car Scrappage Scheme.

We have therefore conducted a calculation that is as conservative as possible.

- We have discounted any leads generated for the Fiat 500, even though the new portal obviously might have worked in favour of generating more leads for the Fiat 500 as well.

- We have discounted 34% of all leads that might have been a direct effect of the Scrappage Scheme, in line with the 34% in sales increase Fiat experienced during its duration.

This dramatic exercise obviously discounts many leads since the Fiat 500 has been the best-selling model for Fiat in recent years.

This overview shows that even when the most significant external factors are excluded, the portal has still doubled lead generation (see Figure 18). This implies that Fiat has doubled leads for all existing old models simply by updating its web portal over the past three years.

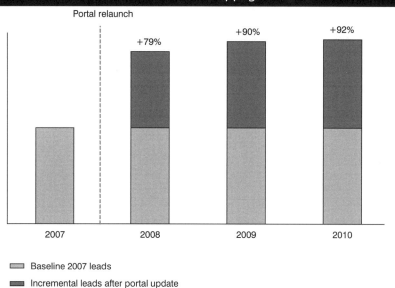

Figure 18: Adjusted lead generation discounting special factors such as Fiat 500 and UK Car Scrappage Scheme

Source: Sophus3, Fiat website analytics solution, 2007–2010; Discovery – Fiat Lead Generation System 2010

Calculating ROI

We calculate the ROI on the basis of the value Fiat are assigning to a qualified lead.

Taking into account the increase in traffic, and looking only at the incremental leads achieved on top, our calculation adds up to an additional value of £5,140,543. This represents a ROI of £5 for every £1 spent.

Within our most conservative estimate (discounting any leads generated via the Fiat 500 or the UK Car Scrappage Scheme), we have achieved an additional value of qualified leads of £1.9m during the past three years.

With an investment of £1m into the portal, this represents a minimum ROI of £2 for every £1 spent.

Conclusions and learnings

Via the update of the portal, Fiat has managed to punch above its weight and has been able to compete with the big media budgets of the big volume manufacturers, by being more insightful and clever in digital.

We have managed to double the conversion of interested users into qualified leads, allowing Fiat to save on media spend. Fiat has now achieved an ROI of at least £2 for every £1 spend.

We have done this by applying behavioural economics and by nudging users towards dealership visits, revealing three key learnings:

1. The traditional linear purchase model is dead: customers buy in associative ways.
2. Marketing should not force customers down a prescribed route, but allow them to pick and choose as they wish.
3. Behaviour drives attitudes as much as the other way round.

Notes

1 'Cars Online 09/10 – Understanding Consumer Buying Behaviour in a Volatile Market', CapGemini, 2009–2010.
2 Ibid.
3 Ibid.
4 AT Consumer Survey, OC&C analysis, 2010; Auto Trader Survey October 2010.
5 Thaler, Richard H.; Sunstein, Cass R.: *Nudge: Improving Decisions about Health, Wealth and Happiness*, Penguin, Yale University Press, 2008.

Chapter 18

Lynx

Using social media to drive brand loyalty – Lynx Facebook campaign

By Selina Sykes, Unilever; Martin Harrison and Susannah Clark, Tullo Marshall Warren
Credited companies: Media Agency: Mindshare; Client: Unilever UK

Editor's summary

It wasn't driving new penetration into the brand and the market that Lynx struggled with, so much as converting this penetration into long-term loyalty. They decided to let go of their ownership of consumer data, and use Facebook and social media as a platform to engage with audiences on their terms in order to significantly influence spending habits. To keep the buzz and conversation going between campaigns, Lynx developed an 'always on' approach, delivering a constant stream of content into Facebook so that the brand could maintain engagement levels. In total Lynx have demonstrated that the Facebook page drove £750,000 of additional revenue. This is one of the first examples of an IPA entry applying rigour to the measurement of a Facebook campaign, going beyond the simple number of 'likes'. The judges appreciated the use of a control sample, and the attempt to link the social media campaign to actual sales.

Using social media to drive brand loyalty

How do you drive loyalty in a commoditised market? And what is the 'value' of a Facebook fan?

In this paper we will provide an answer to an age old and a brand new marketing question. We will demonstrate how, by shaking free of the need to own data and truly engaging on the audience's terms, and by rigorously learning and refining in a new communication channel, Lynx was able to significantly influence spending habits.

We show how Facebook can be used as a powerful platform for brand engagement. We will show that discounts and offers are not the only way to drive sales in social media.

We will show that the value of our Facebook fans is an incremental £4.48 over the monitored six month period and that our Facebook page drove £750,000 additional revenue (an additional £1.4m income over the year).

The problem

The deodorant market is becoming increasingly commoditised with volume growth out-stripping value growth. Heavy price promotions are driving category value erosion. In this context, it becomes more difficult to justify the price premium of a brand like Lynx.

In this context, our large scale campaigns do a good job of driving new penetration into Lynx and the market. What we struggle to do is convert this penetration into loyalty and therefore fully realise the opportunity of our brand acquisition.

We believed that we could drive loyalty through leveraging our brand equity and engaging with our consumers on a longer-term basis. This objective formed the basis of our social media strategy brief.

The objective

Drive brand loyalty through longer-term brand engagement.

The solution

An early strategic shift

In late 2008, Lynx briefed agencies on a Lynx loyalty programme. The aim was to find and recruit a large base of Lynx users, and use them as a defence against price promotion and the erosion of spend in the category.

The initial response focused on email, but the weight of prevailing evidence, plus our own observed response rates, quickly demonstrated the limitations of email to communicate with 16–24 year old males. Social media, on the other hand, provided ample opportunity to communicate with our target audience.

So we took a deep breath and decided to manage our recruitment, communication and management via Facebook. This meant that we let go of ownership of our consumer data. Our assumption was that the quality of interaction we would get through social media would outweigh the additional benefits that owning data confers.

Learn a new communications paradigm

Moving to social media then involved a steep learning curve. We had to define how we communicate with our audience but also how to manage that communication. The open, conversational and 'always on' nature of most consumer Facebook interaction that we observed convinced us that we needed to give ourselves the infrastructure to do the same:

■ we employed a full time 'social editor' to manage interactions on Facebook;
■ we worked with Unilever's legal team to establish 'rules of engagement', but crucially to ensure that our editor could post and converse with no prior approval of content by the brand team or legal team.

We also had to quickly learn what worked. Rigorous analysis of the times we posted, the content and the overall response shaped our communications in real-time (Figure 1).

We discovered that generally the highest number of impressions can be achieved over the weekend (which led to a change in working practices), 5pm is the strongest time to post and overall, on average, Friday is the strongest day to post.

We also found that low level conversation generated higher interaction – the simple question 'Are you getting some digits tonight?' provided a consistently high level of comment and interaction.

Frequency of posting was another learning – we decided to start with the highest frequency of update we could manage (again, we wanted to reflect consumer behaviour rather than received wisdom). We have continued to post several times per day since then with almost no negative feedback or effect on fan growth.

Finally, we were surprised at the enthusiasm with which consumers will talk about the product. Simple discussions such as 'What Lynx are you wearing tonight?' or 'Which Lynx is best?' regularly produced hundreds of comments.

(We were able to leverage this to decide on the name of our new big pack size – a 200ml pack. The two names on the table were XL and Big Boy, so we asked the page which they preferred. XL won fairly comprehensively, so you can now buy it in most retailers).

Committing to the channel

There is a view that social media is not a numbers game, that the social media practitioner should focus on levels of interaction and the value of the interaction rather than raw volume. While this is true to an extent, Lynx has universal awareness and a very high penetration of 23.6% of the UK market. Furthermore, it is a low cost product bought at a relatively low frequency vs. many FMCG categories.

This meant that to make a serious impact on the bottom line, the Facebook page required scale. The Facebook page was put at the centre of the overall marketing strategy, with all other media (TV, outdoor and digital display) featuring the Facebook page as the call to action. Any campaign amplification or content was deployed on

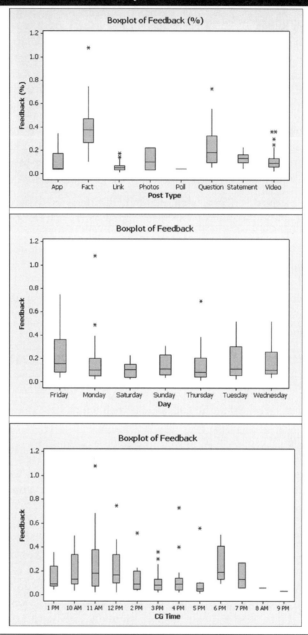

Figure 1: Analysis of feedback based on type of post, time of day and day of week

Source: Facebook Wall data

Facebook. The page became the brand's de facto online presence, with the global website playing a secondary, supporting role (Figure 2).

Figure 2: Mindshare's 'Connections Architecture', showing how the Facebook page was at the centre of communications strategy

Build during campaigns, maintain in between

The 'Connections Architecture' allowed us to use high profile campaigns to drive recruitment to the page. However, Lynx do not have a permanent ATL presence, meaning that there were gaps between campaigns. These gaps created significant weaknesses in the overall programme. Facebook favours pages (and people) with high levels of interaction and activity when populating newsfeeds. A month-long period of inactivity means that you disappear from view, requiring much greater effort to regain ground when a campaign breaks. (This is particularly important if you want to use the base to drive buzz around a campaign – if they haven't heard from you for weeks, the chances are that they won't see you when the campaign starts.)

These gaps made it very important that we had something to talk about all the time. We created a 'conversation calendar' which allowed us to plan content in advance, anchoring our conversations in what was happening in our audience's lives rather than being defined by the Lynx marketing calendar.

This led to a reassignment of budget – away from a campaign by campaign model and more focused on maintaining an 'always on' conversational platform.

Maintaining campaign conversations for sustained periods

There's no need to go into detail about how traditional ATL approaches do not translate well into social media; enough people have made that point. The challenge for us was to take the core idea behind new product launches and global TV advertising and use it to create content that could be delivered over time and a sustained conversation. We developed a model for implementing global campaigns in social media.

All social media assets changed regularly to reflect current Lynx activity (sometimes several times in one campaign). This meant, for example, that we constantly changed our profile picture, without any real rules. Again, we were confident that this reflected consumers' behaviour (Figure 3).

Figure 3: Examples of Facebook profile imagery across the year

Rise – Wake Up and Stay Alert

An example of this approach is the 'Lynx Rise' campaign. Lynx Rise is a shower product. It has lime extract which creates a refreshing sensation when showering. The global insight was that guys can miss the little details that make all the difference in the mating game if they are not alert. BBH created a global campaign, with outdoor and TV executions.

The UK team (TMW, Mindshare, Freud Communications and The Lounge Group) took this concept and translated it into a strong content proposition. Using Jessica Jane Clement, star of *The Real Hustle* and a favourite of our audience, we created 16 *Wake Up Calls* short films, each 10 seconds or so, that showed our hero missing out because he wasn't paying attention. We sweated our assets, creating several compilations of the films, a Jessica Jane Clement special, a behind the scenes film and tailored films for bloggers (Figure 4).

Figure 4: The Lynx Rise Wake Up Calls

The films were released every two or three days over four weeks, allowing us to extend the conversation and buzz around the above the line activity for over two months.

The films generated over 1.4 million views on YouTube and over 350,000 views of their Facebook tab. The average Facebook users watch five films. In total, guys spent over 15,000 hours watching Lynx Rise branded content. This is great news for a product launch and a great digital story, but the key for us was that it provided frequent, high quality, in-depth engagement with our Facebook user base – those guys whose behaviour we are trying to change.

The results

It is notoriously difficult to assess the value of a Facebook fan, particularly if you are not an online retailer and are unable to attribute direct sales to a branded page. Attempts have been made to equate the value of a fan to their equivalent value in other media (*Adweek* – http://bit.ly/d9LlJA). While a blunt instrument, this approach has some merit for us because our strategy is based on twin assumptions – that the high frequency of contact social media allows us can be leveraged to drive behavioural change and that the quality of the content delivered in those interactions will affect brand preference.

To get a view of the actual sales driven by the Facebook page, we engaged Information by Design to build a tracking panel. 400 consumers were recruited from the Facebook page and were then matched demographically and on social media usage to create a control cell (Figure 5).

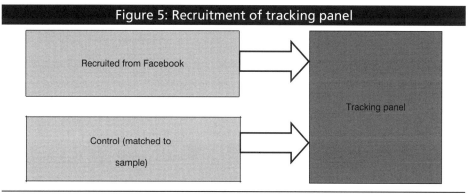

Figure 5: Recruitment of tracking panel

The panel is interviewed on recruitment to establish current usage and attitudes. The control cell was further refined to create a 'matched control' – many of the responders who were on the Lynx Facebook page had very high levels of spontaneous awareness and brand preference (see Table 1). A sub-set of the control cell who demonstrated similar levels of awareness and preference were identified to exclude a natural preference for the brand as an influencing factor.

Table 1: Current usage and attitudes to Lynx	
Statement	**Facebook recruits**
Buy Lynx most often – Shower Gel	82%
Buy Lynx most often – Deodorant	74%
Lynx Body Spray awareness – first mentioned	70%
Lynx Shower Gel awareness – first mentioned	81%
LTR Lynx (likely/very likely)	71%

They are then asked to record everything within the category that comes into their house over a six month period. This allows us to monitor the difference in spend between those who are exposed to the Facebook page and demo7graphically matched consumers who are not.

At the conclusion of the panel study, an exit questionnaire records the same information as the recruitment questionnaire, allowing us to track changes in brand attitudes (Figure 6).

Figure 6: Exit questionnaire

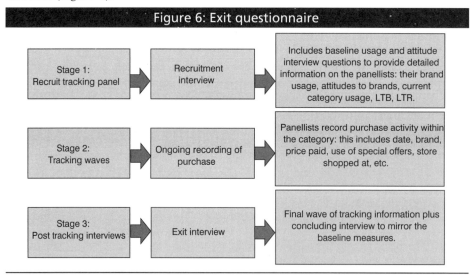

Stage 1: Recruit tracking panel	→	Recruitment interview	→	Includes baseline usage and attitude interview questions to provide detailed information on the panellists: their brand usage, attitudes to brands, current category usage, LTB, LTR.
Stage 2: Tracking waves	→	Ongoing recording of purchase	→	Panellists record purchase activity within the category: this includes date, brand, price paid, use of special offers, store shopped at, etc.
Stage 3: Post tracking interviews	→	Exit interview	→	Final wave of tracking information plus concluding interview to mirror the baseline measures.

Difference in spend

Over the six month period measured, our Facebook exposed group spent £4.86 more than the control cell and £4.48 more than the matched control cell. Their overall spend in the category, however, did not differ significantly – £24.06 vs. £25.16 in the matched control cell. This indicates that we are driving preference for Lynx within the category rather than an increase in spend (see Tables 2 and 3).

Table 2: Difference in spend

KPI	Facebook	Control	Matched control	Difference to control	Difference to matched control
Total Category Spend *	£24.06	£25.02	£25.16	-£0.96	-£1.10
Total spend on Lynx (body spray, antiperspirant, roll on)	£15.50	£10.64	£11.03	+£4.86	+£4.48
Lynx share of spend on category	64%	43%	44%	+22%	+21%
Lynx penetration (proportion of panellists purchasing Lynx)	59%	57%	62%	+3%	-3%

Table 3: What drove the difference?

Brand	Facebook	Control	Difference
AWP	£26.09	£18.78	+£7.31
Frequency of Lynx purchase	7.20	5.69	+1.51
Lynx trip spend	£3.62	£3.30	+£0.32

The Facebook users reported higher average weight of purchase, higher frequency of purchase and higher average trip spend. We achieved the holy trinity of getting them to buy more, more often at a higher price (ie. not on promotion).

What's more, this increase came as brand preference declined in the control group (Figure 7).

Figure 7: Brand preference decline in control group

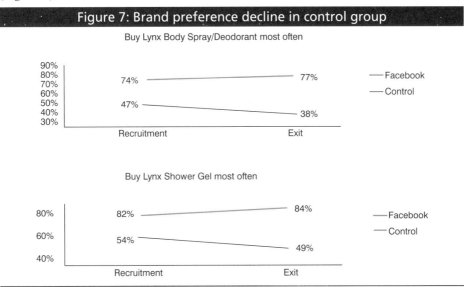

Source: Information by Design

(Note that this is claimed data at recruitment and exit, so will differ from the spend data.)

One of the most important Lynx brand metrics was very positively impacted, again while the control declined (Figure 8).

Figure 8: Response to statement 'Lynx attracts the opposite sex'

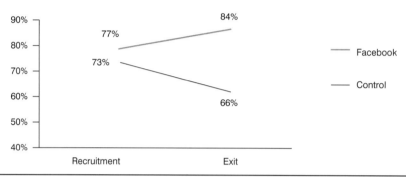

Lynx attracts the opposite sex

Source: Information by Design

We'd like to take credit for this, but we feel it may be an unintended consequence. We didn't set out to get girls to declare how much they like Lynx, but we're glad that it happens (Figure 9).

Figure 9: Example fan post on the Lynx Facebook page

Source: Facebook.com

In conclusion

As marketing fundamentally changes and brands and organisations struggle to respond and react to social media and its implications, we grabbed the bull by the horns. We tackled some hefty questions and committed budget and resource to answering them.

We have proved that Facebook can be a profitable space for brands to operate in and have started to develop a model for entering that space.

We have changed the way clients and agencies collaborate to allow us to make best use of new tools.

We have innovated constantly, but carefully, and with a firm view on the outcome.

While focusing on constant engagement with our audience, we have produced work that has been commended by the Webby's, has won five DMAs and a Revolution award.

Most importantly, we have started to make Lynx an essential part of the teenage landscape again.

Chapter 19

McCain

Driving a Wedge between chips, chips and more chips

By Simon Harwood, PHD Media
Contributing author: David Wilding, PHD Media
Credited companies: Creative Agency: Beattie McGuiness Bungay; Econometric Modelling
Agency: BrandScience; Client: McCain Foods

Editor's summary

McCain Wedges lacked a distinctive identity beyond the occasional alternative to chips. McCain therefore needed to grow the Wedges brand but in a way that didn't cannibalise chip sales. Research unveiled a correlation between Wedges purchase and items bought for barbeques. Taking into account Britain's unpredictable weather, McCain created 'sunshine-activated' executions that were only initiated when the weather forecast looked good. To extend activity beyond the summer months, they also sponsored several movie channels. The thermally activated media and film activity delivered an ROMI of £2.85 and £4.37 respectively. Penetration of Wedges now stands at one in five of all UK households, with frequency at an all time high. The judges appreciated the thoughtful use of channels as a key part of the approach. They also felt this paper demonstrated how solid strategic thinking creates space within a tough marketing context.

Background

This is the story of how marketing insights identified not just one, but two new usage occasions for a product that had been long overshadowed by its bigger, more successful cousins, and as a result grew both penetration and frequency of use.

Most Awards papers open up with a tale of woe to set up the business issue that the campaign has addressed. Ours opens with a tale of success. Chip success.

In the face of a cultural backlash against chips, McCain's 'It's all good' campaign brought to life the simple, natural ingredients which its products have always been made from. At the forefront of this campaign have been uplifting campaigns for McCain's frozen chip products – Oven Chips and Home Fries. By celebrating the chip, McCain had created a zeitgeist-defying brand and sales success story by the end of 2007 (Figure 1).

Figure 1: IAG activity 2006–2007

Today McCain dominates the frozen chip market in the UK, with over 55% penetration of UK households for their frozen chip products, equating to over 165,000 tonnes of chips sold annually in the UK.[1]

So you'd think given the success of chips that the success of potato wedges would be straightforward? Well...

People evidently love chips in this country, but there is a limit to how many chips McCain can sell to any given family in a week. This poses the long-term question of whether the business can move beyond chips into new territories for growth, and gives their non-chip products a unique problem.

Wedges had been an established product within the McCain portfolio for over a decade, but penetration was stuck at a lowly 15.4%.

The reason for this low penetration was that Wedges didn't really stand for much other than the occasional tea-time alternative to chips and lacked a distinctive identity. They were bought when people just fancied a bit of a change, so shared the side of plate with their chip cousins, from whom they were cannibalising share.[2]

Objective

McCain needed to grow Wedges, but crucially do so in a way that didn't cannibalise chip sales. Wedges had to help drive overall McCain sales rather than continue to eat into the existing portfolio (no pun intended).

We had to find a way of putting some clear water between Wedges and chips, by either changing their usage away from side of plate, or by finding a new audience for them away from the core McCain heartland.

Insight

We started by seeking to understand attitudes and purchase behaviour around Wedges. What were the core differences vs. chips that we could build on to develop a winning proposition?

We analysed Dunnhumby data and uncovered a correlation between Wedges purchase and items bought for barbeques. 40% of Wedges shoppers also bought barbeque products in the summer, with items such as marinades, sauces and barbeque flavoured meat in the same basket as Wedges.[3]

To check that the relationship was robust (and not simply a result of summer barbeque seasonality) we found it worked the other way too. Wedges were most popular with those people who had barbeque meats in their baskets, suggesting a genuine opportunity (Figure 2).

We wanted to know why this was. Qualitative groups revealed that people were territorial over chips and hated them being stolen from their plate, but they were much more inclined to share things they were used to seeing on platters – which included skins, chicken wings, prawns... and wedges. In other words, if chips had to be 'dished out' equally, Wedges could be shared more generously because they were seen as social food.

Solution

We had a product that was the perfect barbeque accompaniment: chunky, rustic looking, lightly seasoned for a big taste that was great to share.

Importantly, barbecues offered a use that didn't wander into oven chips' territory (when's the last time you had chips at a barbeque?).

So with a new proposition of 'perfect for sharing', McCain set out to target the home entertainment event of the summer, the great British barbeque (Figure 3).

The 2000s had seen a huge rise in the frequency with which people barbeque, and the growth of a 'British' barbeque culture.

Figure 2: Cross-shopping; BBQ marinades/sauces, BBQ flavoured meat, Total Wedges

Cross-shop group	Spend per customer of Total Wedges	Spend per customer of BBQ-flavoured meat	Spend per customer of BBQ marinades/sauces	Number of customers
Total Wedges only	£1.69			606,340
BBQ flavoured meat only		£6.04		1,019,070
BBQ marinades/sauces only			£1.99	521,180
Total Wedges and BBQ flavoured meat	£1.85	£6.86		167,050
Total Wedges and BBQ marinades/sauces	£1.91		£2.04	81,100
BBQ flavoured meat and BBQ marinades/sauces		£7.74	£2.21	227,250
Total Wedges, BBQ flavoured meat and BBQ marinades/sauces	£2.08	£8.54	£2.24	55,750
Total				2,667,750

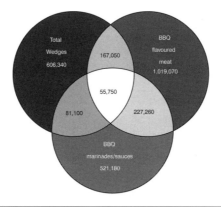

Modern barbecue behaviour is becoming increasingly spontaneous, with Mintel research showing that over 70% of barbecues in the UK are now organised either spontaneously or within two days of the event and, less surprisingly, most occurred at the weekend. In total, that accounted for 92.3 million 'spontaneous' barbecues a year.[4]

These events are easier than ever before to mobilise, thanks to the growth of instant communication via mobile SMS, email and, of course, social networks. They can be planned and executed within hours – very often dictated by the ever unreliable British weather.

2007 had been the wettest summer on record, with beer, burger and barbeque marinade sales plummeting year-on-year. A long hot summer was neither guaranteed, nor expected (Figure 4).

Figure 3: Summer Wedges pack design

Figure 4: Beating the unbeatable foe

The communications strategy needed to be reactive to the elements and poised to capitalise when the going was good.

Our solution was to create a number of 'sunshine-activated' executions which worked together to react quickly to impending good weather.

The first of these was an outdoor innovation, never done before, that harnessed the flexibility of digital formats to ensure that Wedges messages were only activated by McCain when the weather forecast looked good for the weekend (Figure 5).

Activity ran on roadside LED 48 sheets, Tesco TV screens and Transvision screens at key termini stations. We also used ATM screens at supermarkets with a branded, bar coded receipt featuring a 50p product discount to use in store (Figure 6).

Figure 5: Sunshine activated outdoor allowed flexibility to deliver messaging at short lead times

Figure 6: Supermarket ATMs offered a 50p discount coupon

Short copy lead times allowed us to upload creative almost instantaneously, delivering a targeted message to our specific audience at the right time (Thurs–Sat) and in the right mindset (when they were outside in good weather).

The digital outdoor was supported by online advertising which focused on weather sites *ITV Local* and *weather.com*. Here the creative message reacted to the local weather conditions of the user by identifying their location and serving them a relevant barbeque message dependent on the weather forecast – a Wedge as the sun if it was looking good, a Wedge as an umbrella if it wasn't looking great (Figure 7).

Figure 7: When the weather looked good...

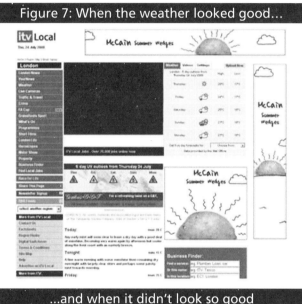

...and when it didn't look so good

Again, this type of dynamic geo-targeted messaging was a real breakthrough in innovation, responding to the exact conditions at the user's locality with the right type of message.

Finally, National press ads ran around key editorial on summer entertaining, and flexible, short-term deals were negotiated with key titles to communicate McCain's BBQ message on the run up to sunny weekends (Figures 8 and 9).

Figures 8 and 9: National press ads

We repeated the activity again in the summers of 2009 and 2010, with further 'sunshine activated' press, outdoor, online and a special Summer Barbeque playlist for Spotify users. The communications strategy created a consistent and innovative campaign which maximised Wedges' exposure and relevance throughout the summer months.

Results

The first summer of activity drove an immediate and sustained impact. Consideration for McCain Wedges had jumped from 74% to 82% by the end of the summer (Figure 10).[5]

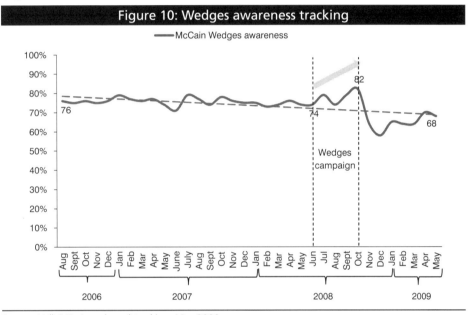

Figure 10: Wedges awareness tracking

Source: Hall & Partners brand tracking, May 2009

The ATM coupons had an enormous 2.24% redemption rate – one of the best ever recorded on this format. Online activity saw a 20% interaction rate with the creative, and 3 million people were exposed to the digital outdoor element.

Econometric analysis has been able to demonstrate the value of the advertising above and beyond seasonal promotions and distribution changes. We were able to isolate the effect of the thermally activated media at ROI of £2.85 (compared to an average £0.61 across all FMCG brands) which equated to £930,000 of additional revenue (Table 1).[6]

Press and outdoor accounted for 92% of this volume giving it a very healthy £5.17 ROI.

Table 1: Wedges returns by medium; Jan08–Apr09					
Wedges	Spend Jan 08–Apr 09	Volume sales	Revenue*	RROI Groc	RROI All**
Press/Outdoor	£0.2m	493	£863	£4.21	£5.17
Online	£0.1m	14	£25	£0.23	£0.28
Halo		23	£42	£1.98	£2.44
Effective media	£0.3m	530	£930	£3.10	£3.81
All media	£0.4	530	£930	£2.32	£2.85

Source: PHD, McCain, 2009. *Assuming average price per kg, Wedges 06–09 = £1.78, Wedges 08–09 = £1.75. **23% higher

The demonstrable payback of the 2008 campaign meant we have been able to successfully repeat the activity for three summers in a row to continue to build the association with barbeques.

The summer of 2009 and 2010 activity drove ROI of £1.19 and £1.97 respectively.[7]

But summer doesn't last forever

Summer only lasts three months, and barbeque opportunities tend to fall away as the cold nights draw in from September onwards.

We knew that our approach in establishing Wedges as perfect for sharing at summer entertainment occasions was working to bring in a new usage occasion for the product.

McCain needed to find a way of encouraging buyers to share Wedges all year round as well as at barbeques.

Insight

We took inspiration from the crisp category where 'dished out' multipacks exist hand in hand with premium sharing brands. There was a clear analogy between our chips which tend to be portion controlled (to stop stealing) and our 'perfect for sharing' Wedges.

We identified that premium sharing crisps were often associated with special nights in and home entertainment platforms.[8]

Research showed consumers were looking for food to deliver a 'big taste' factor for them at these moments and wanted more than they might settle for during the week.[9] The added seasoning in our two permanent skus, Lightly Spiced and Sea Salt & Black Pepper, meant Wedges already had the taste credentials to deliver against these occasions.

With 57% of the UK claiming to go out less,[10] the recession had driven a huge rise in home entertainment and socialising at home, and widened the spectrum of occasions for us to target.

Solution

We identified an opportunity in one particular growth area of home entertainment where we wouldn't be competing with the rest of the McCain portfolio and would be able to communicate Wedges throughout the entire year.

New platforms such as Lovefilm, Sky and Virgin's on-demand devices, and the likes of Playstation 3 and X-box, were making movies more available than ever in the home.

We set out to establish a believable and enduring relationship between Wedges and sharing when watching a film. We knew this approach would take time and that we would need a consistent presence and approach our association from a number of different angles.

We had to find partners who would give us credibility in film and the frequency to explain why Wedges were the perfect accompaniment to watching a movie at home.

We began by sponsoring Sky Movies Comedy which gave us a daily presence in over 1,000 movies including the latest comedy releases and some all-time favourites. Comedy was the perfect antidote to the gloom surrounding the recession, with 40% more comedy DVDs being rented out year-on-year.[11]

Idents featured quotes from celebrated films (amended to include 'Wedges') with the strapline 'Wedges & Movies, a great combination' (Figure 11). The film of the day was also highlighted using TV boxes in national press titles.

Figure 11: Sky Movies Comedy idents

Lovefilm was another platform benefiting from consumers cocooning themselves on the sofa rather than splashing out on evenings out. Lovefilm membership had shot up by two fifths since the start of the recession and offered us a year round presence within a highly relevant environment.[12]

We presented Lovefilm users with a package of quarterly seasonal film collections on the Lovefilm website which included Comedy, Classic, Romantic and Action. User interaction was encouraged through ratings, comments and reviews (Figure 12).

Meanwhile we inserted 400,000 coupons within Lovefilm DVD envelopes to drive trial of Wedges in-home while they planned their next night in.

Figure 12: Lovefilm Classic Collection with Wedges

Source: www.lovefilm.com

We augmented our presence in DVD viewing by partnering with Twentieth Century Fox for the DVD release of *Date Night* featuring an on-pack competition giving away the DVD as prizes – and a top prize of a trip to New York to recreate a Manhattan date night. This ensured we were cementing the association instore by putting the Wedges with Film message prominently on-pack.

Boosted by the success of the first year's association with film, we were confident enough to increase our investment in year two.

Film4 is a big ticket property that could explicitly put Wedges at the heart of the great night in, reaching more ABC1 adults per week than the whole of UK cinema combined, and was the outstanding choice to deliver on our objectives.

We sponsored the flagship 9pm film every day for 12 months, ensuring a presence around the biggest and best films of 2010, from mainstream blockbusters to critically acclaimed award winners (Figure 13).

The partnership gave us access to a film-loving audience which we could inspire to give Wedges a go as a sharing alternative to cold crisps, while encouraging existing buyers to try eating Wedges at a different time.

However, we wanted to go a step further than bumpering content. To hard-wire the film association, we needed to become part of the evening's entertainment.

Figure 13: Film4 idents

We developed a brand new TV format called *4FilmsFor*, a series of 10 x 3 minute episodes broadcast between the films on Film4 over five months. Each episode featured the comedy duo Armstrong & Miller seated in front of a TV and chatting about a familiar situation in life such as planning a holiday, getting a new look, choosing a pet. Scenes from four films were then cut into their conversation.

So in '4Filmsfor Getting a New Look', Ben Miller tries to help Xander Armstrong get a new look as we cut to a top male model, a computerised wardrobe, a weight-lifting newsreader and a cyborg killing machine from the future (Figure 14).[13]

Figure 14: 4Filmsfor; 'Getting a New Look'

In addition to TV, the content was seeded online through editorial across sites such as the *Guardian*, AOL, Yahoo and the *Sun*, as well as via an iPhone app and across Film4's YouTube platform.

The programme brand, together with the Film4 logo, featured with an on-pack promotion where people could share their four favourite films and win a 3D TV.

Film4 were so impressed with the series they launched episode one on Christmas Day before the 9pm film, receiving a quarter of a million viewers.

Results

The *4FilmsFor* series has been viewed by over 3 million people on TV and is guaranteed to be viewed 2 million times online (500,000 views to date).

The association between Wedges and Film has been clearly made and is building. The Film4 sponsorship is the best performing McCain sponsorship to date, with recognition reaching 22% after just nine months – that's one in five frozen food buyers claiming to have seen the activity (Figure 15).[14]

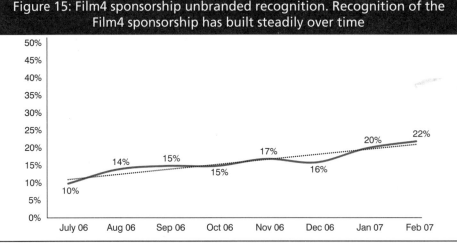

Figure 15: Film4 sponsorship unbranded recognition. Recognition of the Film4 sponsorship has built steadily over time

Source: McCain Wedges Film4 Sponsorship Review, March 2011

40% of recognisers believe that McCain Wedges are 'ideal for eating whilst watching a film' and 36% say they are 'perfect for sharing'.

Awareness of Wedges now stands at 60%, an increase of 11% in the seven months from the beginning of the Film4 sponsorship to February 2011. More crucially there has been a huge increase in conversion from awareness to purchasing with 'ever purchased' measures increasing by 50% in the same period (Figures 16 and 17).

Figure 16: McCain Wedges purchase funnels; an increase in conversion from 'aware' to 'ever bought' (more consumers trialling the products)

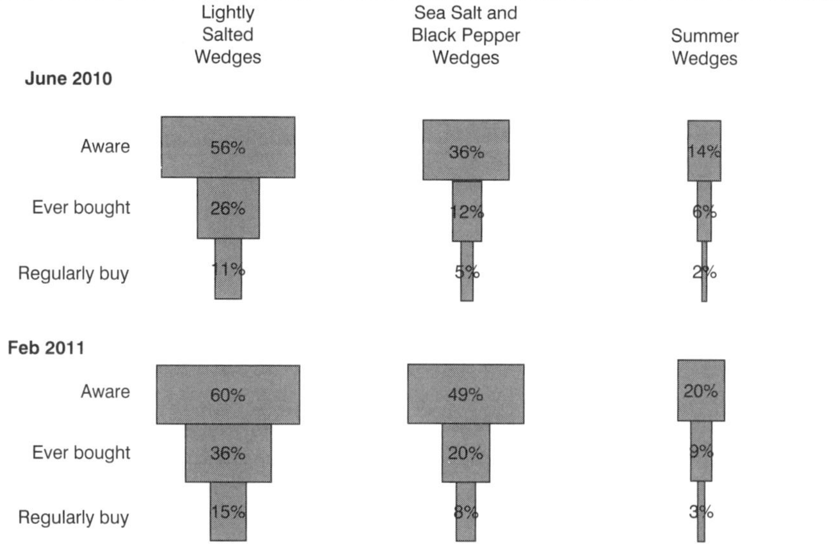

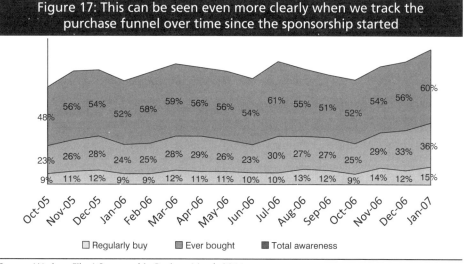

Source: Wedges Film4 Sponsorship Review, March 2011

Figure 17: This can be seen even more clearly when we track the purchase funnel over time since the sponsorship started

Source: Wedges Film4 Sponsorship Review, March 2011

We repeated the econometric analysis and found that this increase in claimed purchase was indeed translating into sales as a direct result of the activity.

The Film activity has delivered a combined ROI of £4.37, equating to £5.13m of incremental revenue for McCain.[15]

We have been able to isolate the component elements, with Sky Movies driving a £5.03 ROI and the Film4 sponsorship £3.36 ROI to date (Figure 18).

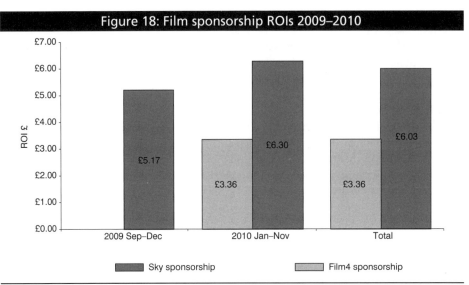

Figure 18: Film sponsorship ROIs 2009–2010

Source: BrandScience; McCain econometric modelling; Sept 2009–Nov 2010

The Lovefilm activity drove £1.23 ROI with 33,176 competition entries, making it one of the most successful branded events to date on Lovefilm.

Not only has the film activity driven directly into Wedges volume, it has resulted in a significant halo effect on both Home Fries and Oven Chips sales.

So Wedges activity hasn't just avoided cannibalising chips sales, it has directly increased them.

Penetration of Wedges now stands at 20.3%, equivalent to one in five of all UK households.[16] We have brought in an incremental 1.55 million new people into the brand since 2007, while frequency is also at an all time high of 2.9, compared to 2.5 in 2007 (Figure 19).

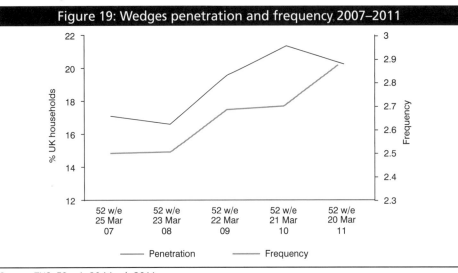

Figure 19: Wedges penetration and frequency 2007–2011

Source: TNS; 52 w/e 20 March 2011

Summary

We created two distinctive contextual usage occasions for Wedges which served to increase penetration by 39% in under three years, equating to an incremental 1,793 tonnes.

At the same time McCain chips sales weren't cannibalised but actually grew via a substantial halo effect from Wedges activity. And we have demonstrated in this paper that this was driven by advertising driving a fundamental change in buyer behaviour.

Wedges were once little more than substitutes for chips but through consistent communication, consumers now recognise Wedges are perfect for sharing, either while helping themselves to platters of food at barbeques or curled up on the sofa watching their favourite new movie.

And for everything else there's always chips.

Notes

1 TNS; 52 w/e 20 March 2011.
2 TNS Switching; March 2008; 102,721kg of Oven Chips volume lost directly to Wedges.
3 Dunnhumby; How many people cross-shop my brands? BBQ marinades/sauces, BBQ flavoured meat, total Wedges; 13 weeks from 5 June to 3 September 2007.
4 Mintel; Barbeques 2008.
5 Hall & Partners brand tracking May 2009.
6 BrandScience; McCain econometric model; Jan 2008–April 2009, BrandScience results vault.
7 BrandScience; McCain econometric modelling; 2009–2010.
8 Project Lounges, 'The role of and opportunity for living room food' *The Cog* 2008.
9 IAG in Potspecs Diagnostics; 19 September 2008.
10 Omnicom Media Group: Evolution of the Consumer (July 2009).
11 'And now the good news', *Marketing*, 4 March 2009.
12 'The staying in crowd', *The Scotsman*, 8 February 2009.
13 Film footage taken from *Zoolander*, *Clueless*, *Anchorman* and *Terminator 2*.
14 McCain Wedges Film4 Sponsorship Review March 2011.
15 BrandScience; McCain econometric modelling; September 2009–November 2010.
16 TNS; 52 w/e 20 March 2011.

Chapter 20

PepsiCo Walkers

Sandwich

By Tom White and George Roberts, AMV BBDO
Contributing authors: Bridget Angear, AMV BBDO; Adam Warner
and Gavin Morgan, PepsiCo; Julia Husband, Ninah; Danielle
Morris, Freud Communications; Alex Pilcher, OMD UK and Karline
Matyjas, Millward Brown
Credited companies: Digital Agency: Jigsaw; Media Agency: OMD UK;
PR Agency: Freud Communications; Social Marketing Agency: The Real
Adventure; Client: PepsiCo Walkers

Editor's summary

In 2009 Walkers was losing share in the single pack segment of the crisps
market. They identified an opportunity to turn this around by prompting
the consumption of Walkers with sandwiches at lunch. Communications
sought to convince consumers, journalists and trade retailers that any
sandwich is more exciting with Walkers, even the town of Sandwich in
Kent. A series of surprise events over three days turned the sleepy town
into the most exciting place in Britain. The campaign resulted in the desired
turnaround in share for the Walkers brand, a change in quality of instore
display, and a 220% long-term profit return on the marketing investment.
The judges appreciated the strength of the strategic insight, leading to a
truly trans-media experiential based strategy. They also felt the paper had
successfully isolated the impact of the activity amidst the broader activity
of the brand.

Introduction

Walkers is an almighty British brand. It stands far ahead of its competitors, the core[1] brand alone capturing roughly £1 in every £5 spent in the crisps and salty snacks category.[2] In 2009 it was having a very good year, with sales up around 9% year-on-year.[3] However, underneath this top-line success lay a problem. One that concerned the most profitable segment of the business: single-pack sales. Walkers was losing share, and the rate of loss was gradually increasing (Figure 1).

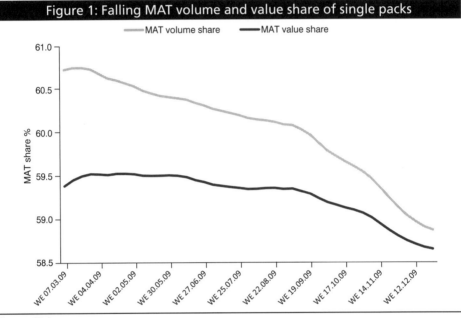

Figure 1: Falling MAT volume and value share of single packs

Source: Nielsen

Towards a solution

We set about finding the best opportunity for singles sales growth. Single packs are an impulse purchase, and research showed us their biggest consumption occasion is as an accompaniment to lunch.[4] We looked at lunchtime crisp eating more closely, and found that there was a significantly lower incidence of Walkers being consumed during 'out of home' lunch occasions, when compared with 'in-home' lunch occasions.[5] In fact the ratio was 1:3 in favour of 'in-home.' It seemed there was significant room to improve Walkers' popularity as an 'out of home' lunchtime accompaniment. This joined up neatly with our objective of increasing singles sales, given singles are naturally orientated towards out of home consumption.

So, we had an objective, but as yet we didn't have an interesting proposition. 'Eat Walkers with your lunch?' We had to find a better creative springboard than that. We found one by looking at what exactly the bulk of our core target for singles consumption – C1C2D men aged 25–34 – were eating for their 'out of home' lunch. The answer wasn't entirely surprising: their staple was the good old sandwich.[6]

But what was more enlightening was the discovery that these men regarded their sandwiches as *'fuel rather than enjoyment'*.[7]

A role for Walkers quickly became apparent. Surely a tasty packet of crisps as an accompaniment could make things more interesting? A quick sense check with the Great British public confirmed that it would. 63% agreed that *'having a bag of crisps with a lunchtime sandwich is more enjoyable than having a sandwich on its own'*.[8]

We now had our proposition: *A sandwich is more exciting with Walkers*.

Moreover, with the long-running 'No More Mr Nice Guy' campaign featuring Gary Lineker, we had a readymade creative vehicle into which to slot this new message. It was just a case of cranking out a TV ad featuring Gary pinching crisps, perhaps in an effort to complete his idea of the perfect 'on the go' lunchtime sandwich.

Job done? Not quite...

The task unfortunately wasn't going to be that easy.

Firstly, 'No More Mr Nice Guy' was perhaps not the best vehicle through which to deliver this very different kind of message from Walkers. The campaign is invaluable, however if it has a weakness, it is in delivering specific brand messages beyond irresistibility.[9]

Secondly, 'just' a TV campaign wouldn't do. Our young male target was not an easy one to reach and engage, especially while 'on the go' or at work. While outdoor might be an obvious partner to TV, it's an expensive medium with which to build national coverage, and our campaign budget wouldn't stretch. Instead, getting their attention by combining TV with news coverage and compelling online content seemed like the smart approach.

Thirdly, the average lunch hour was just 27 minutes long,[10] leaving little time to contemplate which sandwich to choose, let alone what might go well with it as an accompaniment. We needed to get Walkers well and truly on the sandwich shoppers' radar.

And lastly, our observations of the impulse shopping environment revealed another complication. If Walkers were to be bought together with sandwiches on impulse, they would need to be situated near to each other instore. But in many convenience store environments, this wasn't the case. This was particularly true of the rapidly expanding number of Multiple Grocer c-stores.[11] Could communications do anything about this? Gains in quality of distribution resulting from communications are not uncommon, but on the scale we needed them to be, we certainly felt they were. Moreover, with no 'new news' in the traditional sense to speak of – none of the new flavour variants or big prize giveaways that a Walkers campaign would typically involve – PepsiCo would have little to leverage in the daunting task of persuading retailers to make the sweeping merchandising changes we were envisaging.

Much has been said in the communications industry of the power of stories to influence people. But it's rare for marketing communications to create *genuinely* powerful stories. In this case, we knew we might fail if we didn't: the PepsiCo sales force needed a compelling story to take to the retailers, in lieu of traditional marketing 'new news'.

The requirements of the solution

We concluded that our campaign needed to overcome not just one, but two 'saliency' barriers:

1. Mental saliency – it would need to build a top-of-mind association between Walkers and sandwiches.
2. Physical saliency – it would need to play a key role in making the combination physically salient instore.

Generating its own surprising news story would be crucial, in order to ensure we would influence three key audiences:

1. our consumer target, who were perhaps a little too familiar with the 'No More Mr Nice Guy' vehicle;[12]
2. the PepsiCo sales force, and the retailers who would need to be convinced this campaign would make waves;
3. journalists, whose column inches we sought.

The work

Our idea: prove Walkers can make *any* sandwich more exciting, even the town of Sandwich, Kent (Figure 2).

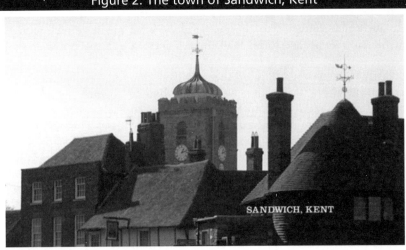

Figure 2: The town of Sandwich, Kent

SANDWICH, KENT

Through a series of surprise events over three days, we turned the sleepy town of Sandwich into the most exciting town in Britain. Each event featured a celebrity fulfilling a typical community role: JLS took the sixth form college assembly, Frank Lampard coached the college football team, Jenson Button got behind the wheel of a black cab, Marco Pierre White sold gourmet sandwiches from a market stall, and Pamela Anderson pulled pints at the local pub while Al Murray hosted the quiz. Gary adopted the role of compere, rather than his usual role as protagonist (or antagonist!).

The idea was to capture the genuine surprise and excitement of the locals on film, to produce television commercials and online video content (Figure 3). To ensure reactions were genuine, a great deal of effort went into keeping our plans under wraps, and the events were filmed unscripted, and unrehearsed.

A campaign with an event at its heart helped us to influence our key audiences, because it allowed us to get them involved. We arranged for journalists to be 'embedded' in Sandwich over the course of the three days, and we invited along members of the sales team and representatives from Walkers' key retail customers too.

Channel strategy

The communications model

At its basic level, the communications model was this: the events generate content, which is then released through a focused set of channels, according to a phasing plan designed to maximise the campaign's buzz creation and longevity.

Phasing plan

Our phasing plan, which formed the basis for all our media thinking, involved three discrete stages: tease à reveal à extend. It was guided by the tactics major motion picture houses use when distributing their content: preview with trailers à reveal the feature-length version à offer DVD extras for those who want to engage more deeply.

In phase one, teaser stories from our embedded journalists in Sandwich were in the news the very next day. And just 24 hours later, 10" teaser adverts were broadcast on TV and released online, creating the opportunity for viewers exposed to both the news stories and the adverts to connect up the dots. After just a further five days, the reveal phase began, with full feature stories in the news and the release of a 60" advert, again on TV and online.

The extend phase then comprised a 30" follow-up TV ad, further PR content and the steady release and seeding of 26 pieces of video content across the web. The content was also housed on our YouTube channel, which functioned as our main content hub (Figure 4).

Figure 3: Sandwich 60" TV storyboard

Music: piano Intro to JLS' 'One shot'.

We see scenes of a sleepy little British town.

Super: Sandwich, Kent

Gary Lineker VO: We believe that Walkers can make any Sandwich that little bit more exciting. Even this one (Nods towards the sign).

JLS get ready back-stage.
Headmistress VO: As you might have guessed, this isn't a normal assembly...JLS!!!

[Screams of excitement, music vocal begins]

We see Pamela Anderson serving pints in a pub.

Al Murray VO: Pamela's actually been in training as a bar maid this afternoon [cheers]

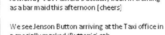

We see Jenson Button arriving at the Taxi office in a specially marked 'Button's' cab.

A lady in the office is so surprised she screams.

We see Al Murray in the pub.

Al Murray VO: This is a special Walkers Pub Quiz. Right, you up for this?!?

Gary arrives in the town square with his Girlfriend. He's wearing a giant sandwich.

We see Marco Pierre White mingling with the Sandwich locals outside his Sandwich stall.

Marco Pierre White VO: I've got some sandwiches, and some Walkers crisps.

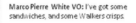

Frank Lampard surprises the local College football team. He and Gary take penalties in front of a crowd of locals.

The music (JLS' One Shot) moves up a gear as the chorus begins.

We see the Sandwich Tech students go crazy with excitement, as JLS appear and perform on stage.

We then see Gary and Pamela in the pub.

Gary VO: Your Sandwich could be more exciting too, so next time you stop for lunch, don't forget the Walkers.

Super: Any Sandwich is more exciting with Walkers.
[Fireworks explode over the town in the distance]

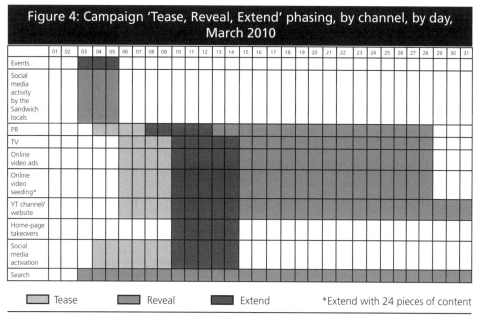

Figure 4: Campaign 'Tease, Reveal, Extend' phasing, by channel, by day, March 2010

Source: OMD/AMV BBDO/Freud Communications

Viral take-up of the campaign was aided by our strategy of reaching out to our celebrities' Twitter fan-bases (Figure 5). Our choice of celebrities was guided by the size of their social media following.

Figure 5: Celebrity tweets

Source: Screen-grabs taken at the time from celebrities' official Twitter channels by Freud Communications

Results

In this section, we will explore the journey from campaign to business results (Figure 6).

Figure 6: The journey from campaign to business results

1. The events were a success with the locals

⇩

2. Journalists responded as intended

⇩

3. The content was a viral success

⇩

4. The advertising stood out and was liked

⇩

5. The campaign was a popular and critical success

⇩

6. The sales-force & retailers were influenced

⇩

7. The right message was received by consumers

⇩

8. Consumer behaviour changed

⇩

9. Sales and share turned around

1. The events were a success with the locals

Success with the Sandwich locals was critical: without their very positive reactions (Figures 7 and 8), the campaign would have flopped.

Figure 7: Surprised locals

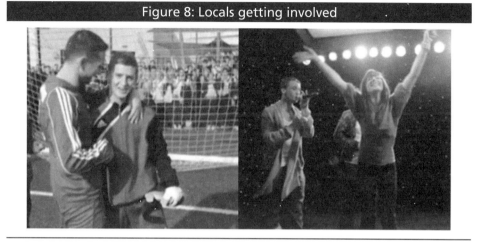

Figure 8: Locals getting involved

As we had hoped, they were inspired to post user generated content on social networking sites (Figure 9).

Figure 9: Locals capturing content and sharing with friends online

Caroline Rose, Sandwich Tech student, said:

Thanks for making my little town of Sandwich more exciting!! I had a fab week meeting all the celebs especially bumping into JLS on my lunch break :) come back again soon x.[13]

To show the town our appreciation, we ran a thank you ad in the local press (Figure 10).

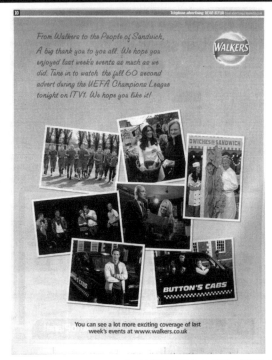

Figure 10: 'Thank You' ad which ran in the Sandwich local press

2. Journalists responded as intended

The campaign generated 353 pieces of news coverage across print (Figure 11), TV and online,[14] delivering 94,725,000 opportunities to see.[15]

- 99.7% of the coverage was positive in terms of sentiment.[16]
- The key words 'Walkers + Sandwich' appeared in the same sentence in 86.1% of the pieces of coverage, helping to build the association between the two.[17]
- The value of this coverage has been calculated at £3,261,819 in advertising equivalent value.·

An embedded *Now Magazine* Journalist said of the campaign:

Sandwich was such a brilliant idea. At one point I feared for my life as a small group of girls suddenly grew into a mob as word got out that the hottest boys in pop were actually in the town![19]

Figure 11: Consumer PR coverage

The coverage unfolded according to the phasing plan, with strong peaks at the Tease and Reveal stages, running just in advance of the matching TV phasing, as planned (Figure 12).

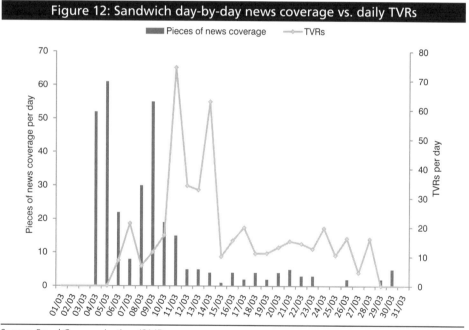

Figure 12: Sandwich day-by-day news coverage vs. daily TVRs

Source: Freud Communications/OMD

The content was a viral success

- 1.7 million complete video views were registered (3.3 million minutes in total viewing time).[20]
- JLS were so pleased with our videos, they posted one on their YouTube channel – *'JLSOFFICIALMUSIC'* – contributing 91,831 video views.[21]
- The *'walkerssandwich'* YouTube Channel became the #1 most viewed sponsored channel in the UK in March.[22]

We also saw a surge in Google searches for the term 'sandwich walkers' (Figure 13).

Figure 13: Google searches for 'sandwich walkers'

sandwich walkers   1.00

Search Volume index			Google Trends
30.0			
20.0			
10.0			
0	Apr 2010	Jul 2010	Oct 2010

Source: Google Trends: scale is a volume index based on the average traffic of search term 'sandwich walkers' from the United Kingdom in 2010

And general brand buzz picked up significantly, with peaks in line with the Tease and Reveal phasing (Figure 14).

Figure 14: Brand buzz: number of social media mentions per day

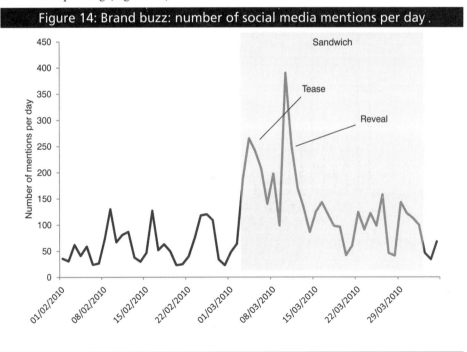

Source: The Real Adventure (Social Media monitoring agency)

4. The advertising stood out and was liked

Marketing magazine's analysis of advertising recall, *Adwatch*, listed Walkers Sandwich at number three (Figure 15), beating the likes of Marks & Spencer, Microsoft and NatWest along with several others who all spent more than twice as much as Walkers.[23]

Figure 15: Adwatch

Adwatch 14.04.10

Marketing's unique weekly analysis of advertisement recall in association with tns

Q Which of the following TV commercials do you remember seeing recently?

	31.03	Brand	Agency/TV Buyer	%
1	(-)	Dyson	In-house/Walker Media	58
2	(1)	Sky	Brothers & Sisters/MediaCom	57
3	(-)	Walkers	Abbott Mead Vickers BBDO/OMD UK	53
4	(-)	Confused.com	Beattie McGuinness Bungay/PHD	50
5	(-)	Santander	WCRS/Carat	48
6	(-)	BT	Abbott Mead Vickers BBDO/MediaVest	45
7	(-)	Asda – George	Saatchi & Saatchi/Carat	42
8	(-)	Microsoft	Crispin Porter & Bogusky/Universal McCann	41
9	(-)	Wickes	MWO/Mediaedge:cia	40
10=	(-)	NatWest	M&C Saatchi/MediaCom	38
10=	(-)	Marks & Spencer	RKCR Y&R/Walker Media	38
10=	(-)	Disneyland Paris	Euro RSCG BETC/ZenithOptimedia	38
13	(6)	Tesco	The Red Brick Road/Initiative	37
14=	(-)	Kingsmill	M&C Saatchi/ZenithOptimedia	36
14=	(4)	B&Q	McCann Erickson/ZenithOptimedia	36
14=	(-)	Visa	Saatchi & Saatchi/Mediaedge:cia	36
17=	(-)	Cushelle	Fallon London/Carat	34
17=	(-)	Nissan Qashqai	TBWA/OMD UK	34
19	(-)	Bing	JWT London/Universal McCann	33
20	(2)	Morrisons	DLKW/Mediaedge:cia	32

Adwatch research was conducted from 25-29 March 2010 by TNS as part of its twice-weekly OnLineBus omnibus among 1000 adults aged 16-64. For details of the survey, contact sue.homeyard@tns-ri.co.uk (020 7160 5550). Advertisements were compiled by Xtreme Information (020 7575 1800) and Mediaedge:cia UK (020 7803 2000).

Walkers

The crisp brand makes up for a joke at Sandwich's expense by creating a social spectacle

Walkers 'Sandwich' ad blends celebrity endorsement with reality-show excitement

Source: *Marketing*, 14 April 2010, p. 23

Millward Brown diagnostics help us to explain this success: the advertising was significantly more distinctive and involving than the norm (Figure 16).

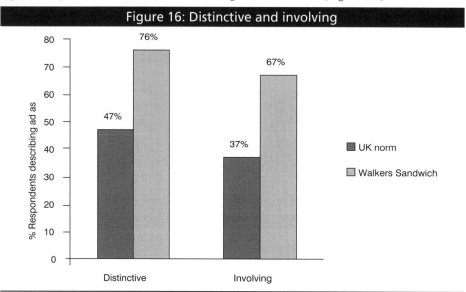

Figure 16: Distinctive and involving

Source: Millward Brown Post-Test Diagnostics, May 2010; statistically significant with 95% or higher confidence. UK norm is the 'Online Total (Seen Ad) Norm', as at April 2011

Furthermore, consumers reported finding the advertising highly enjoyable and worthy of talking about with their friends (Figure 17).

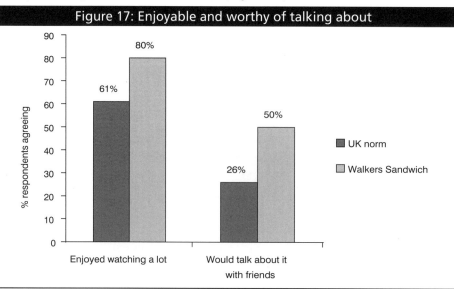

Figure 17: Enjoyable and worthy of talking about

Source: Millward Brown Post-Test Diagnostics, May 2010; statistically significant with 95% or higher confidence. UK norm is the 'Online Total (Seen Ad) Norm', as at April 2011

5. The campaign was a popular and critical success

A panel of 8000 members of the public[24] voted Sandwich in the top 10 for ITV's 'Ad of the Year 2010' show.[25]

Mark Hurst, Creative Director, MWO, wrote in *Marketing*:

It's the sheer excitement Walkers has created that does it...The tone is perfectly judged, and we feel that what Walkers did was very real for the people there.[26]

Sandwich was one of the most creatively awarded campaigns of 2010, scooping Gold and two Silver Cannes Lions in 2010, among a host of others.[27]

It was also acknowledged by the Chartered Institute of Marketing, who named it best FMCG campaign of 2010.[28]

6. The sales-force and retailers were influenced

Jason Richards, Vice President of Sales, PepsiCo UK, commented:

The unique and exciting nature of the campaign really captured the imagination of our sales teams and our customers, leading to fantastic execution of Walkers meal deals across multiple channels.

In total, more than 10,000 new meal deals were activated.[29] Table 1 details the key gains.

Table 1: Instore gains in quality of distribution	
Tesco	Addition of permanent stackers at front of store
Sainsbury's	Meal deals at front of store
Co-op	Replaced McCoy's in meal deals
ASDA	8 box at front of store
Morrisons	Walkers launches meal deals
Impulse	Meal deals secured with strong POS support

Source: PepsiCo

Even though we know the campaign was instrumental in delivering these gains, Ninah's econometric analysis has *eliminated* their impact from the campaign's sales contribution and ROMI figures discussed below, in order that we can understand the campaign's ability to influence consumer demand in isolation.

7. The right message was received by consumers

Despite this being a very different model of Walkers advertising to that the public are used to, and with Gary in only a peripheral role, the branding was phenomenally strong, with more than double the normal number of people agreeing they '*couldn't fail* [top box] to remember it was for Walkers' (Figure 18).

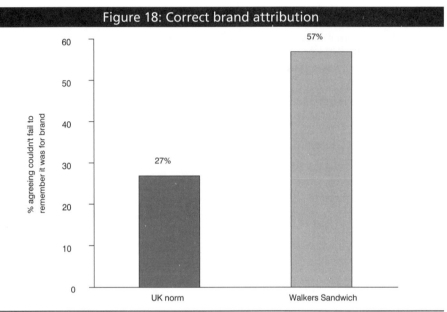

Figure 18: Correct brand attribution

Source: Millward Brown Post-Test Diagnostics, May 2010; statistically significant with 95% or higher confidence. UK norm is the 'Online Total (Seen Ad) Norm', as at April 2011

Crucially, it also communicated the message we intended, building a salient association between Walkers and sandwiches, with an 86% increase in the number of consumers agreeing that a packet of Walkers '*makes my sandwich more enjoyable*' (Figure 19).

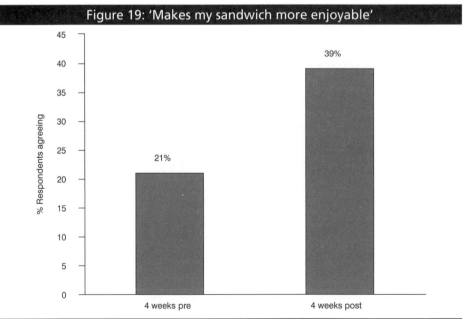

Figure 19: 'Makes my sandwich more enjoyable'

Source: Millward Brown brand tracker

8. Consumer behaviour changed

The percentage of all out of home sandwiches eaten at lunch *with* a packet of Walkers stopped declining, and indeed increased in 2010 (Figure 20).

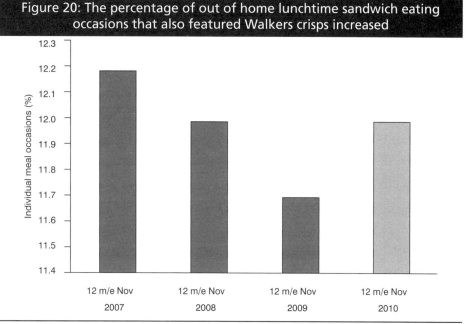

Figure 20: The percentage of out of home lunchtime sandwich eating occasions that also featured Walkers crisps increased

Source: Kantar Consumption panel

And looking at lunchbox occasions in isolation, in 2010 there were 10 million more of these featuring sandwiches consumed *with* Walkers crisps than there were in 2009.[30]

9. Sales and share turned around

Prior to the campaign, Walkers single-pack unit and value sales were steadily shrinking, however a turnaround commenced in the weeks the campaign was on air (Figure 21).

The same is true of unit and value share (Figure 22).

Moreover, looking at MAT share of single packs, Sandwich marked the start of a *long-term* change in fortunes (Figure 23).

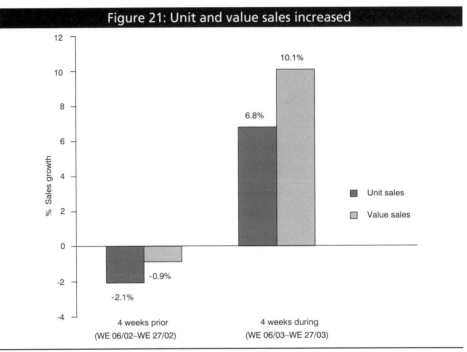

Source: Nielsen

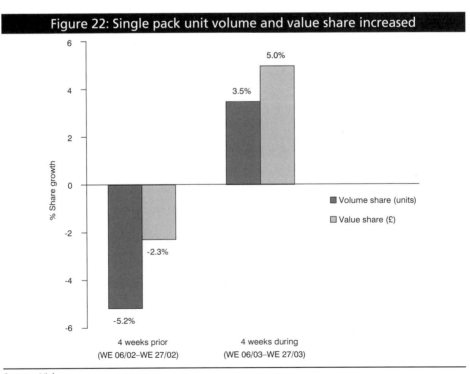

Source: Nielsen

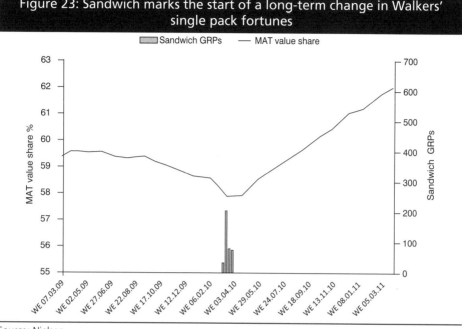

Figure 23: Sandwich marks the start of a long-term change in Walkers' single pack fortunes

Sandwich GRPs — MAT value share

Source: Nielsen

Evidence that communications were responsible

Preface

Walkers typically has a fairly packed annual communications calendar. Sandwich was just one campaign amongst a procession. Throughout January 2010, Walkers *Baked* was advertising.[31] And from 5 May, the 'Flavour Cup' Walkers core campaign was on air. Moreover, it was preceded by the launch of a suite of new 'Flavour Cup' flavour variants instore, which delivered a big incremental distribution kick starting in mid-April.[32] All this makes it extremely difficult to demonstrate conclusive proof, using non-econometric methods, of Sandwich's contribution to the bottom line, *except* within the constraints of a narrow band of time. The narrow band we have therefore used is w/e 6 February 2010, to w/e 3 April 2010. This is our 'evaluation period' (not withstanding our econometric evidence, which looks at a much longer time-frame). The campaign ran from w/e 6 March to w/e 27 March 2010.

Rate of sale

Unit rate of sale clearly responded to the campaign activity (Figure 24).

Econometrics

Econometric modelling by Ninah[33] has isolated Sandwich's powerful contribution to single pack volume sales (Figure 25).

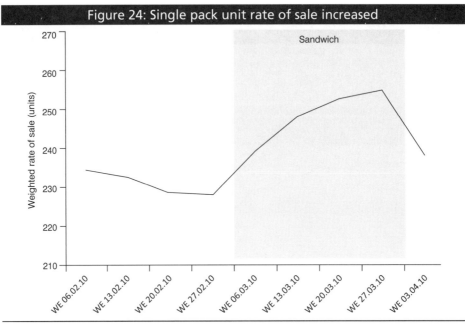

Figure 24: Single pack unit rate of sale increased

Source: Nielsen

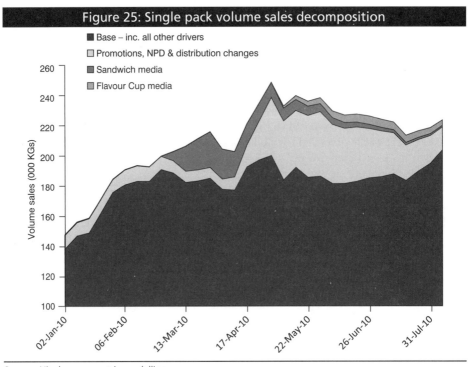

Figure 25: Single pack volume sales decomposition

Source: Ninah econometric modelling

Eliminating other factors

Was it price?

No. During the campaign, Walkers' average price per unit actually increased relative to the single pack market average (Figure 26). Given that we have shown volume sales grew during this time, it appears the advertising more than supported this increase.

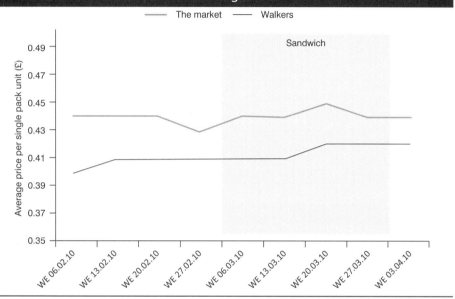

Figure 26: Walkers' single pack price increases relative to the market average

Source: Nielsen

Promotional activity?

No. Percentage volume sold on promotions fell during the campaign, while unit sales rose (Figure 27).

Was it distribution?

No. In quantity terms, distribution was flat during the evaluation period (Figure 28).

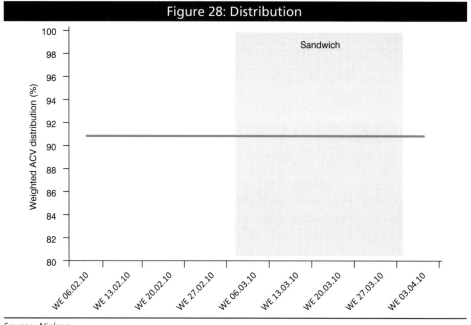

Figure 27: Volume sold on promotion declined as unit sales rose

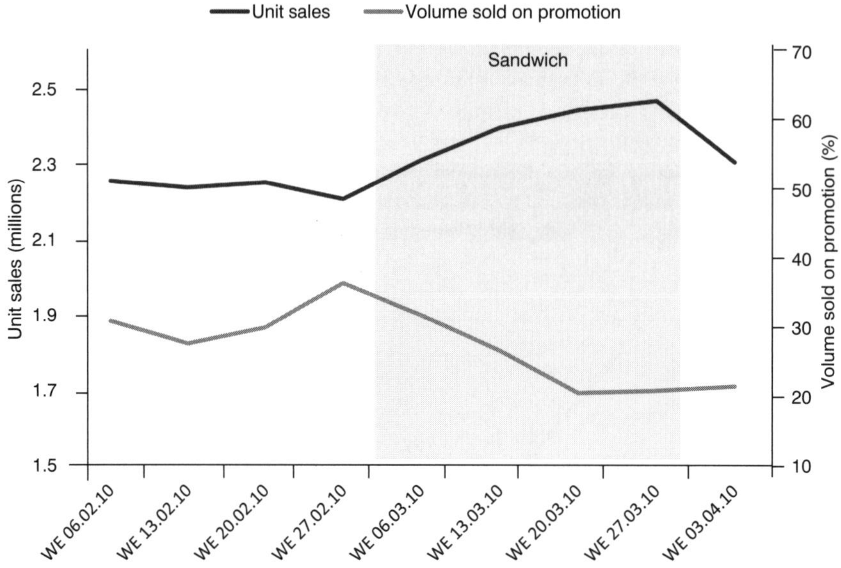

— Unit sales   ▬▬ Volume sold on promotion

Source: Nielsen

Figure 28: Distribution

Source: Nielsen

Was it all down to those gains in quality of distribution that the campaign helped deliver?

No. Ninah have eliminated these from their modelling of Sandwich's contribution to sales. Furthermore we can show that, in Waitrose, an account where *no* gains in distribution quality were made,[34] rate of sale responded to the advertising with a high degree of correlation (Figure 29).

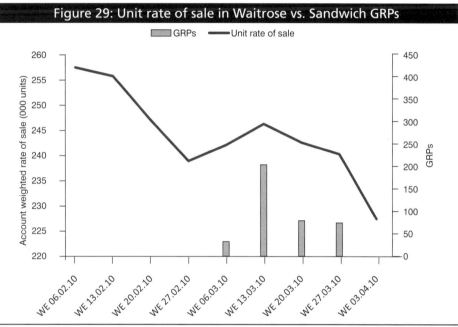

Figure 29: Unit rate of sale in Waitrose vs. Sandwich GRPs

Source: Nielsen/OMD

Was it the market?

No. We have accounted for the market by citing share data.

The season?

No. Walkers sales show little seasonal variation, except in the build up to Christmas. Moreover, sales in February (the 'prior' comparison period used above) are typically *higher* than they are in March (when the campaign ran) (Figure 30).

The economic climate?

No. Ninah's econometric modelling examined this in detail and found evidence to suggest that sales were significantly affected by the economic climate.

The World Cup?

No. The Football World Cup took place between 11 June and 11 July, months after the end of the campaign.[35] Moreover, Ninah's econometric model accounts for this (when looking at the long-term effect) as well as other sporting events.

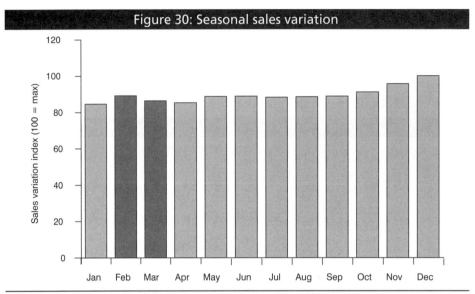

Figure 30: Seasonal sales variation

Source: Ninah econometric modelling

Was it a new product launch?

No. While there were two new permanent flavours launched in February 2010, these were only available in a *multipack* format (6pack).[36] Our analysis above looks at *single* pack sales. Aside from these, several temporary new flavour variants launched as part of the 'Flavour Cup' campaign, but they did not reach shelves until w/e 17 April 2010.[37]

A change in packaging?

No. The 'Flavour Cup' campaign was cross-promoted on existing variants, but this change did not reach shelves until w/e 17 April 2010.[38]

Another Walkers campaign?

There were no other Walkers, or Walkers sub-brand communications during the evaluation period.[39]

Did Walkers benefit from weak competition?

No. Seabrook Crisps were in very strong growth, and made distribution gains in Q1 2010.[40] Moreover, McCoy's and Kettle were both active in media with significant spends in and around the Sandwich campaign period (Figure 31).

Was there less 'healthy snacking' or anti-obesity advertising?

No. Advertising spend in these areas in Q1 2010 was significantly higher than in the surrounding months (Figure 32).

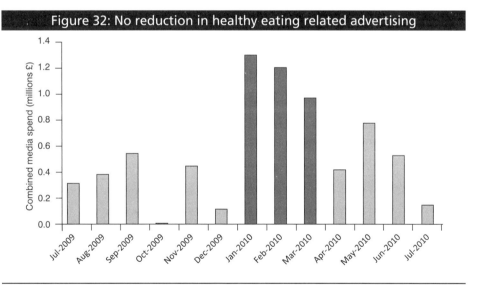

Figure 31: Walkers' competitors were active around the time

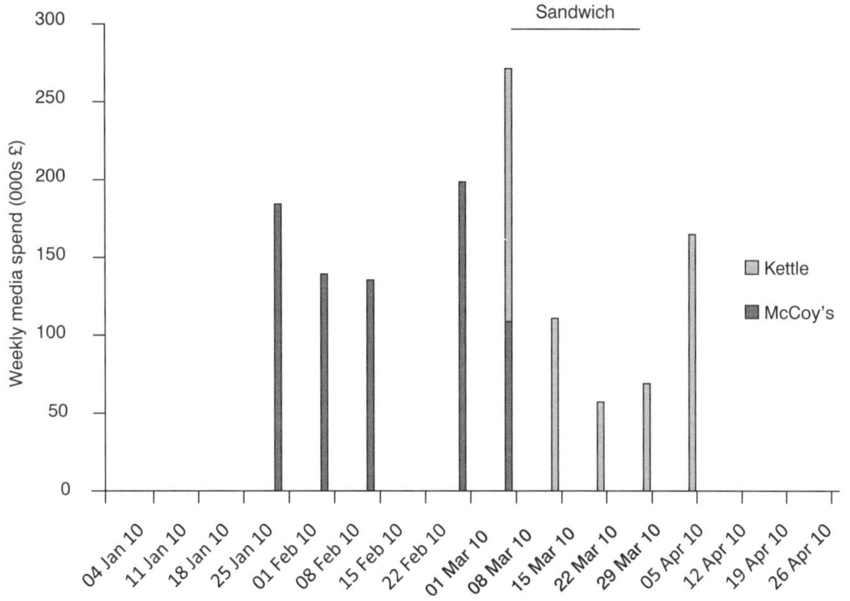

Source: Nielsen

Figure 32: No reduction in healthy eating related advertising

Source: Nielsen. Includes the following brands: COI 'Change 4 Life'; Weight Watchers; Ryvita; McVities 'Go-Ahead'; Kellogg's Special K; Quaker Oats; Marmite snacks

Return on marketing investment

PepsiCo do not disclose their margins, or those of their retail customers. Neither do they publicly reveal the total profit generated by their marketing.[41] But we can present here the campaign's short and long-term ROMI (Table 2).

Table 2: ROMI	
	Net profit generated by every £ spent (ROMI)
Short-term (1 year)	£0.60
Long-term (3 years)	£2.20

Source: Ninah Consulting Econometric Modelling. These figures include the campaign's substantial impact upon Walkers' core multipack sales, in addition to single pack sales. They exclude the gains in quality of distribution which the campaign played a major part in delivering. ROMI has been calculated as follows: (incremental profit – total campaign cost)/total campaign cost

The campaign has proven itself profitable even in the short term, which is rare for an FMCG brand. Moreover, the ROMI figures are approximately 30% higher than would be expected for a brand the size of Walkers.[42]

However, Walkers campaigns do typically perform well in terms of ROMI, so perhaps a true test of Sandwich's performance is a benchmark versus these other Walkers campaigns. The result? Sandwich is the *second highest performing Walkers campaign that Ninah have ever modelled.*[43]

It is possible that the campaign's ROMI is in fact higher still, due to halo effects on sub-brands such as Baked, Max and Lights.

New learning and conclusion

This paper has shown the value of building scope to influence multiple key audiences into the very fabric of an idea. In this case the audiences were journalists, the sales-force, and most crucially the trade, as well as consumers.

It also stands as further proof that bold, strategically sound communications deliver better than average returns.

Perhaps Greg Lyons, Walkers Vice President of Marketing, said it best when he said:

Sandwich was a risky campaign, but ultimately one that delivered remarkable rewards. It exceeded all of its objectives and our expectations. A brilliant idea, executed flawlessly.

Notes

1 Walkers 'core' excludes Walkers sub-brands such as Lights, Baked, Max and Extra Crunchy. This applies wherever the term 'Walkers core' is used in the paper. In this paper, wherever 'Walkers' is mentioned, 'Walkers core' is the subject. 'Core' is simply dropped for the sake of brevity.
2 Source: Mintel. Nearest competitor Pringles has only 7% share of crisps and salty snacks, versus Walkers core's 21%.
3 Source: Mintel.
4 Source: Mintel – Sandwiches and other Lunchtime Foods report, UK, March 2009.

5   Source: Kantar consumption panel.
6   Source: Mintel – Sandwiches and other Lunchtime Foods report, UK, March 2009.
7   Source: AMV BBDO Qualitative Research, October 2009.
8   Source: TNS Omnibus.
9   Source: Millward Brown post-test results; various campaigns.
10   Source: Eurest Lunchtime Report 2008.
11   Source: Mintel – Sandwiches and other Lunchtime Foods report, UK, March 2009.
12   This was the case even back in 2002. The Walkers IPA paper from that year includes the following quote from a young male in qualitative research by AMV BBDO: "Oh look Lineker ends up with the crisps again. That's a surprise."
13   Source: walkerssandwich YouTube channel comments.
14   Source: Freud Communications. Key wins included articles in *The Sun*, *The Guardian*, *The Daily Star*, and on The BBC and SKY TV news.
15   Source: Freud Communications; Print: figures for national titles come from NRS, regional titles come from JICREG; Broadcast: figures come from Accenture; Online: where ABC e-figures are published, these figures are used. In other cases, Mediaproof estimate according to the evidence available.
16   Source: Freud Communications sentiment analysis.
17   Source: Freud Communications coverage analysis.
18   Source: Freud Communications. The advertising equivalent value is $3 \times$ rate card cost to account for editorial impact. Freud then rates the piece of coverage on a scale of 1–10 depending on the messaging quality within it, factoring this in to the calculation to arrive at a realistic final figure.
19   Source: Freud Communications.
20   An aggregation of YouTube video views, views on walkers.co.uk, and views from the numerous other video hosting sites which we seeded content to.
21   Source: YouTube.
22   Source: YouTube.
23   Source: Nielsen, March 2010 Expenditure. Walkers' TV spend was £960k.
24   Source: http://www.thinkbox.tv/server/show/nav.1380.
25   Broadcast on ITV, 30 December 2010, 9–10pm.
26   *Marketing*, 14 April 2010, p.23.
27   Sandwich's creative awards: Cannes (Gold, 2 Silver, 1 Bronze); Eurobest (Grand Prix, 2 Silver); Creative Circle (Bronze); Kinsale Sharks (3 Silver).
28   Source: Marketing Excellence Awards 2010.
29   Source: PepsiCo.
30   Source: Kantar Consumption panel.
31   Ninah's econometric modelling has shown Baked advertising to have a significant halo effect on Walkers' core sales.
32   To be clear, this refers to gains in distribution quantity, as distinct from the distribution quality gains we attribute to the Sandwich campaign in point 6 above – 'Success with the retailers, as intended'.
33   Ninah's econometric model accounts for the following sales drivers: price; distribution; promotions and display for products across the Walkers portfolio; the economy and consumer confidence; seasonality and public holidays; temperature; other Walkers media; competitors' price, distribution, promotions and media.
34   Source: PepsiCo.
35   Source: FIFA.com. Ninah accounts for the World Cup in their longer term modelling of the campaign's ROMI.
36   Source: PepsiCo. The two new flavours were Cheddar Cheese and Bacon, and Sour Cream & Chive.
37   Source: PepsiCo. The Flavour Cup ATL activity took place from w/e 09 May 2010 to w/e 27 June 2010.
38   Source: PepsiCo.
39   Source: OMD. Outside of the evaluation period, the Flavour Cup campaign aired in May 2010, and the Walkers Baked campaign aired in January 2010 (as previously discussed).
40   Source: Mintel – Crisps and Salty Snacks Market Report, January 2011.
41   We are also not able to show total campaign cost here as it would reveal the net profit generated. It is however shown alongside the ROMI in the technical appendix.
42   Source: Ninah Consulting archive analysis.
43   Ninah have modelled 10 Walkers campaigns; Sandwich is second only to 'Do Us a Flavour'.

Chapter 21

The Economist

By Jeff Lush and Magali Barreyat-Baron, AMV BBDO
Contributing author: Craig Mawdsley, AMV BBDO
Credited companies: Media Agency: PHD Media; Client: *The Economist*

Editor's summary

As growth slowed for the 167-year-old *Economist*, they needed to recruit new readers. For many years *The Economist* had built a reputation as the publication of choice for finance professionals, yet this was a narrow representation of its range and style. An engaging and 'interactive' outdoor campaign sought to convince people to consider the newspaper in a different light, and not as a publication filled with dry content and solely focused on finance. Tube commuters were given a 'mini experience' of reading an *Economist* article, where the 'Where do you stand?' thought was brought to life whilst they absorbed the poster. This campaign more than paid for itself from incremental subscriptions alone, with a conservative ROI of £1.96. The judges felt this case demonstrated a thorough understanding of evaluation methods and revealed an interesting national impact from regionally focused activity.

Introduction – tough times, but not for all

It is a commonplace idea that traditional publishers of news and analysis are having a tough time of it, and it is almost as widely known that *The Economist* has managed to buck this trend.

Not only has it been tremendously successful in terms of global expansion, but also with domestic growth in the UK, where *The Economist* had entered the new century with double-digit growth (see Figure 1).

Figure 1: *The Economist* circulation in the UK

Source: ABC UK bi-annual data JJ=January to June, JD=July to December

These Audit Bureau of Circulations figures are the industry standard, and we shall be using them throughout this paper. Just as sales in FMCG markets are monitored by Nielsen, sales in newspapers and magazines are audited by ABC, who report a year in two halves: January to June and July to December.

The figure given for each 6-month period is the *average* circulation per issue, including subscriptions, newsstand sales and bulks (copies taken by hotels and airlines, etc., for distribution to their customers).

Back to our story

Unfortunately, over the last few years *The Economist*'s UK growth had slowed to not much more than 1% – perhaps not surprising, given the maturity of the brand and the continuing malaise in the wider market (Figure 2).

A major impact here is the industry-wide decline in newsstand sales, from which even *The Economist* was not immune. Between July–Dec 06 and July–Dec 09 its newsstand sales had declined by 13.9%, versus an industry estimate (by Comag) of News and Current Affairs titles declining by 20.7%.

Circulation growth is of course critical, not only for the revenue it generates through cover price, but also as the currency of advertising sales. It is oxygen for media companies, and by the end of 2009 it looked like even for *The Economist* the air was getting a little thin. It was time for a rethink.

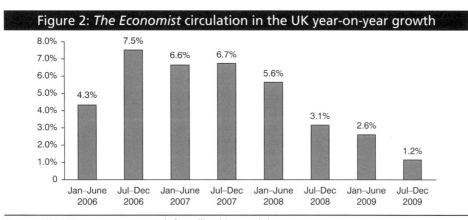

Figure 2: *The Economist* circulation in the UK year-on-year growth

Source: ABC UK, year-on-year growth for rolling bi-annual data

The need for a new recruitment strategy

Clearly if we wanted to accelerate our growth, we needed to revitalise how we recruit new readers. We had spent twenty years talking rather smugly about the cleverness of those who read *The Economist*. It was time for a new approach.

Our first step was to run a piece of TGI analysis across our audience in order to identify specific traits that could help us reach and engage with potential new readers.

We found out that our readers were significantly more interested than the general population in finding out about other cultures, lifestyles and global events, and generally speaking, getting new ideas from all sorts of disciplines and sources.

Further qualitative research amongst readers revealed that what they had discovered and valued in *The Economist* was an analysis-based, broad-ranging, thought-provoking read which prompted them to consider issues in a way which helped them to feel like informed participants in the world rather than bemused spectators.

When we recruited people for qualitative research with similar motivations, but who had never read *The Economist*, the results were tremendously enlightening. At first they described *The Economist* as dull, focused solely on finance and written for bankers. But as we gave them an opportunity to read articles on subjects they would never have expected even to see covered by the publication, we saw their attitudes literally change before our eyes. Were it not for the MRS code, we could have sold subscriptions on the night!

And we then knew that the most persuasive thing we could do with our communications was to find an engaging way of bringing to people who had never considered us a 'mini-experience' of reading a typical *Economist* article.

We summarised *The Economist*'s promise as:

- agenda-setting fresh perspectives;
- unexpected content;
- views tested through analysis and debate.

This new focus on the editorial experience, and the belief that surfacing content was the key to future success, was the key to the whole marketing strategy.

Focusing our communications

Whilst our ambitions were high, we had to be realistic about the scope of the ATL budget – £733k for the year – and recognise that a degree of audience focus was inevitable. The TGI figures revealed that London, already an area of existing strength for *The Economist*, also provided significant growth potential with access to 42% of our motivationally-defined audience. The analysis also revealed their high propensity for Underground use with 25% using it at least once a month with an impressively low wastage: 47% of rush-hour travellers fitting our profile.

In terms of developing a media strategy, London Underground obviously provides a very poster-focused environment, echoing the approach that had brought much fame and success to *The Economist* previously. However, despite the attractiveness of the poster audience data, we wanted to find a new way to engage an intellectually curious audience who mistakenly believed that *Economist* editorial content would be dry, stand-offish and narrowly focused on finance.

The guiding thought

The strategic thought that unlocked the engagement potential of Underground posters was 'Where do you stand?' – inspiring both creative and media strategy in equal measure (see Figures 3 and 4).

Amplifying the strategy through media

The campaign was designed to be 'interactive', in the sense that it would give people a 'mini-experience' of reading an *Economist* article. But the real genius of the campaign was how the message and media moment combined harmoniously to bring the strategic thought of 'Where do you stand' to life for the commuter whilst they consumed the poster. How? By juxtaposing provocative, but contrary, arguments on high dwell time cross-track double 48-sheets, the commuter was implicitly invited to complement their intellectual engagement with physical participation – quite literally, where would they stand?

Surprising subject matter, stimulating debate, interactivity – all this constituted a major change in 'body language' for *The Economist*, designed to invite people into what had always presented itself as an exclusive club.

Figure 3: An example from the June 2010 burst

PRISONERS SHOULD BE ALLOWED TO VOTE

Voting is a fundamental right. Even those who break the law have rights.

The European Court of Human Rights has ruled that the ban on prisoners voting is unlawful. Among European countries, only Britain and Luxembourg impose this ban.

The ban isn't consistent. Those in intermittent custody, who spend some days at home and some days in prison, may vote if the election falls on a day when they are at home.

WHERE DO YOU STAND?

The Economist

For a free copy text PRISONER to 80801.

PRISONERS SHOULD NOT BE ALLOWED TO VOTE

People who break laws should not have a say in making them.

The suspension of the right to vote, along with the rights to freedom and privacy, is part of the punishment for committing a crime.

Banning prisoners from voting is one of the ways in which society sends out the message that serious crimes have serious consequences.

WHERE DO YOU STAND?

The Economist

For a free copy text PRISONER to 80801.

Figure 4: An example from the October 2010 burst

PROSTITUTION IS A CRIME, NOT A BUSINESS

It exploits vulnerable people, so society should not condone it.

If sex has a price, it loses its value.

If Britain legalised brothels, it would become a centre for seedy sex tourism. London can do without its own version of Amsterdam's red light district.

WHERE DO YOU STAND?

The Economist

For a free copy text LEGAL to 60300.

PROSTITUTION IS A BUSINESS, NOT A CRIME

People should be allowed to buy and sell whatever they like, including their own bodies.

The idea that most prostitutes are victims of sex-trafficking is nonsense. In a recent study of migrant sex workers in Britain, only 6% said that they had been deceived or coerced into selling sex.

It provides good money for hard-up people. A study of street prostitutes in Chicago showed they earned about four times as much as they could expect from other jobs.

WHERE DO YOU STAND?

The Economist

For a free copy text LEGAL to 60300.

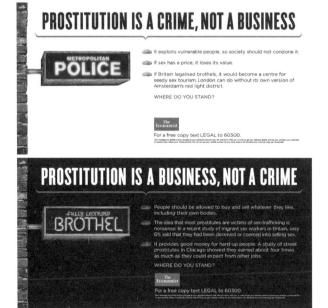

Campaign activity

The first burst launched in June 2010, with an investment of £374,415, followed by an October burst costing £279,376. 92% of the media budget was devoted to outdoor poster formats, the vast majority within London Underground but with some specific London commuter rail sites that were able to provide the cross-track juxtaposition experience. In total, the campaign ran on 310 cross-track 48-sheets (155 pairs of debates) in June and 260 panels in October (130 debates). Commuters who engaged with the campaign could be expected to have seen it, on average, 12 times.

We also took the opportunity to introduce some innovative and progressive tactical measures into the campaign, further differentiating it from previous *Economist* outdoor brand activity:

- Each poster offered a text response mechanism offering a free copy of the magazine, the first time *The Economist* had employed a direct response mechanism on outdoor brand media. There were some initial reservations about blurring the line between DR and 'pure' brand advertising (as well as questions about whether text response mechanisms could work on the Underground!).

- However, reading a real copy of *The Economist* was the obvious next step on from the mini-experience offered by the posters, and so justified the mechanic. This understanding of the customer journey was vindicated by the results, as we shall see later.

- *The Economist* also used digital OOH for the first time, with cross-track projections in Zone 1 and 11 Transvision screens at 10 London rail stations.

Response – anecdotes

From the beginning there was a positive buzz about the campaign. Each 'debate' topic generated over 1,000 comments on *The Economist*'s Facebook page and Twitter; the campaign was very well received by staff and relayed by bloggers (Carole Wurzelbacher, Edward Boches and Minuteman Press) and in the media (Figure 5).

Figure 5: Examples of media coverage

Source: www.guardian.co.uk and www.independent.co.uk

Several schools requested copies of the ads to debate the issues with students in their classroom.

As one of our objectives was to show that we offered agenda-setting fresh perspectives, it was also particularly satisfying to see one of our topics becoming front-page news soon after the ad went live (Figure 6).

Figure 6: One of the campaign topics makes the headlines

Source: *The Daily Telegraph*

Response – attitudes

Clearly we were hoping to see shifts in attitudes towards the publication as a result of the campaign, and the tracking study led by TNS Research International did not disappoint. 29% of the sample recognised at least one of the posters from the June 2010 burst, and this increased to 38% for the October 2010 burst.

'Consider reading' increased significantly across the sample from 34% to 40%, whilst a whole host of brand image statements, such as 'a stimulating read', 'covers a broad range of subjects', 'gives a different point of view' also improved significantly (see Figure 7).

Figure 7: Recognition of at least one execution; consider reading

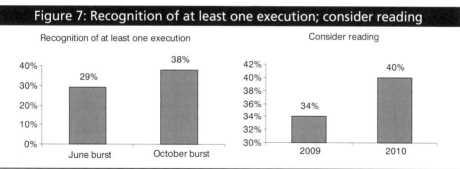

Source: TNS brand tracker, Dec 2010

Interestingly, the percentage of current readers who said they would actively recommend the publication to others increased significantly, from 42% to 51%, perhaps suggesting that the less restricted and more genuine view of the magazine promoted by the campaign facilitated this crucial advocacy (Figure 8).

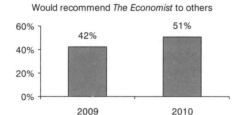

Figure 8: Would recommend *The Economist* to others

Would recommend *The Economist* to others

Source: TNS brand tracker, Dec 2010

So we had certainly achieved what we set out to in terms of the 'softer measures'. What about some hard sales results? First of all, back to those texts.

Response – texts

These turned out to be a very good investment as an additional element to what was essentially a brand-building campaign.

The first burst produced 4,859 text responses, whilst the second produced 5,412 for 25% less spend, suggesting, as with the recognition scores, a cumulative creative effect in addition to a successful refinement of the media strategy. Each texter was called back for their full details, was sent a free copy and offered a subscription at an initial offer price of 12 issues for £1. After the first three months, pricing returns to the normal level of £30 per quarter.

Historical data shows that across the first 12 months of a typical subscription, around half of new subscribers renew at each quarter. Those who have renewed through a full year then generally stick around for some time – after the first (discounted) year, the average length of a subscription is seven years.

So far we have been able to analyse the data from the first burst, through to their third renewal.

Roughly half of the texters simply took up the free copy offer, while the other half (2,406) the three-month trial subscription. Over half of those new subscribers paid for a second quarter (1,344). And 43% of those subsequently paid for a third quarter. If we apply this performance to the second burst, and apply a 50% anticipated conversion to a fourth quarter, then we see direct subscription revenue in the 12 months after the two bursts of £146,000.

After the first discounted year (at £91), a normal subscription costs about £120. *The Economist* calculates a conservative revenue benefit of £406,000 over seven years (see Table 1).

Which means that 62% of our brand campaign was paid for out of the direct response generated alone!

Another interesting insight into how the campaign was working was provided by subsequent regional analysis of the text code responses and the resulting subscriptions. We had theorised that, given the attitudinal profile of our target, a London Underground-focused campaign would nevertheless spread its influence beyond London, as so many potential readers would visit London for work or leisure even if they did not live or regularly work there.

Table 1: Brand campaign – subs from text messages				
		Subs volume	Revenue per sub £	Revenue £
Year 1	Q1	5,112	1	5,112
	Q2	2,856	30	85,680
	Q3	1,228	30	36,842
	Q4	614	30	18,421
				146,056
Year 2		522	120	62,632
Year 3		444	120	53,237
Year 4		377	120	45,252
Year 5		321	120	38,464
Year 6		272	120	32,694
Year 7		232	120	27,790
				406,125

Source: *The Economist*

The map shows addresses of subscriptions taken up which were initiated by texting the numbers on the London posters, and confirms our theory (Figure 9).

Figure 9: Map of addresses of new subscriptions

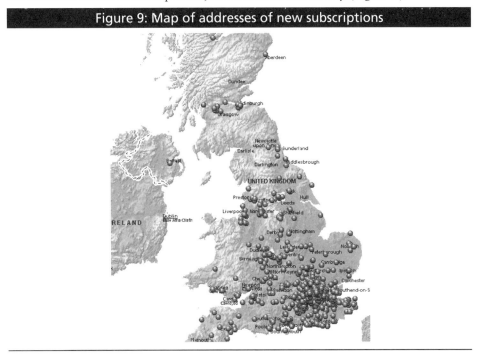

To a degree, the London sites delivered a 'national' audience fitting our profile, with subscriptions way beyond London, but without having incurred the wastage and cost of a national campaign.

Response – sales and subscriptions

The turnaround in circulation growth was striking (see Figure 10).

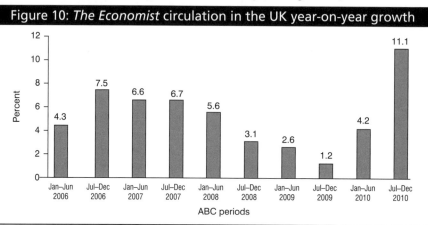

Figure 10: *The Economist* circulation in the UK year-on-year growth

Source: ABC UK bi-annual data JJ=January to June, JD=July to December

There is no doubt at all that the combined effect of the marketing activity in 2010 produced a dramatic improvement in circulation growth, but of course we are not about to claim all of this as a brand advertising effect.

Firstly we need to discount any changes in the product: there had been no redesigns or editorial policy shifts aimed at attracting new readers. *The Economist* was what it had always been.

Whilst retail trade marketing actually went down slightly from 2009 to 2010, throughout the year we had substantially increased the budget for subscription marketing – mainly inserts in the magazine itself, and in 'affinity' publications such as *The Guardian* or *The Times*. The absolute amount that *The Economist* spends on inserts is confidential, but we can disclose the magnitude by which subscription-driving spend increased to enable us to compare the effect in 2010 with previous years.

In the first half of the year, we invested 2.2 times as much in subscription marketing as in the previous year. The advertising campaign had barely begun in the last month of the period covered by the Jan–June ABC figures, and as these are averaged over the whole period, clearly the effect of the campaign will be heavily diluted.

Even though the text message responses tell us that the advertising was working hard at driving interest and subscriptions from the start, it is unarguable that the lion's share of the 4.2% increase in Jan–June (a 7,903 increase in circulation) must be ascribed to the increase in subscription marketing.

If, however, we pass to the second half of the year, once the advertising campaign has had the chance to get underway, then we can fairly start to disentangle an incremental effect for the advertising, over and above what is being achieved by the increase in subscription marketing.

As can clearly be seen from the chart above, the second half of the year was a phenomenal improvement on even the turnaround first half. The year-on-year growth was an astounding 11.1%, equating to an increase in circulation of 21,003.

As ABC numbers are cumulative, rolling data, we need to take off the growth in the first half to isolate the impact of the second half's activity: 21,003 minus 7,903 = 13,100.

Now, to get to the advertising effect only, we also need to take off the subscription spend impact.

The increase in subscription marketing for the second half of the year was actually a little lower than for the first – 1.8 times versus 2.2 times – but we have made the conservative assumption that subscription marketing delivered the same level of growth in the second half than in the first: i.e. 7,903.

So the growth in the second half that is down to the advertising is: 13,100 minus 7,903 = **5,197**.

So how much is that worth?

As we have said before, the value of circulation increase is two-fold – on the one hand, the increased revenue through sales, and on the other, the increase in advertising revenue through increases in rate card.

The Economist's ongoing commitment to an attractive CPM for our clients meant we did not transfer the full ABC circulation increase onto the rate card. Nevertheless, 11.1% growth enabled us – alongside other factors such as media inflation and competitors' activity – to drive our rate card by 5.1%.

In terms of revenue through sales, we have already mentioned that the newsstands channel is in decline, and whilst the decline slowed in June to December 2010 (to 8% from nearly 14% the previous year), it had by no means stopped. All of the sales revenue growth from the increased circulation derives from the increases in subscription, although we must discount the figures for bulks.

Increases in bulks account for 16% of the year-on-year circulation growth, July to December 2010, and so discounting this from the 5,197 increase driven by our advertising campaign, we would need to calculate revenue from 4,365 subscriptions.

Applying the same assumptions as before, these subscriptions generate £2.2m of additional revenue over seven years (Table 2).

Table 2: Brand campaign – wider growth impact			
	Subs volume	**Revenue per sub £**	**Revenue £**
Year 1	4,365	91	397,215
Year 2	3,710	120	445,230
Year 3	3,154	120	378,446
Year 4	2,681	120	321,679
Year 5	2,279	120	273,427
Year 6	1,937	120	232,413
Year 7	1,646	120	197,551
			2,245,960

Source: *The Economist*

With an operating margin of 57%, and a media investment of £653,791, that gives an **ROI** of (1,280,197/ 653,791) **1.96.**

A few possible quibbles

1. Consumer confidence

One might imagine that *Economist* subscriptions would somehow be related to consumer confidence. Perhaps sales go up as confidence goes down and people look for help, or maybe sales go up with consumer confidence as people spend on luxuries like magazines. In fact, there is no relationship either way.

Consumer confidence was on the rise in 2010. But this trend started in 2009, and even with adding a reasonable lagged effect of six months, we could not see a direct correlation with subscription effectiveness (Figure 11).

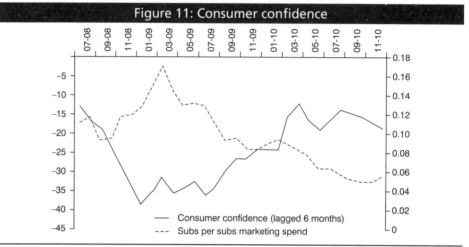

Figure 11: Consumer confidence

Source: GFK Consumer confidence barometer study

2. Competitors spend

The Economist share of voice amongst its closest competitive set was actually in slight decline between 2009 and 2010: from 25% to 23% (Figure 12).

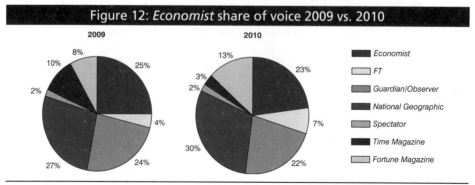

Figure 12: *Economist* share of voice 2009 vs. 2010

Source: Billets

3. News content and *Economist* covers

As financial news is more at the centre of world events (as it has been since 2008) one might imagine that *Economist* sales would go up. This may indeed be the case, but almost all of this short-term increase would go to casual purchase at newsstand, and as our analysis shows, all our increase has come from the deeper commitment of subscription sales.

Conclusion

We have shown that a radical change in marketing strategy on the part of an 167-year-old newspaper led to a new chapter of growth in the publication's history. Fresh analysis of our readers' motivations and a hard-headed look at the editorial offering uncovered a welcome truth: that shining a spotlight on our writing would attract new readers.

Subscription revenue from texts alone virtually paid for the campaign, which will be nearly paid for once again by the incremental advertising revenue from just one year, gained by the rate card increases directly driven by the advertising. If we ignore all this and simply consider the net present value of the subscribers we have recruited, then we get an ROI of 1.96.

We think this is an achievement to be proud of, although, perhaps, our proudest moment was when we noticed that even the *Economist* editorial team seemed to think we were onto a good idea (Figure 13).

Figure 13: *Economist* **article after the campaign began**

The Economist August 7th 2010   Leaders 13

Berlusconi on the ropes

Signor Fini, where do you stand?

Italian politics has entered a new, unstable phase. Time for its most talented politician to show his true mettle

VICTORY for Silvio Berlusconi can rarely have tasted so bitter. On August 4th a junior minister from his People of Freedom party (PdL) faced a vote of censure in parliament over an alleged scheme to rig judicial and political posts. The prime minister's man won, but thanks largely to the abstention of 25 PdL deputies allied to Gianfranco Fini, who had ended months of bickering by breaking with Mr Berlusconi a few days earlier. Mr Fini did not need to press home his advantage to spell out that the PdL can no longer count on winning a majority. Only two years into his five-year term, Mr Berlusconi now governs at Mr Fini's pleasure. The question is, what does Mr Fini plan to do with his power?

leader). He has also taken a stand against corruption. Whereas Mr Berlusconi has repeatedly attacked the judiciary and sought to frustrate their inquiries by tinkering with the law, Mr Fini has argued that any office-holder who becomes a formal suspect should always stand aside—which arguably gives magistrates too much power. Most of all, Mr Fini wants a party that is not just a vehicle for Mr Berlusconi, but one that can weave policy from the hopes and ideas of all its members.

Yet doubts remain. Although Mr Fini says some of the right things, does he say them for the right reasons? The easiest worry to put to rest is over his origins as a neo-fascist. His praise long ago for Mussolini was indeed contemptible, but if there is such a thing as redemption in politics Mr Fini deserves his chance. In a political journey lasting many years, Mr Fini has trekked to the centre-ground. In the process he has visited Israel and Auschwitz, jettisoned neo-fascist true believers, includ-

How to access the IPA Effectiveness Awards Databank

The IPA Databank represents the most rigorous and comprehensive examination of marketing communications working in the marketplace, and in the world. Over more than 30 years of the IPA's Effectiveness Awards competition, we have collected over 1,100 examples of best practice in advertising development and results across a wide spectrum of marketing sources and expenditures. Each example contains up to 4,000 words of text and is illustrated in full by market, research, sales and profit data.

IPA Effectiveness Awards Search Engine (EASE)

You can use the EASE search engine at www.ipa.co.uk/ease to interrogate over 1,100 detailed case studies from the IPA Databank. You can search the case studies by keywords and/or filter by any parameter from questions asked in the Effectiveness Awards Entry Questionnaire. EASE is free to use and is the first search engine on the web which allows you to do this. IPA members can also contact the Information Centre directly where more complex searches can be commissioned and the results supplied by e-mail.

Purchasing IPA case studies

Member agencies are entitled to download a maximum of 12 case studies in any given calendar year, free of charge, after which they can download additional case studies from the IPA website at www.ipa.co.uk/cases for £25 each. Alternatively members can sign up to warc.com (see overleaf) at a beneficial IPA rate and can then download case studies as part of that subscription. Non IPA members can purchase case studies from the IPA website (www.ipa.co.uk/cases) at £40 per copy.

Further information

For further information, please contact the Information Centre at the IPA, 44 Belgrave Square, London SW1X 8QS
Telephone: +44 (0)20 7235 7020
Fax: +44 (0)20 7245 9904
Website: www.ipa.co.uk
Email: info@ipa.co.uk

warc.com

Warc is the official publisher of the IPA Effectiveness Awards' case histories. All IPA case studies are available at warc.com, alongside thousands of other case studies, articles and best practice guides, market intelligence and industry news and alerts, with material drawn from over 50 sources across the world.

Warc.com is relied upon by major creative and media agency networks, market research companies, media owners, multinational advertisers and business schools, to help tackle any marketing challenge.

IPA members can subscribe at a 10% discount. To find out more, visit warc.com.

www.ipaeffectivenessawards.co.uk

On our dedicated Awards website you can find out everything you need to know about the annual IPA Effectiveness Awards competition, including how to enter, and who's won what since 1980.

As well as viewing case study summaries and creative work, you'll also find a series of mini brand films, including a selection produced in 2010 celebrating some of the top cases from 30 years of the Awards:

- Audi
- Orange
- PG Tips
- Tesco
- Tobacco Control

IPA Databank case availability

NEW ENTRIES 2011

2011	Anchor Squirty Cream
2011	Aquafresh Kids*
2011	California Travel & Tourism Commission
2011	CrossCountry Trains
2011	Department for Transport
2011	Depaul UK*
2011	Doro Mobile Phones
2011	East Midlands Trains*
2011	Fiat*
2011	first direct*
2011	Hiscox
2011	Johnnie Walker
2011	Jungle Formula*
2011	Liverpool ONE
2011	Lynx*
2011	Marie Curie Cancer Care*
2011	Marmite XO
2011	McCain*
2011	Organ Donor Register*
2011	Ovaltine*
2011	Panasonic Toughbook
2011	PepsiCo Walkers*
2011	Program of Humanitarian Attention to the Demobilised*
2011	Promote Iceland*
2011	Rubicon
2011	Smokefree North West
2011	*The Economist**

NUMERICAL

2003	55 Degrees North**
2006	100.4 smooth fm
2000	1001 Mousse*

A

2004	AA Loans*
1982	Abbey Crunch
1990	Abbey National Building Society
1990	Abbey National Building Society
1980	Abbey National Building Society Open Bondshares
1990	Aberlour Malt Whisky*
2004	Ackermans (SA)
2008	Acquisition Crime*
2006	Actimel*
1996	Adult Literacy*
2002	Aerogard Mosquito Repellent (Australia)
1999	Agri Plan Finance**

1986	AGS Home Improvements*
1988	AIDS
1994	AIDS*
1986	Air Call
2010	Albert Bartlett Rooster Potatoes
1990	Alex Lawrie Factors
1980	All Clear Shampoo*
1988	Alliance & Leicester Building Society*
1990	Alliance & Leicester Building Society*
1992	Alliance & Leicester Building Society*
1984	Alliance Building Society
1990	Allied Dunbar
1984	Allinson's Bread
1984	Alpen
1990	Alton Towers
2003	Alton Towers 'Air'**
1999	Alton Towers 'Oblivion'**
2010	Always
1990	Amnesty International*
1992	Amnesty International
2009	Ancestry.co.uk
1990	Anchor Aerosol Cream
1988	Anchor Butter
1994	Anchor Butter
2011	Anchor Squirty Cream
1986	Andrex*
1992	Andrex
1994	Andrex Ultra
1986	Anglia Building Society
1996	Anglian Water
2006	Anti-Drugs (Scottish Executive)
2007	Anti-Drugs (Scottish Executive)*
2002	Anti-Drink Driving*
1997	Anti-Drink Driving (DoE Northern Ireland)**
1990	Anti-NHS Reform Campaign (BMA)
1994	Anti-Smoking
2011	Aquafresh Kids*
2007	Aqua Optima*
2000	Archers*
2006	Ariel
2007	Army Cadet Force
1998	Army Recruitment*
2004	Army Recruitment*
2005	Arriva Buses*
1996	Arrol's 80
1994	Arthur's (cat food)
2005	ATS Euromaster*
1988	Audi
1990	Audi*
1998	Audi*

C

1996	Cable Television
2008	CABWISE (Transport for London)*
2008	Cadbury Dairy Milk
2010	Cadbury Dairy Milk (India)
2010	Cadbury Dairy Milk*
2008	Cadbury's Biscuits*
1994	Cadbury's Boost*
1992	Cadbury's Caramel
1984	Cadbury's Creme Eggs
1988	Cadbury's Creme Eggs
1998	Cadbury's Creme Eggs
1992	Cadbury's Crunchie
1984	Cadbury's Curly Wurly*
1980	Cadbury's Dairy Box
2004	Cadbury's Dream (SA)
1982	Cadbury's Flake
1984	Cadbury's Fudge*
1994	Cadbury's Highlights
1999	Cadbury's Jestives**
1990	Cadbury's Mini Eggs
1994	Cadbury's Roses*
1986	Cadbury's Wispa
1988	Café Hag
2009	California Travel & Tourism Commission
2011	California Travel & Tourism Commission
1996	Californian Raisins
1980	Campari*
1992	Campbell's Condensed Soup
1988	Campbell's Meatballs*
1994	Campbell's Soup
1996	Cancer Relief Macmillan Fund
1984	Canderel
2008	Capital One
1994	Car Crime Prevention
1992	Caramac
1997	Carex**
1998	Carex
2003	Carex**
2007	Carex*
2008	Carex
2010	Carling
1994	Carling Black Label
1996	Carling Black Label
1984	Carousel
1998	Carrick Jewellery
1986	Castlemaine XXXX*
2006	Cathedral City*
1992	Cellnet Callback
1988	CenterParcs
2004	Central London Congestion Charge*
1992	Central Television Licence Renewal
2010	Change4Life
2000	Channel 5
1990	Charlton Athletic Supporters Club*
1980	Cheese Information Service
1996	Cheltenham & Gloucester Building Society
1988	Chessington World of Adventures
1998	Chicago Town Pizza
2002	Chicago Town Pizza
2003	Chicago Town Pizza**
1994	Chicken Tonight

2000	Chicken Tonight Sizzle and Stir*
2007	Child Protection on the Internet (Home Office)
1994	Child Road Safety
1992	Childhood Diseases Immunisation
2004	Children's Hearings (Scottish Executive)*
2005	Children's Hearings System*
1990	Children's World
2001	Chiltern Railways (Clubman Service)**
1984	Chip Pan Fires Prevention*
1990	Choosy Catfood*
1992	Christian Aid
1998	Christian Aid*
2007	Churchill Square (Shopping Centre)
1994	CICA (Trainers)*
1992	Citroen Diesel Range
2010	Civic
1988	Clairol Nice n' Easy
1988	Clarks Desert Boots*
1996	Classic Combination Catalogue
1994	Clerical Medical
1992	Clorets
1984	Clover
1988	Clover
2007	Coca-Cola Zero*
1980	Cointreau
1998	Colgate Toothpaste*
1990	Colman's Wholegrain Mustard
2010	Comfort Fabric Conditioner*
2010	Commonwealth Bank
2000	Confetti.co.uk*
2005	Consensia/Police Service of Northern Ireland
2000	Co-op*
2004	Co-op Food Retail
1994	Cooperative Bank*
1996	Cooperative Bank
1990	Copperhead Cider
2007	Cornwall Enterprise
2010	Corsodyl*
1982	Country Manor (Alcoholic Drink)
1986	Country Manor (Cakes)
1984	Cow & Gate Babymeals*
1982	Cracottes*
2004	Cravendale (Milk)*
2000	Crime Prevention
2003	Crimestoppers Northern Ireland**
1980	Croft Original
1982	Croft Original
1990	Croft Original*
2011	CrossCountry Trains
1999	Crown Paint**
2002	Crown Paint
2003	Crown Paint**
2000	Crown Paints*
2004	Crown Paints
1990	Crown Solo*
1999	Crown Trade**
1999	Crown Wallcoverings**
1984	Cuprinol*
2007	Curanail
1999	Cussons 1001 Mousse**
1986	Cyclamon*
2009	Cycling Safety*

D

1996	Daewoo*
1982	*Daily Mail**
2002	Dairy Council (Milk)*
2000	Dairylea*
1992	Danish Bacon & Meat Council
2008	Danone Activia*
1980	Danum Taps
2003	Data Protection Act
1990	Data Protection Registrar
2008	Dave*
1980	Day Nurse
1994	Daz
2006	Daz*
2008	De Beers*
1996	De Beers Diamonds*
2002	Debenhams
1980	Deep Clean*
2005	Deep River Rock - Win Big
2000	Degree
2003	Demand Broadband**
2011	Department for Transport
2011	Depaul UK*
2006	Dero*
2008	Dero
1980	Dettol*
2009	Dextro Energy
2002	DfES Higher Education
2010	DH Hep (C)
1984	DHL Worldwide Carrier
1998	Direct Debit
2004	Direct Line*
1992	Direct Line Insurance*
2008	Direct Payment*
2007	Direct Payment (Department of Work and Pensions)*
2006	Disability Rights Commission
2003	District Policing Partnerships (Northern Ireland)
1990	Dog Registration
2006	Dogs Trust
2000	Domestic Abuse*
2002	Domino's Pizza*
2009	'Don't be a Cancer Chancer'*
2011	Doro Mobile Phones
2008	Dove*
2010	Dove Deodorant*
2002	Dr Beckmann Rescue*
2001	Dr Beckmann Rescue Oven Cleaner**
1980	Dream Topping
1988	Drinking & Driving
1998	Drugs Education*
1994	Dunfermline Building Society
1980	Dunlop Floor Tiles
1990	Duracell Batteries
1980	Dynatron Music Suite

E

1988	E & P Loans*
2007	E4 Skins (Channel 4)*
2011	East Midlands Trains*
2004	East of England Development Agency (Broadband)*
2000	easyJet*
2009	Eden and Blighty*

1994	Edinburgh Club*
1990	Edinburgh Zoo
1980	Eggs Authority
2004	Electoral Commission (Northern Ireland)
2003	Electoral Commission/COI (DoE Northern Ireland)
1992	Electricity Privatisation
2009	Elephant Chakki Gold (ECG)
2009	Ella's Kitchen
1980	Ellerman Travel & Leisure
1996	Emergency Contraception
1986	EMI Virgin (records)*
1980	English Butter Marketing Company
1986	English Country Cottages
1992	Enterprise Initiative
2003	Equality Commission of Northern Ireland
1992	Equity & Law
2007	Erskine*
2010	essential Waitrose*
1990	Eurax (Anti-Itch Cream)
1999	EuroSites (continental camping holidays)**
2004	Eurostar*
2006	Eurostar
2008	Eurostar
1994	*Evening Standard* Classified Recruitment
2010	Everest*
2004	Evergood Coffee (Norway)
1984	Exbury Gardens

F

2008	Fairy Liquid
2008	Fairy Non Bio
1990	Family Credit
1998	Famous Grouse, The
2006	Famous Grouse, The*
1982	Farmer's Table Chicken
1996	Felix*
2000	Felix*
2006	Felix*
1980	Ferranti CETEC
1990	Fertilizer Manufacturers' Association
2011	Fiat*
1982	Fiat Auto UK
1980	Findus Crispy Pancakes
1988	Findus French Bread Pizza & Crispy Pancakes
1992	Findus Lasagne
1982	Fine Fare*
1984	Fine Fare
2005	Fire Authority for Northern Ireland*
2005	First Choice*
1996	First Choice Holidays
1998	first direct*
1992	first direct
2004	first direct
2011	first direct*
2005	First Great Western and First Great Western Link
2007	First Scotrail
2003	Fisherman's Friend**
1992	Flowers & Plants Association
2002	Flowers & Plants Association

2003	Flymo Turbo Compact**
1994	Fona Dansk Elektrik
1980	Ford Fiesta
1998	Ford Galaxy*
1986	Ford Granada*
1982	Ford Model Range
2010	Forevermark*
1984	Foster's
1995	Fox's Biscuits**
2005	Fox's Rocky*
1998	French Connection
2000	Freschetta*
1999	Freschetta Pizzas**
2009	FRijj*
1982	Frish*
1996	Frizzell Insurance*
2002	Fruitopia
1994	Fruit-tella
2000	ft.com*
2005	Fybogel

G

1997	Gala Bingo Clubs**
1999	Gala Bingo Clubs**
2004	Garnier
1986	General Accident
2003	George Foreman Grills
2009	ghd*
1992	Gini (Schweppes)*
2010	Ginsters
2007	Glasgow City
1986	Glasgow's Lord Provost
1986	GLC's Anti 'Paving Bill' Campaign*
2000	Glenmorangie*S
1995	Glow-worm Boilers (Hepworth Heating)**
1996	Glow-worm Central Heating
2001	GoByCoach.com (National Express)**
1996	Gold Blend*
1988	Gold Spot
1984	Golden Wonder Instant Pot Snacks*
1980	Goodyear Grandprix
1984	Grant's Whisky
1992	Green Giant
1988	Green Science
1988	Greene King IPA Bitter
1990	Greenpeace
1982	*Guardian, the*
2004	*Guardian, the**
1990	Guinness (Draught) in Cans
1996	*Guinness Book of Records*

H

1990	H. Samuel
1992	Haagen-Dazs*
2009	Halifax*
2006	Halifax Bank of Scotland
1982	Halifax Building Society
1992	Halifax Building Society
1994	Halifax Building Society
2002	Halifax Building Society*
1980	Halifax Building Society Convertible Term Shares
1994	Halls Soothers*
1982	Hansa Lager

1999	Hartley's Jam**
2007	Hastings Hotels
2002	Hastings Hotels (Golfing Breaks)*
2001	Hastings Hotels (Golfing Breaks in Northern Ireland)**
2000	Health Education Board for Scotland
1994	Heineken Export
2010	Heinz*
2008	Heinz Beanz Snap Pots
1980	Heinz Coleslaw
1984	Hellman's Mayonnaise*
1982	Henri Winterman's Special Mild
1996	Hep30 (Building Products)
1990	Herta Frankfurters
1992	Herta Frankfurters
2008	Hewlett Packard Personal Systems Group (PSG)
2005	Hidden Treasures of Cumbria*
2005	Highlands and Islands Broadband Registration Campaign
2011	Hiscox
2007	Historic Scotland*
2006	HM Revenue & Customs (Self Assessment)*
1980	Hoechst
1992	Hofels Garlic Pearles
1984	Hofmeister*
1982	Home Protection (Products)
1984	Home Protection (Products)
2006	Homebase
1990	Honda
2004	Honda*
1986	Horlicks
1994	Horlicks
2006	Horlicks
1986	Hoverspeed
1992	Hovis
1996	Hovis
2002	Hovis*
2010	Hovis*
2010	HSBC*
1984	Hudson Payne & Iddiols
1996	Huggies Nappies
1994	Hush Puppies

I

1996	I Can't Believe It's Not Butter!*
2008	Iceland
1992	Iceland Frozen Foods
1980	ICI Chemicals
1984	ICI Dulux Natural Whites*
1992	IFAW*
1998	Imodium
2001	Imperial Leather**
2002	Imperial Leather
2003	Imperial Leather**
2004	Imperial Leather*
1990	Imperial War Museum
1998	Impulse
1988	*Independent, the*
2006	ING Direct*
1998	Inland Revenue Self Assessment
2005	Inland Revenue Self Assessment*
1988	Insignia
1982	International Business Show 1981

1992	Lucozade
2008	Lucozade Sport*
1988	Lurpak
2000	Lurpak*
2008	Lurpak
2002	Lynx*
2011	Lynx*
2004	Lynx Pulse*
1994	Lyon's Maid Fab
1988	Lyon's Maid Favourite Centres

M

2004	M&G
1988	Maclaren Prams
2003	Magna Science Adventure Centre**
2007	Magners Irish Cider*
1999	Magnet Kitchens**
2004	Magnum
2009	Make Poverty History
2006	Make Poverty History (Comic Relief)
1990	Malibu
2006	Manchester City*
1999	Manchester City Centre**
2001	Manchester City Centre**
2002	*Manchester Evening News* (Job Section)*
2003	*Manchester Evening News* Job Section**
2003	ManchesterIMAX**
1982	Manger's Sugar Soap*
1988	Manpower Services Commission
2011	Marie Curie Cancer Care*
1994	Marks & Spencer
2006	Marks & Spencer*
2004	Marks & Spencer Lingerie*
1998	Marmite*
2002	Marmite*
2008	Marmite*
2011	Marmite XO
1998	Marmoleum
1988	Marshall Cavendish Discovery
1994	Marston Pedigree*
2001	Maryland Cookies**
2006	Mastercard
2008	Mastercard
2009	Maximuscle*
1986	Mazda*
1986	Mazola*
2008	McCain
2011	McCain Wedges*
1996	McDonald's
1998	McDonald's
2010	McDonald's
2008	McDonald's Eurosaver
1980	McDougall's Saucy Sponge
1988	Mcpherson's Paints
1990	Mcpherson's Paints
2000	McVitie's Jaffa Cakes
2004	McVitie's Jaffa Cakes
2010	Medicine Waste
1992	Mercury Communications
2005	Metrication
1988	Metropolitan Police Recruitment*
2003	Microbake
1988	Midland Bank
1990	Midland Bank

1992	Miele
1988	Miller Lite*
2000	Moneyextra*
2010	Monopoly
2006	Monopoly Here & Now*
2006	More4*
1999	Morrisons**
2008	Morrisons*
2009	Morrisons*
2010	Morrisons
1988	Mortgage Corporation*
2008	Motorola*
2002	Mr Kipling*
1984	Mr Muscle
2010	MTR*
1995	Müller Fruit Corner**
1994	Multiple Sclerosis Society
2010	Munch Bunch
1996	Murphy's Irish Stout*
2000	Myk Menthol Norway*

N

2005	Nambarrie Tea^S
2000	National Code and Number Change
1980	National Dairy Council - Milk
1992	National Dairy Council - Milk
1996	National Dairy Council - Milk*
1992	National Dairy Council - Milkman*
1996	National Lottery (Camelot)
1999	National Railway Museum**
1996	National Savings
1984	National Savings: Income Bonds
1982	National Savings: Save by Post*
2007	National Trust (Northern Ireland)
1986	National Westminster Bank Loans
1982	Nationwide Building Society
1988	Nationwide Flex Account
1990	Nationwide Flex Account
2006	Naturella*
1990	Navy Recruitment
1988	Nefax
1982	Negas Cookers
1982	Nescafé
2000	Network Q
1992	Neutrogena
1982	New Man Clothes
1994	New Zealand Lamb
1980	New Zealand Meat Producers Board
2003	Newcastle Gateshead Initiative
2001	NHS Missed Appointments**
2006	Nicorette*
1994	Nike
1996	Nike
1994	Nissan Micra*
2000	No More Nails*
1986	No.7
2005	Noise Awareness*
1988	Norsk Data
1998	North West Water
1997	North West Water (drought)**
1998	North West Water (drought)
2007	Northern Bank
2007	Northern Ireland Fire and Rescue Service
2009	Northern Ireland Fire and Rescue Service

1992	Prudential
2008	Public Awareness Campaign for Helmet Wearing*

Q

1984	QE2
2003	Qjump.co.uk
1988	Quaker Harvest Chewy Bars*
1982	Qualcast Concorde Lawn Mower*
1986	Quatro
1986	Quickstart
1996	Quorn Burgers

R

1982	Racal Redec Cadet
1990	Radio Rentals
1994	Radio Rentals
1990	Radion Automatic*
2008	Radley*
1980	RAF Recruitment*
1996	RAF Recruitment
2004	Rainbow (evaporated milk)*
1994	Range Rover
2000	Reading and Literacy*
1992	Real McCoys
2000	Rear Seatbelts*
1984	Red Meat Consumption
1998	Red Meat Market*
1988	Red Mountain*
1996	Reebok*
1990	Reliant Metrocabs
1994	Remegel
2010	Remember a Charity*
1998	Renault
1990	Renault 19*
1986	Renault 5
1992	Renault Clio*
1996	Renault Clio*
1984	Renault Trafic & Master
2009	Resolva 24H*
2005	ResponsibleTravel.Com
2010	Retail OTP
1982	Ribena*
1996	Ribena
2001	right to read (literacy charity)**
2001	rightmove.co.uk**
2002	Rimmel*
1986	Rimmel Cosmetics
2008	Road Safety*
2009	Road Safety
2006	Road Safety -- Anti-Drink Driving (DoE Northern Ireland)
2006	Road Safety --THINK! (Department of Transport)
1999	Road Safety (DoE Northern Ireland)**
2003	Road Safety (DoE Northern Ireland)
2004	Road Safety (DoE Northern Ireland)*
2007	Road Safety (Republic of Ireland Road Safety Authority/DoE Northern Ireland)
2010	Robinsons Fruit Shoot*
1996	Rocky (Fox's Biscuits)
1988	Rolls-Royce Privatisation*
2004	Roundup
2005	Roundup Weedkiller*
1988	Rover 200

1982	Rowenta
1990	Rowntree's Fruit Gums
1992	Royal Bank of Scotland
1986	Royal College of Nursing
2002	Royal Mail
1986	Royal Mail Business Economy
1997	Royal Mint**
1990	Royal National Institute for the Deaf
1996	RSPCA
2011	Rubicon
1988	Rumbelows
2006	Ryvita Minis
2007	Ryvita Minis*

S

2004	s1jobs
1994	S4C
1988	Saab*
2004	Safer Travel at Night (GLA)*
1996	Safeway
2002	Sainsbury's* (Jamie Oliver)
2002	Sainsbury's* (Promotion)
2006	Sainsbury's
2008	Sainsbury's*
2010	Sainsbury's*
2008	Sainsbury's magazine
2001	Salford University**
2003	Salvation Army, the**
1996	Samaritans
1980	Sanatogen
1986	Sanatogen
1988	Sandplate*
1986	Sapur (Carpet Cleaner)
1992	Save the Children*
1988	Schering Greene Science
2001	Scholl Flight Socks**
2000	scoot.com*
1980	Scotcade
2005	Scotch Beef ˢ
1984	Scotch Video Cassettes
1992	Scotrail
1992	Scottish Amicable*
2008	Scottish Government: Teacher Recruitment
2005	Scottish Power*
1998	Scottish Prison Service
2005	Scruffs Hard Wear
2002	Seafish Industry Authority
2006	Seeds of Change (Masterfoods)
1980	Seiko
2010	Self Assessment*
1992	Sellafield Visitors Centre
2001	Senokot**
2002	Senokot
2005	Senokot
1999	Seven Seas Cod Liver Oil**
1980	Shake 'n' Vac
1984	Shakers Cocktails*
2009	Shell
2002	Shell Optimax
1999	Shippam's Spread**
1980	Shloer*
1986	Shredded Wheat
1990	Silent Night Beds*
2005	Silent Night My First Bed*ˢ

2009	Simple
2002	Skoda*
1982	Skol
1992	Skol
2008	Sky
1999	Slazenger (cricket bats)**
2009	Slendertone*
1980	Slumberdown Quilts
1990	Smarties
1980	Smirnoff Vodka
1980	Smith's Monster Munch
1982	Smith's Square Crisps
1992	Smith's Tudor Specials
1992	Smoke Alarms
1994	Smoke Alarms*
2011	Smokefree North West
1996	So ...? (Fragrance)
2006	Sobieski (Vodka)
1986	Soft & Gentle
1996	Soldier Recruitment
1995	Solpadol**
1994	Solvent Abuse
1996	Solvite
1999	Solvite**
2000	Solvite*
1988	Sony
1992	Sony
2006	Sony BRAVIA
1992	Sony Camcorders
2006	Sony DVD Handycam
2006	Sony Ericsson K750i/W800i*
2004	Sony Ericsson T610*
1996	Springers by K (Shoes)
2006	Sprite
1984	St Ivel Gold*
2004	Standard Bank (SA)
2005	Standard Life^S
2009	Stanley Tools UK
2000	Star Alliance
1992	Stella Artois*
1996	Stella Artois*
1998	Stella Artois
2000	Stella Artois*
2002	Stella Artois*
2002	Strathclyde Police
1994	Strepsils*
2010	Stroke Awareness*
1990	Strongbow
2009	Strongbow
2007	Subway*
1982	Summers the Plumbers
1980	Sunblest Sunbran
1990	Supasnaps
2000	Surf*
2010	Surf*
1980	Swan Vestas*
1984	SWEB Security Systems
1992	Swinton Insurance
2009	Swinton Taxi Division*
1996	Switch
1998	Switch
2003	Syndol (painkillers)**

T

1992	Tandon Computers

1990	Tango
2010	Tango
1986	TCP*
2010	TDA Teacher Recruitment*
2006	Teacher Recruitment*
2001	Teacher Training Agency**
2003	Teacher Training Agency**
1986	Teletext
1986	Territorial Army Recruitment
2000	Terry's Chocolate Orange*
1980	Tesco
2000	Tesco*
2002	Tesco*
2007	Tesco (Green Clubcard)
1990	Tetley Tea Bags
2010	The Army
2010	The Co-operative Food*
1992	*The Economist**
2002	*The Economist**
2011	*The Economist**
2010	The Happy Egg Co.
2004	The Number 118 118*
2010	thetrainline.com*
2010	THINK!*
1984	Thomas Cook
2008	Thomas Cook
1990	Tia Maria
1992	Tia Maria
1990	*Times, The*
1994	Tizer
2005	Tizer*
1980	Tjaereborg Rejser*
2010	T-Mobile*
2004	Tobacco Control (DH)*
2010	Tobacco Control*
1980	Tolly's Original
2002	Tommy's: The Baby Charity*
1984	Torbay Tourist Board*
1986	Toshiba*
1986	Touche Remnant Unit Trusts
1992	Tower of London
2004	Toyota Corolla
1996	Toyota RAV4
2008	Toyota Yaris
1982	Trans World Airlines
2003	Translink CityBus
2007	Translink Metro
2003	Translink Smartlink
2005	Travelocity.co.uk*
2006	Travelocity.co.uk*
1984	Tri-ac (Skincare)
2009	Tribute Ale
2008	Trident*
2007	Trident (Metropolitan Police)*
2004	Tritace
1980	Triumph Dolomite
2006	Tropicana Pure Premium*
1986	TSB*
1988	TSB*
1994	TSB
2004	TUI (Germany)
1982	Turkish Delight*
1986	TV Licence Evasion*
2006	TV Licensing*
2000	Twix Denmark

U	
1984	UK Canned Salmon
1986	Umbongo Tropical Juice Drink
2003	UniBond
1999	UniBond No More Nails**
2005	UniBond Sealant Range*
2005	University of Dundee*ˢ
1998	UPS
2003	UTV Internet
1990	Uvistat*
V	
1988	Varilux lenses
1994	Vauxhall Astra
1990	Vauxhall Cavalier
1996	Vauxhall Cavalier
1999	Vauxhall Network Q**
1996	Vegetarian Society
2006	Vehicle Crime Prevention (The Home Office)*
2004	Vehicle Crime Reduction (The Home Office)
2001	Vimto**
1986	Virgin Atlantic
2008	Virgin Atlantic*
2010	Virgin Atlantic*
2004	Virgin Mobile*
2004	Virgin Mobile Australia*
2004	Virgin Trains*
2006	Virgin Trains*
2010	Virgin Trains
1994	Visa
2006	Visit London
1986	Vodafone
1998	Volkswagen*
2002	Volkswagen (Brand)*
2004	Volkswagen Diesel*
2006	Volkswagen Golf*
2006	Volkswagen Golf GTI Mk5*
2002	Volkswagen Passat*
2008	V-Power
1992	VW Golf*
W	
1980	Waistline
2002	Waitrose*
2007	Waitrose*
2008	Waitrose*
2003	Wake Up To Waste (Northern Ireland)**
1992	Wales Tourist Board
2010	Walkers

1996	Walkers Crisps*
2002	Walkers Crisps*
1980	Wall's Cornetto
2006	Wall's Sausages
1984	Wall's Viennetta*
1996	Wall's Viennetta
1998	Wallis
1984	Walnut Whips
2003	Warburtons
1990	Warburtons Bread*
2005	Waste Awareness
1984	Websters Yorkshire Bitter
2004	Weetabix*
2007	Weetabix*
1988	Weight Watchers Slimming Clubs
2002	West End Quay
2005	West Midlands Hub of Museums*
1990	Westwood Tractors
1992	Whipsnade Wild Animal Park*
1980	Whitegate's Estate Agents*
2010	Wickes
1990	Wilson's Ultra Golf Balls
1988	Winalot Prime*
2010	Wispa*
2006	Women's Aid*
1994	Wonderbra*
Y	
2000	Yellow Pages Norway
1980	Yeoman Pie Fillings
1980	Yorkie
1982	Yorkshire Bank
2002	Yorkshire Forward/Yorkshire Tourist Board
2008	Yorkshire Tourist Board – Make Yorkshire Yours
Z	
1984	Zanussi*
1994	Zovirax

In compiling this list the IPA has made every effort to ensure an accurate record of all cases currently available in the IPA Databank. However, there may be instances where cases are currently missing from file and as a result have not been listed here.

Index